Women of the Bible and God's Redeeming Love

ANNE NICHOLSON

WESTBOW PRESS
A DIVISION OF THOMAS NELSON
& ZONDERVAN

Copyright © 2018 Anne Nicholson.

All rights reserved. No part of this book may be used or reproduced by any means, graphic, electronic, or mechanical, including photocopying, recording, taping or by any information storage retrieval system without the written permission of the author except in the case of brief quotations embodied in critical articles and reviews.

Scripture taken from the New King James Version®. Copyright © 1982 by Thomas Nelson. Used by permission. All rights reserved.

THE HOLY BIBLE, NEW INTERNATIONAL VERSION®, NIV® Copyright © 1973, 1978, 1984, 2011 by Biblica, Inc.® Used by permission. All rights reserved worldwide.

Scripture taken from the Amplified Bible, Copyright © 1954, 1958, 1962, 1964, 1965, 1987 by The Lockman Foundation. Used with permission.

WestBow Press books may be ordered through booksellers or by contacting:

WestBow Press
A Division of Thomas Nelson & Zondervan
1663 Liberty Drive
Bloomington, IN 47403
www.westbowpress.com
1 (866) 928-1240

Because of the dynamic nature of the Internet, any web addresses or links contained in this book may have changed since publication and may no longer be valid. The views expressed in this work are solely those of the author and do not necessarily reflect the views of the publisher, and the publisher hereby disclaims any responsibility for them.

Any people depicted in stock imagery provided by Getty Images are models, and such images are being used for illustrative purposes only.
Certain stock imagery © Getty Images.

ISBN: 978-1-9736-3720-2 (sc)
ISBN: 978-1-9736-3721-9 (e)

Library of Congress Control Number: 2018910813

Print information available on the last page.

WestBow Press rev. date: 12/03/2018

Dedication

This book is dedicated to my husband, Jimmy, who loves God with all his heart, soul, mind and strength. Through the years, his sacrificial commitment to serve Jesus has not only changed my life but countless others along the way. He has taught me how to give all things freely because all we have belongs to God. He is fully persuaded what's impossible with man is possible with God. He hopes more, prays more, and loves me more than I deserve. Even in my most unlovable moments, he remains faithful to His promise and loves me as Christ loves His church. I am who I am today because he loves me in a way that honors God.

Table of Contents

Acknowledgements ix

Introduction And Author's Note xi

About The Study xiii

Eve: Mother Of All Living 1

Sarah: Believing The Promise 37

Hagar: A Woman Of Flight 73

Rebekah: A Bride For Isaac 113

Miriam: Sister Of Moses 153

Rahab: A Woman On The Wall 189

Ruth: Blessed Submission 225

Esther: Destiny Fulfilled 265

Gomer: Perpetual Prostitute 303

Mary: Virgin Mother 345

Acknowledgements

I'd like to thank women everywhere, and especially the women of the Bible, for without them there would be no book. Who knew, beginning with Eve in the garden these women could have such an influence in our lives thousands of years later? God did, and somewhere deep within, I knew it too. I have long been captivated by their lives and the beauty of God's redemptive work in them.

I didn't do this alone. As with any first-time author, many people have been a part of this marvelous journey. Of course, the highest debt of gratitude I owe is to Jesus. He saved my wretched soul! From that moment, I have had an insatiable love and desire for His Word and His presence. Thank you, Jesus. Otherwise, I would be forever lost, overwhelmed and consumed by sin.

Next, I'd like to thank my husband and partner in life and ministry who has journeyed right along with me. He is, to this day, my favorite Bible teacher. His wisdom and keen insights have kept me on the edge of my seat for years. His teaching has inspired my writing and pushed me to reach new heights. I most admire his openness and commitment to share God's Word and abundant grace - truthfully and unashamedly. After Jesus, Jimmy is my hero.

Next, I owe a tremendous debt of gratitude to the Board of Open Heavens Ministries, Inc. Thank you Bill, Jerry, Lynne, and Dorenda! And, to many others, including our prayer partners and ministry advisors, thanks to you as well. God has used all of you mightily, and your collective efforts since 2004 have enabled us to "go with God." Without your prayers and partnership, we couldn't have made it. As we begin the publishing journey, may God expand His kingdom and add much fruit to your accounts. You're all incredible.

A special thank you is extended to my Mother-in-law, Gloria Nicholson. She has faithfully served as an honorary board member since the beginning. She has encouraged our lives and ministry, as only a mother can - through thick and thin - including and most importantly, her prayers. As a mother myself, I know how this goes - much prayer, and often little results, but faithfulness nonetheless.

To my Father-in-law, James L. Nicholson, III – a particular note of thanks. He proved to be a marvelous preliminary editor. It's nice to have a former teacher in the family whose life work has been teaching authors to write. As a published author in his own right, his great eye for a "good word" and encouragement proved invaluable.

A loving thank you to my reader and dear friend, Jean Giglio. Her keen insight and attention to detail helped keep me focused. She has prayed over every word in this manuscript, sometimes with laughter and sometimes through tears. Her encouragement and ceaseless prayers are worth more than gold. And, to her husband Bobby, a heartfelt thanks for loaning her to me on short notice - often.

And last, but not least, to all the women in Mexico who originally attended my Bible college classes, studied with me, and test drove my material – thank you. Your participation was invaluable. Each of you is special to me, and you know who you are. This book and study guide, as well as the others: *Disciplines of a Godly Woman; Who's God and What's That to Me? Behold, the Bride; Seeing Jesus; A Journey of Faith; Becoming a Mary in a Martha World, and To Rome With Love,* is a reality because of your love for Jesus, your hunger for His Word, and your faithful commitment to study. Hopefully and God willing, these will take print form sometime in the future. Thanks to you all, and most especially Linda Flores Gordon, my teaching partner and closest friend. You mean more to me than words can adequately express. May our collective tears and prayers bear much fruit for His Kingdom. Until we teach together again - blessings and Godspeed!

Introduction and Author's Note

People watching can be exciting. Some might confess it's a favorite pastime; I'm a fan myself. On a recent vacation, my husband and I spent several hours simply sitting in the sea-breeze observing God's creation doing life.

Because I'm a woman, I particularly enjoy observing women. As a missionary couple, over the last fourteen years, we've had the esteemed privilege of being moved by God in and out of unique locations, both foreign and domestic. As you might imagine, our travels have provided the backdrop for some priceless people watching along the way. We have served in danger and peril, in peace and tranquility, among those in plenty, as well as those in need, all at the Lord's pleasure. It's been particularly thrilling to see the beauty of God revealed through the lives of ordinary women.

You may find it fascinating to learn women are fundamentally the same. Although we might not all look alike or speak the same language, we have much more in common than not. Women are women, and we are uniquely created by God, on purpose - with purpose, and in His very image. I have realized over time, no matter where we call home, the same issues and concerns plague our hearts. It was not surprising to discover everyday things also provide our greatest joys. Things like holding our new baby for the first time, or the announcement of a long-awaited engagement. Women everywhere delight in the victories and successes of those we love most - our husbands and children. The size of the winnings is irrelevant - to a wife and mother, a win's a win! Sometimes, we celebrate their triumphs and achievements more than they do, because seeing God work in and through their lives still satisfies and brings us indescribable joy. Believing women worldwide not only pray for their husbands and children but praise God for them as well.

God is into people! We're His focus and passion – His work and mission! His electing love rests on us – exclusively. That's why I've particularly enjoyed watching Him raise women from the trash heap or elevate them from abject poverty to positions of notoriety and influence – again and again. He gave them hope and dignity. He saved them! I've seen Him restore families, repair marriages, even raise the most hopeless, helpless soul right off the deathbed. He has the final say! He exchanges ashes for beauty in crumbling lives and delights to do so. In fact, He does His best work in our messes! Sometimes the messier, the better. He has saved me from peril and wrong choices many times. In hindsight, I can see I needed rescuing from myself, first and foremost! Thankfully, He put me back on the path of His choice. He is the master of restoration and redemption. I consistently stand in awe of His grace and mercy. Quite frankly, I am astounded He can and will use me at all. I still feel much like a diamond in the rough!

Not because of us, but because of who He is, we are continually being redeemed. After all, Jesus is our Redeemer and King! That brings us to the focus of our study. Not only did God envision all women, He lovingly created them. He called them into existence, at the appointed time, to plant them where He desired, and love them through it all. Then as needed, He redeemed the whole of their lives to accomplish His will and purposes. That's what our study will reveal. In every one of their lives God redeemed the good, the bad, and as needed, the ugly! What an awesome God!

About the Study

This study is a scriptural journey which invites us deep into the lives of women of the Bible. We will step back in history to examine their successes and failures. In the process, we will discover how God has revealed Himself in and through their lives. He has not changed, and He will deal with us similarly. Albeit true, times have changed, but His primary focus has not and it never will. Redeeming humanity is paramount in His mind. Having true and passionate worship of Him and experiencing intimate fellowship with Him is still His goal. Revealing Jesus, God the Son, as Savior of the world who died so we might be forgiven and reconciled to God is always His plan.

We have much to learn through the women of the Bible's victories and defeats. I sometimes wonder what it must have been like to live during those times in history. Where did Sarah get the strength to submit to Abraham? How did she leave everything she had ever known behind without resentment, bitterness, and heartache? How did Esther stand uninvited before the King without her knees buckling beneath her? Where did she find her resolve and passion? Was she indeed prepared to die for her people? What did Hagar think about Abraham and his God when she was cast out into the wilderness? Why and how did God use Rahab, a harlot, to accomplish His plan? Moreover, why were the supporting walls to Rahab's home left standing while the remaining walls of Jericho lay crumbled in a pile of rubble at her feet?

Questions like these and many more will be answered in our course of study. We will examine the lives of Eve, Sarah, Hagar, Rebekah, Miriam, Rahab, Ruth, Esther, Gomer, and Mary, the Virgin Mother. Our scriptural journey will reveal where these women are in God's redemption story, what they got right, what they got wrong, and how God's love redeemed it all. Overall, we might inquire, "What made these ordinary women useful to our extraordinary God?"

Each lesson will highlight one woman and God's detailed redemptive work in and through every facet of her life. Thanks to our merciful God, He won't leave them as He finds them! How encouraging for us. You will be amazed as He takes their sin, their mistakes, and blunders and creates something beautiful, and of lasting significance. Woman after woman, week after week, He will create something unique, worthwhile and meaningful. The Bible says, "All Scripture is given by inspiration of God and is profitable for doctrine, for reproof, for correction, and for instruction in righteousness." (2 Timothy 3:16).

Real Women.

All of them were real women merely doing life. That's what makes this study so beautiful. From God's perspective, they are just like us! The women of the Bible, without exception, had plans, hopes, and dreams. They each loved, they laughed, and they cried. They had good days and bad days. Some had kids; some didn't. Some were married, some weren't. Some were wholesome and good, and others were decadent. They feared, they sacrificed, and they nurtured. They experienced significant victories and shameful defeats, all of them. How do I know? Well, first of all, I've read the book, but women are women, always have been and always will be.

I am so thankful their lives are included in the Bible for us to study. Take heart; this is an opportunity for us to ask and answer questions like:

- What is God speaking to my heart through their redemptive stories?
- How might I trust God in deeper measure and finish strong for the benefit of the gospel?
- How might studying their lives enrich mine for the benefit of my family, my church, and my community?
- How might I make a lasting difference?
- What legacy will I leave?"

I'm so excited for us. If you've never studied the women of the Bible, you're breaking new ground. At the heart of our journey, we want to know God better. Deep within, we desire to know what He thinks about us. After all, we've heard all our lives we're flawed and defective. But, He says otherwise. In His sight, we are perfect! We are His daughters in whom He is well pleased. Will we believe it in our hearts? That's the real question and the challenge before us. We have an opportunity through this study to discover how He has loved these women and effectively used their lives, through the good times and bad, as an expression of His grace and for His glory.

Finishing Strong.

If you're a woman who wants to finish strong, desiring to grow in faith and practice, this study is for you. Do you want to strengthen your family and marriage? Do you love your husband in a way that honors God? That's our hardest challenge as wives, you know. Loving your husband in a way that honors God. Each week, we will dig into God's Word to discover what He says on many matters, including these. After all, He is our ultimate authority. In so doing, we will endeavor to know His will so that we might finish strong. We want to know the God of the Bible more intimately. We want to know the women of the Bible, too. Why? Because that's God's plan, and because quite frankly, there is nothing new under the sun. Women are women, always have been and always will be. I see bits of myself in all of their lives. I'll just bet you will too!

It's Your Study.

Take the time to make the most of it. To achieve the maximum, complete your lessons. If possible, set a designated time to meet with Jesus every day. Make that appointment and keep it. Pray before you begin and ask the Lord to speak powerfully to you through their lives, as you wait upon Him. Ask Him to bring healing where healing is needed and correction likewise. Unburden your heart and anticipate His presence. He will surely meet you there. Remember, we want God's best for ourselves and our families – nothing else will do. But the bottom line in this. We will never know what God wants to share about their lives and how they intersect with ours unless we study what His inspired Word tells us. He has spoken to me through every woman and every lesson. We have much to glean from God.

The Format.

Each lesson begins with an in-depth story highlighting the woman of the week. An accompanying study guide follows. It will help us navigate the appropriate scripture. I have used the same five-day format for both. They will reveal: Day One: Who They Are; Day Two: Where They Are In God's Redemption Story; Day Three: What They Got Right; Day Four: What They Got Wrong; and Day Five: How God's Love Redeemed It All. You may decide to read each story at one sitting or break it down over a day or two. Or, you may choose to read the first section and work through Day One of the study guide, and so on. Whatever you decide is ok. It's your study! Complete all questions of the study guide. God will use the questions to speak to your heart. Answer the questions honestly and allow His Spirit to work deep within you. Additionally, the daily lessons are important because they will reinforce the teachable elements from each of their lives.

If We Seek Him, We Will Find Him.

It is my prayer you will get up each day eager to see what the women of the Bible are up to, and how God redeemed them. I hope as you go about your daily life, they will come to mind. I pray you will think about them and ask God to speak to you plainly through their lives. Remember, we get out of Bible study in direct proportion to the time we invest. Set aside quiet time each day to get alone with Jesus! You will grow proportionately! He will bless your time and faithfulness indeed! I am praying for you. Enjoy the journey.

Faithfully His,

Anne Nicholson

Note: Unless otherwise stated, all scripture comes from The New King James Version of the Bible. (1982). Nashville: Thomas Nelson.

All calligraphy by Kate Gwin @ www.haintbluecollective.com

Eve

Eve: Mother Of All Living

We begin our study of women of the Bible with Eve. It's most appropriate since Eve was the first woman who ever lived. Can you imagine? She was the first woman lovingly created by God. You might say she was the prototype or pattern of all women to come, including us! When God created Eve, He made a creature of inner and outer beauty, one of substance and character, and one with a soul which would live forever. She was a keeper, through and through! Undoubtedly, God's model has stood the test of time.

Sometimes, we make things we can improve upon, but that was not the case with Eve. God doesn't make junk or mistakes. He didn't need a "do-over." Eve was all God desired right from the beginning, precisely what He had planned. From the moment she drew her first breath and gazed into Adam's eyes, she was a lovely vision of God's making. Pause for a moment and think about it. Can you imagine what it must have been like to stand in God's presence and meet your future husband for the very first time? And, naked no less? Neither of them had on clothes, not a stitch. Nonetheless, what they beheld was stunning, beautiful, and perfect. How thrilling for them, especially Adam. Seeing Eve for the very first time, someone like him, yet uniquely different in all the appropriate places! It's interesting to note they didn't know their nakedness or shame until after sin entered the garden. But, let's not get ahead of ourselves. We'll revisit their sin, and its painful consequences further along in our study.

All We Truly Need.

Eve was the first bride, the first wife, and the first mother. Unlike us, Eve didn't have the luxury of role models, sisters, self-help books, or "how to" guides. Thankfully, she didn't have cable TV and a myriad of self-proclaimed advice-giving experts either. Life was simple. She had God and His word, and Adam. That was it, and undoubtedly it was enough! We can know it was enough because God always provides what we need. Surely, He would not have left Eve inadequately prepared or void of needed supply to accomplish her tasks. Our Creator and God of detail had provided everything Eve required for success.

We can rest in the comfort of knowing He is not only our Creator and a God of detail, but an intentional God of purpose, order, and completion. The Bible assures us, God is "merciful and gracious, longsuffering, and abounding in goodness and truth" (Exodus 34:6). He is all this, yet, this impromptu description of God remains incomplete without love. The apostle John affirms, "…God is love" (1 John 4:8;16). Love is an attribute of God's very nature. We can sum it up by saying, "God who loves us does not leave us alone, undone, or without all we need to accomplish His plan." The issue lies with us. Essentially, it's learning to separate our needs from our wants, recognizing God's perfect provision, and being thankfully satisfied with it. As we shall see, although Eve had everything she needed, she didn't think so. How utterly human! We'll be looking closer at this in our study guide. In the meantime, be encouraged! In Christ Jesus, we have all we truly need. And remember, if God asks something of you, provision is

Eden: garden of delight

either there or coming in short order. He has or will provide everything necessary for your success. He has never failed to provide, nor will He. What a generous, loving God; He wants you to succeed! Ladies, that's the plan. <u>Where God guides - He provides!</u>

Who Was Eve, And Where Is She In God's Redemption Story?

As we've already noted, Eve was the first woman of the human race. She and her husband, Adam, lived in the garden of Eden. (Genesis 2:15). The word *Eden* means *paradise; a place of delight; delight; pleasantness.* According to God's creative account, His work was accomplished and complete with her formation. In the beginning, Eve was the last living thing created by God. You might say, <u>with Eve, God added the feminine element</u>, thereby placing the finishing touches on creation. Seeing the results, God was satisfied. After blessing His image-bearers, He instructed them to be fruitful and multiply. (See Genesis 1:28.) Indeed, God's creation was "very good." Moses inspired words, "Then God saw everything that He had made, and indeed it was very good. So the evening and the morning were the sixth day." (Genesis 1:31).

Fashioned By God.

In Genesis 3:20, Eve was named by Adam. Her name appropriately means "mother of all living." She was not born in the traditional sense, nor was Adam. Both were fashioned or formed by the hand of God. They were uniquely brought forth as mature adults, wholly man and wholly woman from day one of their existence. From their beginning, they were walking, talking, and preparing for marriage, while enjoying resplendent fellowship with God.

God's creative activity in Genesis 2:7 is translated or expressed in the English word *formed* in most versions of the Bible, including the New King James Version (NKJV). The verse states, "And the Lord God formed man of the dust of the ground, and breathed into his nostrils the breath of life; and man became a living being." Notice the word *formed* in this passage. From the original text, the Hebrew word translated *formed* is yāṣar.

In this context, *formed* conveys the idea of a potter shaping or squeezing its conceived object into being by molding it into existence. That's where we get the idea God is the potter and we are the clay. The loving hands that would one day bear the wounds of our atonement held humanity in them. That should cause us to consider even in the beginning God enjoyed an unrivaled affection for people. His "hands-on" involvement at this creation event would be an indication He had exceptional plans for us. We were chosen to bear His image. That, alone, should be enough to indicate our relationship with God would be unlike any other. Not only has He designed us for the esteemed privilege of bearing His image, but He has also given each of us a soul that will live forever.

To further grasp the depth of our formation, we must understand the first act of this creative event would have taken place in the mind of God. Long before your birth, God had you in His mind - He thought of you! Is that not riveting? God thought of you! Before you were a twinkle in your father's eye – Our Creator, the great I AM – Lord of all, had purposeful and intentional thoughts of you! Therefore, we see embedded in the word, *yāṣar - formed*, the preordained purposes of God.

The Creative Power Of God.

The prophet Isaiah well understood the creative power of God. He has used this same word to define God's forming the nation of Israel in the sense of bringing it into existence or calling it forth from nothing. Let's review the prophet's words:

But now, thus says the LORD, who created you, O Jacob, And He who formed you, O Israel: "Fear not, for I have redeemed you; I have called *you* by your name; You *are* Mine..." (Isaiah 43:1).

God *formed* the nation of Israel; He chose a people. First, God saw or conceived Israel in His mind. Then, He called them forth. Similarly, in the beginning, God formed Adam and Eve. He saw them, and at the appropriate time, He brought them forth. He has formed you and me – all of humanity. You have life today because God first conceived you in His mind. Then, He formed or fashioned you and placed you in your mother's womb for safekeeping, growth, and development. God kept you there until the appointed time. When He determined, He brought you forth and introduced you to the world. That's the day you were born. The psalmist understood the rich meaning of this word, too. Notice the word *fashioned* in the following verse. From the original text, it's the same Hebrew word, with the same meaning. Psalm 139:16 says, "Your eyes saw my substance, being yet unformed. And in your book they all were written, the days fashioned for me, when as yet there are none of them." Long before we were ever formed and placed in the security of our mother's wombs, God saw the totality of our lives. Our Lord God saw all of it.

God Created Eve.

Unbeknownst to Adam, he needed Eve. Let's take a look at Genesis 2:18; and 2:20-25.

Genesis 2:18: And the Lord God said, "It is not good that man should be alone; I will make him a helper comparable to him."

20 - So Adam gave names to all cattle, to the birds of the air, and to every beast of the field. But for Adam there was not found a helper comparable to him.

21 - And the Lord God caused a deep sleep to fall on Adam, and he slept; and He took one of his ribs, and closed up the flesh in its place.

22 Then the rib which the Lord God had taken from man He made into a woman, and He brought her to the man.

23 And Adam said: "This is now bone of my bones And flesh of my flesh; She shall be called Woman, because she was taken out of Man."

24 Therefore a man shall leave his father and mother and be joined to his wife, and they shall become one flesh.

25 And they were both naked, the man and his wife, and were not ashamed.

From verse 18, whose idea was Eve? Was it Adam's or God's? Eve was God's idea; not Adam's.

Look at verse 20. There is no indication Adam even knew he was alone. He was not clamoring or yearning for a mate. There is no evidence in scripture he ever considered his circumstances. In fact, it appears in our text Adam was not aware of his needs. Nonetheless, God knew. He is aware of all our needs – always. Even now, at this very moment - if you are in need, God knows it.

Notice in verse 20, as Adam names the animals, something happens. The state of Adam's singleness becomes apparent to whom? Look at the verse. It becomes clear to God - Adam is alone and without a mate. He needs a comparable mate. What did God make for Adam? Eve, a suitable *helper* (*'ēzer*). From the original language guess what *helper* means? It means helper! The definition is *one who provides aid or relief,* most notably the Lord. This same word, *'ēzer*, in the original language, is also used to describe the help or assistance the Lord provided to the psalmist over and over again. For example, Psalm 121:1-2 says, "I will lift up my eyes to the hills—From whence comes my *help* (*'ēzer*)? My *help* (*'ēzer*) comes from the Lord, who made heaven and earth.

We see this *help* in the New Testament as well. Notice the words of Jesus in John 15:26, "But when the *Helper* (*paraklētos*) comes…" same idea - one coming alongside. In this verse, we discover the Hebrew word, *'ēzer*, has a Greek counterpart - *paraklētos*. These words share the same meaning. The overarching idea? God sees the help we need and comes to our aid. He is our help and ultimate provider.

God Creates A Comparable Helper For Adam.

God sent Adam "help" through Eve. Let's take a minute to examine this help. It embodies the material, physical, and spiritual. It's the complete and total package. Eve was created to complete Adam. The couple had much to accomplish. Adam and Eve were to subdue the earth and have dominion over it, that is - under God's watchful eye, steadfast leadership, and guidance. The task was not left solely to Adam. God blessed them and instructed them – together. Reading Genesis 1:28, "Then God blessed them, and God said to them, 'Be fruitful and multiply; fill the earth and subdue it; have dominion over the fish of the sea, over the birds of the air, and over every living thing that moves on the earth.'"

From the original text, God issued an imperative command. They were to be fruitful and multiply. They were instructed to subdue the earth and have dominion over it. Adam couldn't do this alone. Eve's creation speaks to Adam's deficiency without her help. It never speaks of her insufficiency as a person apart from Adam. In God's mind, she has no insufficiency at all. Eve did not lack in any measure! God's loving hands purposely formed both man and woman. Please note the intentionality here. They were of equal importance to God, but they had different roles to play. We might sum it up by concluding, Adam and Eve were created by God's loving hands, equal but different, each having a unique and distinct call or preordained purpose from God.

Eve Was Never Inferior To Adam.

Eve was never an interior being to Adam. There is nothing in the creation story which speaks of Eve's inadequacy or deficiency in any manner. That is not what this means. Instead, Adam could not accomplish all God required because He lacked provision. What did God say? Look back to the last few words of Genesis 2:20. According to God, Adam was found lacking. What was missing? A comparable helper! Being a helper is not a punishment. Women have not been demoted somehow in God's mind. We are not less than. In fact, it's quite the opposite. Looking back to our uniqueness, God planned to involve women in His creation story tenderly and extraordinarily. With every conception, the mother partners with God to store, protect, nurture, and nourish His creation – His future image bearers. That's right, whether she's aware of it or not, God uses her in His creation story. No man can or ever will partner with God in this specific way. Yes, they are a part of the process, but they do not dominate the event. It is biologically impossible for them to do our work in God's creation story, and vice versa. As women, we have the esteemed privilege of holding the hope and future of God's glory within our mortal bodies; lest we forget no child is conceived apart from divine assistance. Pregnancy - all pregnancies require the preordained purposes of God. Remember, God envisions every life and all of its days before it is placed securely within the appointed womb.

Being A Woman Is A Divine Call From God.

That's right! To be a helper is an abundant blessing from God. You might find it interesting to learn the Holy Spirit is called the *comforter* as well as the *helper*. In addition to comfort, He brings the physical and spiritual help, direction, peace, and aid to every situation. In that context, it is one in the same. Let's look at that again. In addition to comfort, the *helper* brings the physical and spiritual help, direction, peace, and aid to every situation of our lives. If you are married, does this describe your relationship with your husband? You are called by God to be a *comparable helper* within your marriage. As you consider those words, let's take a closer look.

A helper, *ēzer* - comparable to him. What does that mean? It means, *able to be likened to another; similar; of the equivalent.* We are equal but different. All women are created or made in the image of God. Eve was the female counterpart to all Adam was. She was not ever inferior, nor was she an afterthought. God knew well before the world began what woman would bring to the equation. She was just as important to God's plan as Adam. The bottom line is this. To be complete, Adam needed Eve. Honestly, they needed each other. Neither of them could do what God required apart from the other. It would require both of them, and submission to accomplish God's overall plan. Adam needed a mate, the one God would have for Him. Although we could devote an entire study to God's plan for marriage, this lesson is not written with that purpose in mind. Instead, we will get an overview of God's original plan for marriage as we journey through our entire study.

God's Plans Have Not Changed.

In light of God's redemptive love, we are examining the lives of women of the Bible. To achieve our goal, we are doing so with specific questions in mind. The bottom line in the creation story is God had a plan for marriage, and it has not changed. One day soon, we will be held accountable for our marriages. Not what's politically correct, not what our surrounding culture dictates or popular opinion would have you believe. When the mountains melt like wax, only God's Word will remain. At the end of time, just what God determined truly matters. That's why it's so crucial for us to know what God has said in His Word - the Bible. We will never find the right answer if we don't start by asking the right question. "What does God say?" On all matters. Remember, God's Word is where we discover the pattern to shape our lives – including our marriages. The Bible is where we recognize and learn about our respective God-ordained roles. Everything we need for life and godliness is there. His Word is our blueprint for life. Not only is it sweet like honey, but it's our guide and a lamp unto our feet.

God Did Not Need Adam's Help.

In Genesis 2:21, God placed Adam in a deep sleep. God did not need Adam's help to create a suitable mate. He was more than able to accomplish all He has purposed to do on Adam's behalf. God knew far better than Adam what Adam needed, after all, He created him. We must remember, God can accomplish everything He pleases. However, we are invited to partner with Him in acts of obedience, serving, faithfulness, and prayer, etc. But if we prove to be uncooperative, stubborn, unwilling, or unavailable, God can and will accomplish His plan in spite of us - whatever He deems necessary. Either way, His divine purposes will be accomplished just like we see here. From eternity past, it was always God's plan to create Adam and Eve and unite them in marriage. When Adam awakened from his God-imposed slumber, he saw Eve for the very first time. Can you imagine what he must have thought? I have a vivid imagination, but I cannot fathom the delight and wonderment he must have felt when he first beheld her. Beauty is in the eye of the beholder and what Adam beheld captured the whole of his heart in an instant. You might say it was love at first sight in the garden called delightful. It appears Adam had no trouble recognizing his rib when he glanced at Eve. Bible scholars agree Eve was a creature of unsurpassed beauty. God is a God of detail, and He thought of everything! Nothing, absolutely nothing, was left to chance.

In your study guide, this week's memory verse is 1 Corinthians 11:9. The passage comes from Paul's instructive letter to the church at Corinth. He declares emphatically in 1 Corinthians 11:8 and 9, "For man is not from woman, but woman from man. Nor was man created for the woman, but woman for the man." Reading 1 Corinthians 11:9 from *The Amplified Bible* (Copyright © 2015 by The Lockman Foundation, La Habra, CA 90631), "…for indeed man was not created for the sake of woman, but woman for the sake of man." The amplified rendering should make it abundantly clear to us. For the sake of man, the woman was created. Although times have changed, God's plan has not. Women are still divinely created by God and called into being for the sake and benefit of man. We were made under the watchful eye of God to become the *comparable helper* - *ēzer* - man has always needed. God's plan goes back to the beginning of recorded time. Eve was the first, but God's plan for creation remains the same.

In Genesis 2:23, Adam describes Eve as "bone of my bones and flesh of my flesh." We must notice Eve was not fashioned from dirt like Adam. She was divinely created from living flesh and bone. From the rib of Adam God fashioned Eve. In her creation God completed humanity. From Adam's side, God *fashioned* (yāṣar) a *comparable helper* (ʽēzer) called Eve. In woman's creation, the circle of marital love was defined and identified. She was taken from Adam's side to be at his side, cradled under his arm and nestled close to his heart. She was to complete him and walk in step with him. She was not to be found running ahead of him or lagging behind. She was not his boss or leader, nor was she his slave or doormat. She was his *comparable helper* divinely *fashioned* by God.

Marriage And The Trinity.

Regardless of what men might say, a man without a woman is incomplete. He is never whole, and he knows it. If they were complete, without a woman, they would be self-sufficient apart from a comparable helper, which God determined Adam needed – not Adam! Eve was God's ideal completion and comparable helper for Adam. She was just what Adam needed! You might say it was a match made in heaven. They lived in a delightful garden called Eden, securely nestled in a love triangle with God. In this picture, we see a reflection of the Godhead, known as the Trinity.

Earthly marriage should reflect the Godhead's unique oneness, love, intimacy, submission, and fellowship. Ideally, it should reflect the never-ending unity and love which is shared perpetually between God the Father, God the Son, and God the Holy Spirit. That's the Godhead - the Trinity - sometimes referred to as the Three in One - equal in nature and importance, yet still three persons. They are united in a common goal or purpose, each with a uniquely important role, yet always supporting each other and the common goal.

Similarly, through our marriage union, and under God's headship, we are united as one flesh and operate in love and unity with a common goal and purpose. Each spouse endeavoring to fulfill his and her God-ordained roles and purposes with God's help. Each partner is faithfully supporting, nurturing, and protecting the gifts and individual uniqueness which makes their spouse who God created them to be. Submission within the Trinity was and is always present. Jesus submits to God, and the Holy Spirit submits to Jesus and also to God.

In a Godly marriage, the husband submits to God's authority, and likewise, the wife submits to her husband as God has commanded in scripture. The wife's submission to her husband is "…as to the Lord" (Ephesians 5:22). We will examine these Godly principles throughout our weeks of study. Generally speaking, we enhance each other's lives through thick and thin, remembering our perfection is found in Christ and Christ alone. Our perfection is complete in what He has accomplished on our behalf. None of us is perfect. Nonetheless, we are to love each other in a way which pleases God. That's the key. We accomplish this through Godly submission – by His grace and for His glory. Not to oversimply, but instead, to get a visual, let's look at two examples:

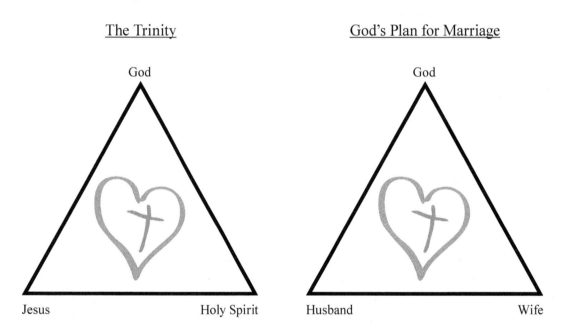

As we examine the illustrations, the left triangle represents The Trinity. The right triangle represents God's plan for marriage - a reflection of the Trinity. Notice God at the top of each diagram. He is God the Father within the Trinity, and within the scope of marriage, He is the ultimate authority. After all, marriage was and is His plan. He created it to bless us and fulfill His purposes. The second member of the Trinity is Jesus, God the Son, and He submits to the authority of God. Although Jesus is one with the Father and equal in power along with God and the Holy Spirit, scripture reminds us in John 5:19 and 1 Corinthians 15:28, Jesus is submitted to the Father. Likewise, the Holy Spirit, equal in purpose and power submits to both Jesus and God the Father and draws no attention to Himself. It is His purpose and pleasure to perpetually point everyone to God the Son, who is our Lord Jesus. Another of His distinct roles is to awaken God's Word within us. He opens up scripture to us so we can understand what God's Word says. He also protects it, seals it within our hearts, and brings it to performance in our lives. How so? He lovingly convicts us of sin and leads us to repentance. He empowers us to long for righteousness and pursue it. It's interesting to note; He was there hovering over God's Word, protecting it, and empowering it, from the very beginning – "In the beginning God created…" Genesis 1:1. Notice the power in creation. Search Genesis 1, and you will discover His work. The apostle John reminds us, "It is the Spirit who gives life" (John 6:63). He resides within us, and we have a witness or testimony of His presence. Therefore, we can know with certainty; we are a child of God.

In our natural marriage, the husband is a picture and type of Christ. He is submitted to God, and although equal to you, his role and responsibilities are somewhat different. He is called to lead and guide the family under God's headship and will be held accountable for the outcome. The Holy Spirit represents you, the wife as the *comparable helper*. Remember, the Holy Spirit brings the physical and spiritual help in addition to comfort, direction, peace, and aid to every situation. We carry out the will of God by coming alongside our husbands to aid them as they accomplish the work God has prepared for them before the world's foundation.

The cross and heart occupy the middle of each trinagle as a reminder of the love, unity, fellowship, and sacrifice at the center of both the Trinity and every ideal marriage. Love always calls for sacrifice and Jesus paid the premium - the ultimate price. In fact, all of the members of the Trinity sacrificed on our behalf. It is a Trinitarian plan and miracle from God every time a sinner comes to faith. To that end, we owe a debt which can only be satisfied through our faith, love, and devotion. We must yeild to Him. Paul says we have a reasonable service to present our bodies "as a living sacrifice, holy, acceptable to God…" (Romans 12:1). We will not know this side of heaven the full measure or depth of sacrifice our salvation cost each member of the Trinity. Scripture has provided through the inspiration of God's Holy Spirit, what we need to know about God and His eternal plan. Namely, the unveiling or ever-increasing revelation of Jesus Christ as our Lord and Savior who died so we could live and be reconciled to God.

So that was the beginning, in the beginning. A man and woman uniquely created by God existed in a love triangle with Him. He ordains marriage and officiates the first wedding in Genesis 2:24-25. Who designed marriage and called it into existence? Our Lord God! And then, tragically, our struggles began. The original sin is man's rebellion against God. We will unpack this in our study guide. Not to oversimplify, but we have pushed against God by rebelling against His word from the garden. We have wanted to be god and make our own decisions instead of obeying God and following His instructions. The truth of it is this. The faithful are obedient. People of great faith obey God – regardless! They do so without regard to the circumstances or consequences. They trust God, respond obediently, and leave the results to Him. Jesus said, "If you love Me, keep My commandments." (John 14:15).

What Did Eve Get Right And Wrong?

She got it all right except biting the apple. Scripture does not record any other sin or rebellion concerning Eve. She bought into the lie of the enemy, and everything changed in a second. From the garden, right at the beginning of God's creation story, we messed up. Your study guide will help you navigate this remarkable segment of scripture. It will be an exciting exercise. Suffice it to say, you will be amazed as you study. Throughout history, people have blamed this entire event on Eve, but that's not how God saw it.

The Enemy In The Garden.

In Genesis 3, Eve encountered an enemy lurking in the garden. The chapter begins:

Now the serpent was more cunning than any beast of the field which the Lord God had made. And he said to the woman, "Has God indeed said, 'You shall not eat of every tree of the garden'?" (Genesis3:1).

Do you see the enemy's subtle tactic? Satan sets the bait by calling God's motives into question. Just so you know, he is still calling God's motives into question, even today. That's why it's critical for us to know and understand God's Word. When we hear the truth, we know it! If we move one small measure from the truth, it is no longer true. As believers, we must know God's Word, receive it in our hearts, and respond accordingly. Remember, the faithful are obedient! God has provided all we need for life and godliness in His word. Quite frankly, everything else is mere commentary!

Eve's Response.

Genesis 3:2-3, And the woman said to the serpent, "We may eat the fruit of the trees of the garden; but of the fruit of the tree which is in the midst of the garden, God has said, 'You shall not eat it, nor shall you touch it, lest you die.'"

Eve takes the bait, literally, and bites the apple. Then, Adam follows suit and bites too. The apple is twice bitten. Two wrongs never make a right. Ultimately, a merciful God casts them out of the delightful garden called Eden.

Back To The Trinity.

Commentators agree Adam and Eve were both out of order when they bit the apple. First, Eve assumed the lead, ignoring Adam's authority and God-ordained headship. Next, Adam willfully ignored the voice of God, following his wife into sin, instead of leading her to safety. But, I believe it went beyond these basic statements. First, Eve was determined. Once she transgressed outside the protective covering of Adam, the tasty fruit was simply too alluring to pass up. In other words, she had to have what her eye coveted. She wanted to see beyond what God had provided. Essentially, she wanted to be god instead of yielding to God. That's the original sin. When the fruit proved to be tasty, she delighted to share it with her husband. So, Adam ate it. But I believe in so doing, Adam sacrificed on her behalf. He deliberately chose to eat the forbidden fruit, whereas, Eve was deceived. Surely he understood there would be consequences associated with his actions. How could he not? God had given him clear instruction. Your study guide will help you navigate these passages. Tragically Adam sinned, too. Undoubtedly, God exposes marital authority, by calling Adam to account for Eve's sinful behavior. Could it be Adam's love for Eve was so great that he chose to bite the apple? Although He enjoyed resplendent fellowship with God, Eve made him complete and attended his physical and emotional needs as well. Perhaps Adam couldn't bear the thought of his beautiful Eve becoming an outcast. Surely, Adam could not consider his Eve outside the delightful garden alone. For Adam, it was simply unthinkable.

The First and Second Adam.

What imagery! It's a beautiful picture of our Lord Jesus - God the Son of the Trinity, who did not leave us alone to shoulder the responsibility of our sins - either. He was willing to vacate His throne, the majesty and glory of heaven, and the presence of God so we could be saved. Do you remember what He feared most? Not the pain, abuse, insults, or ridicule. Jesus feared being separated from God when He hung on the cross. Nonetheless, He came into agreement with God in the Garden of Gethsemane praying, "Father, if you are willing, take this cup from me; yet not my will, but yours be done." (Luke 22:42) (NIV). It's the most beautiful sacrifice; the greatest act of love, ever - since the beginning of time. Jesus died for our sins. His death on Calvary radically changed the course of history. Not only finishing Satan, and opening our communication with God in heaven, but reconciling us to Him, and altering our eternal destiny as well. Undoubtedly, a divine Trinitarian plan straight from God's throne. Only a loving Godhead could unite to bring everlasting life from the death of a sacrificial lamb – Jesus. But it's true. United in love, passion, and purpose, this was their plan from eternity past. To reconcile sinful man to God and love us into the kingdom.

How Did God's Love Redeem It All?

God is in the business of redemption. That's His job. In essence, it's who He is. He is a Redeemer - Our Redeemer! Week after week, we will examine His redemptive love in the lives of woman in our study. Not if we mess up, but when we mess up, He will redeem. Paul reminds us of God's redemptive work. "And we know that all things work together for good to those who love God, to those who are the called according to His purpose." (Romans 8:28). This verse could well be the theme for our entire study. Incidentally, you will find an appropriate memory verse at the beginning of each lesson. You are encouraged to commit them to memory. If they are written on your heart, they will remain and can never be taken from you.

A Promise-Keeping God.

As Adam and Eve departed the garden, God gave Eve a promise to store in her heart. Then He graciously gave her the faith to believe it. How incredibly merciful is God's work? Let's take a look at the "first gospel" message in scripture:

> "And I will put enmity
> Between you and the woman,
> And between your seed and her Seed;
> He shall bruise your head,
> And you shall bruise His heel." (Genesis 3:15).

Eve heard good news! Not to oversimply the gospel message, but Eve heard God's plan of redemption. He would redeem her, bless her with children, and a descendant of hers would defeat Satan. God had made a way, not only for Adam and Eve but for all who believe. Notice, she had sinned, and Adam, too, but God's grace abounded more!

A merciful God never leaves us or abandons us in our despair. God was not surprised when the serpent lurking in the garden deceived Eve. He knew Adam and Eve would mess up. He knows we will mess up, too. Nevertheless, from before the foundation of the world, God has planned to redeem us – to save us! He is still saving to the uttermost and redeems us daily. He is a faithful, promise-keeping God!

On that note, has God given you a promise and the faith and confidence to believe it? I think He has. We will go over all this in your study guide. If you are doing this study within a group, you will have many opportunities to share. Your testimonies are welcome in this study! You are encouraged to do the work. It's when and where we grow. We can anticipate thrilling victory and personal growth as we explore God's redemptive work throughout our study.

It's Your Turn.

Before you turn to your study guide, complete the blank love triangle which follows. If you are married, you may refer back to the illustration of Adam and Eve's marriage. If you are not married, do the same thing, but place Jesus in the second place of the Trinity. Until God brings you a mate, you are married to Him. Next, draw a heart and cross to fill the interior. The love of Jesus, the sacrifice of Jesus, and submission of Jesus must fill your heart. He must be the center and the heart of all Christian marriages. We must look to the cross daily and recall all He has done on our behalf. In light of that, is there anything you cannot give or forgive, whatever the situation might require, for the sake of harmony, fellowship, and unity within your marriage? Remember Jesus has paid it all. He has forgiven you all things and desires you and your husband enjoy intimate love and fellowship. As as well as peace and unity that reflects the Trinity. After all, until His return, we are God's chosen purveyors of truth, love, and goodness on the earth.

In the beginning of the Bible, God revealed His plan for marriage, and the study of Eve includes that plan. If you're married or have the desire to marry, thank God for His perfect plan. Remember, marriage is a divine gift from heaven. Regard it as such and protect it under His watchful eye and instruction from scripture. It's as close to heaven as we will get on earth!

With that in mind, enjoy your husband and love him unreservedly. Pray for him, and submit to his God-ordained authority. Not married yet? Pray for your future husband. It's never too early to pray for God's will and blessings – start today. Many women have used Colossians 1:9-12 to guide these prayers. Remember, it is not your job to make your husband a better man. Let God do His perfect work and trust Him. Then you are at liberty to love and enjoy your husband and serve him with gladness, minus anxiety or fear. Allow God to use your submission and faithfulness in his life as He sees fit. He will do it. As troubles come, refer to scripture. Take all matters to the cross, and prayerfully submit yourself accordingly. It's God's will for your life and marriage in Christ Jesus! Please complete your love triangle below.

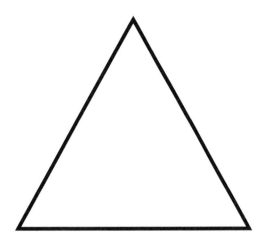

Be blessed this week as you study Eve: Mother Of All Living

Next Week – Sarah: Believing The Promise

Eve's story unfolds in Genesis 2 – 3. She is referenced in 2 Corinthians 11:3; and 1Timothy 2:13

Eve: Mother Of All Living

Day One: Who is Eve?

Memory Verse: 1 Corinthians 11:9 Nor was man created for the woman, but woman for the man.

Eve has the distinction of being the first woman ever known and loved by God. She was explicitly made for Adam. Adam had absolutely no difficulty recognizing his rib when he saw her. Adam loved Eve, and God welcomed marriage into the universe. God not only attended this wedding, He officiated over it.

1. Read Psalm 139:14, how are we made? What does this verse suggest we are to do in light of that?

fearfully & wonderfully made. We should have great love & respect for ourselves.

2. Reflecting more on Psalm 139:14, what does the soul know? What does that mean? Does it bring another scripture to your mind?

that God's works are wonderful. Everything he does is good. When He made Adam & Eve in Genesis & it was good.

3. Genesis 1:27 defines an element of purpose in our creation. What did God intend to do?

To create man & woman in His image. "male & female" were to both reflect the image of God.

4. From Genesis 1:27 complete this thought: "... __male__ and __female__ He created them." It appears from this verse God had a plan to create Eve all along. She was certainly no afterthought. How does this reassure you?

That God had equally planned + purposed women, as much as man.

5. Thinking biblically, why do you suppose God made Adam first? Is this significant to you, personally? Why or why not? If possible, please link your thought or idea to a verse of scripture.

Because he was to be the "head", just like Jesus Christ is the head of the church (the bride)

Col 1:18 "Christ is also the head of the church, which is his body..."

6. In Genesis 2:16, God desired a comparable helper for Adam. What does helper mean in this scripture?

helper

7. We know God makes no mistakes, and He's a God of love. With a biblical understanding of helper, how does this make you feel? Is your heart in line with God's plan? Why or why not?

I feel good about it because He still intended Adam + Eve to be a team + together multiply + subdue the earth. Yes because I know Ryan is to love me like Christ loves the church

8. Paul spoke with passion and authority about the marital structure. Read 1 Corinthians 11:3-9 and answer the following questions:

a. Review 1 Corinthians 11:3. Can you identify the Godhead? Who are the members? For further confirmation, read and record John's words from 1 John 5:7.

(Father, Son + Holy Spirit) God is the head of Christ, Christ the head of man, man the head of woman. There are three.

b. Can you identify the divine design reflected in the order of God's creation of male and female in 1 Corinthians 11:7-8? What is it?

He created male first, then female from male

c. According to Paul, what is the purpose of woman in regards to man in 1 Corinthians 11:9?

woman was created "for man"

Meditation
Ephesians 1:4 …just as He chose us in Him before the foundation of the world, that we should be holy and without blame before Him in love

Eve: Mother Of All Living

Day Two: Where Is Eve In God's Redemption Story?

Memory Verse: 1 Corinthians 11:9 Nor was man created for the woman, but woman for the man.

As we look at Eve's place in the grand redemption story, what about yours? Where are you, physically and spiritually, in God's immense redemption story? Wherever you are, it is no surprise to our Heavenly Father. In fact, it is by His sovereignty you are where you are. Once we grasp the fact we are not independent of Him, even in our decisions, it lightens our load. Today's lesson will focus on the delightful garden called Eden and the enemy lurking in the bushes.

1. Read Genesis 2:8-14. Although the exact location of Eden is unknown, what do these verses tell us about the garden and its location? List its boundaries.

There were all kinds of trees w/ the tree of life in the middle & tree of the knowledge of good & evil; a river watering the garden was separated into 4 head waters

2. There are two trees located in the midst of the garden. What were they? And what did they represent? List your scripture reference with your answer.

Tree of life: eternal life w/ God
Tree of the knowledge of good & evil: the tree they were forbidden to eat (to be like God)
vs. 9

3. Thinking biblically, why do you think God set these limitations? Are the boundaries excessive?

To give them a choice

4. The enemy entered the Garden some place between Genesis 1:31, when God saw everything was very good and Genesis 3:1. How did he appear to Eve?

He approached her about the tree — questioning God. "Did God really say...?" Ch 3 v 1

5. How do 1 Peter 5:8 and Revelation 12:9 describe Satan? Write the verses, underlining all the words which define him.

1 Peter 5:8 - *"Be self-controlled and alert. Your <u>enemy</u> the <u>devil</u> prowls around like a <u>roaring lion looking</u> for someone to devour."*

Revelation 12:9 - *"The great <u>dragon</u> was <u>hurled down</u> — the <u>ancient serpent</u> called the <u>devil</u>, or <u>Satan</u>, who leads the whole world astray. He was hurled to the earth + his angels with him."*

We have an adversary. Eve found this out the hard way. We have been forewarned. Read Ephesians 6:10-18 to answer the remaining questions:

6. From Ephesians 6:10, where does our help come from and in what form?

the Lord ~ in his mighty power

7. From Ephesians 6:11, what are we recommended to do and why?

put on the full armor of God to take a stand against the devil's schemes.

8. From verse 6:12, how is our enemy defined?

- *the rulers, authorities, + powers of this dark world*
- *spiritual forces of evil*

9. How has he deceived you or hindered your walk? The most hurtful attacks sometimes come from family. Has the enemy used your family to attack your faith?

He has accused me + lied to me about who I am. He's used my weaknesses to try to define me.

10. Fill in the appropriate blanks from Ephesians 6:13-18 (NKJV).

Therefore take up the whole armor of God, that you may be able to withstand in the evil day, and having done all, __to stand__. 14 __Stand firm__ therefore, having girded your waist with __the belt of truth__ having put on the __breastplate__ of __righteousness__, 15 and having shod your feet with the preparation of the __gospel__ of __peace__; 16 above all, taking the __shield__ of __faith__ with which you will be able to quench all the fiery darts of the wicked one. 17 And take the helmet of ___salvation___, and the ___sword___ of the Spirit, which is the word of God; 18 ___On all occasions___ with all prayer and supplication in the Spirit, being ___alert___ to this end with all ___prayer___ and ___supplication___ for all the saints -

Meditation
Psalm 119:114 You are my hiding place and my shield; I hope in Your word.

Eve: Mother Of All Living

Day Three: What Did Eve Get Right?

Memory Verse:1 Corinthians 11:9 Nor was man created for the woman, but woman for the man.

Eve's journey began extraordinarily. From her beginning, she was a full-grown woman, in every regard. She was called forth, equipped, and fitted for everything God desired, including marriage, which took place almost immediately. I can promise you; nothing was lacking in Eve. Nothing was left to chance. Her creator, Our Lord God, had provided all she needed to be successful. She and Adam existed in a love triangle with God in the midst of a garden called delightful. Sounds like paradise, indeed!

She had a strong start. Commentators agree it was not long before the serpent deceived her. While tomorrow's lesson focuses on the deception, today's lesson encourages our spiritual fitness as we prepare to stand firm against the enemy. It's a valuable lesson.

Read Matthew 4:1-11 and answer the questions:

1. What happended in Matthew 4:1?

2. If Jesus could be tempted, how much more can we? What did the enemy say and how did Jesus respond? Matthew 4:2-4. Where did Jesus' words come from?

3. Satan planned to lure Jesus away from the purposes of God. It's His plan for us as well. How has the enemy lured you away from the purposes of God? Use one or two words to describe his tactics. Did he succeed? Ex.: pleasure (passion), position, or possession.

4. The tempter's tactics fall into three categories. They are lust of the flesh (verses 2, 3); lust of the eyes (verses 8, 9); and pride of life (verses 5, 6). After review of these verses, in which category do you believe you would most likely fall?

5. Jesus battles His adversary with the word of God. In this exercise, write a verse below which will protect you from the category you listed in question 4 above.

6. The enemy can never have you. You are secure in Christ. The mighty grip of God holds you securely! Thinking biblically, list the steps you could take to strengthen yourself in preparation for the enemy's work? Use scripture. Please identify the verse.

7. The enemy cannot read our minds; he does not possess the omniscience of Christ. He can, however, hear our words, observe our body language, and see the way we live. What does the book of James tell us about our lives and the importance of living out what we confess with our lips?

8. Willful disobedience and sloppy living will destroy our testimony. And, what is at stake? The Gospel. How do you plan to safeguard yourself going forward? What three steps will you take?

1.

2.

3.

Meditation
Philippians 4:13 I can do all things through Christ who strengthens me.

Eve: Mother Of All Living

Day Four: What Did Eve Get Wrong?

Memory Verse:1 Corinthians 11:9 Nor was man created for the woman, but woman for the man.

We all make mistakes, none of us is perfect. All thanks and glory to God, we have the righteousness of Christ Jesus. Because of all Jesus has done we are as pure as the driven snow. Our sins have been cast as far as the east is from the west. God remembers our sins no more. What a marvelous gift for us.

Day four is about a fall - a hard fall. A fall that is still being talked about more than 6,000 years later. Without God's remedy, we would forever be falling, hopelessly, and reeling from sins' repercussions. The bottom line is, Eve was deceived. The good news is God provided a promise and gave her the faith to believe. We will get to the promise in tomorrow's lesson. For now, let's look at what happened that fateful day in the garden called delightful.

1. Reading from Genesis 3:1, what words describe the serpent who entered the Garden? Thinking biblically, did this surprise God? Yes or no? Give a scripture reference to support your answer.

2. What did the serpent ask? What was Eve's response? verses 1-3

3. What does 1 John 3:8 tell us about the Christ-child born in Bethlehem? About Satan's motivation?

4. Eve was deceived. Using a dictionary, write a definition for *"deceive."* Have you ever been deceived? What was the outcome?

5. We know Eve was deceived. List a safeguard we have at our disposal as believers. Identify the appropriate scripture to support the safeguard.

6. Why do you think Eve was the object of Satan's attack? Was she better prey? Do you believe the enemy's attack was avoidable? If so, what does your belief demonstrate regarding the sovereignty of God?

Anne Nicholson

7. Satan called God's word into question. He cunningly represented himself as an angel of light, better equipped to interpret God's Word. Beware of those who would try to deceive you concerning God's word. How did Paul describe them in 2 Corinthians 11:13-15?

8. Read Genesis 3:2-3. God has provided all we need. Why do you think Eve felt the need to embellish on God's already generous provision?

9. Satan's motivation has always been to challenge God's authority. We do the same thing. It's the original sin. Having embraced the deception, Eve bit the apple. Next, she did the unthinkable and offered it to Adam. The New Testament confirms Eve was deceived. However, Adam ate! It was a direct transgression without deception. What was Adam thinking? Why do you think Adam bit the apple?

Satan: Genesis 3:6 tells it all. Eve saw the tree appeared to look good to the eye, yielded tasty fruit and was desirable to make one wise. In other words, the apple looked satisfying to the flesh in every way. It met all three criteria: lust of the eyes, (it was pleasing to the eye), lust of the flesh (it looked good for food - it appeared tasty), and pride of life (it was desirable to make one wise). Check, check, check! How cunning, indeed! Satan had met all the criteria to deceive his victim. The apple was enticing and appeared gratifying, worthy, and pleasurable in every sense. Beware of the enemy, he is out to deceive you as well. Get up each day and clothe yourself in the full armor of God. And, when he comes, your defense is God's Word. The enemy is no match for the Word of God.

10. In closing, prayerfully read the words of Jesus from John 8:44. Beginning with the second sentence of the verse, complete the following.

John 8:44 ...He was a _____ from the beginning, and does not stand in the _____, because there is _____ _____ _____ _____. When he speaks a _____, he speaks from his own _____, for he is a _____ and the _____ of it.

Meditation
Mark 13:5 And Jesus, answering them, began to say: "Take heed that no one deceives you."

Eve: Mother Of All Living

Day Five: How Did God's Love Redeem It All?

Memory Verse:1 Corinthians 11:9 Nor was man created for the woman, but woman for the man.

1. Read Genesis 3:7-9. List the five occurrences after Adam and Eve bit the apple from verses 7-8. What did God ask in verse 9?

1.

2.

3.

4.

5.

v. 9 –

2. Read Genesis 3:10-12. Notice, Adam was afraid, but there was no confession. Without confession there is no repentance, without repentance, there is no forgiveness. Sin is not what condemns us; it is our unconfessed, unrepentant sin. God can never restore us in an unrepentant state. That has been humanity's prideful sin from the garden. We see it here. If needed, take a minute to confess and receive forgiveness. It is always the appropriate time to confess before the Lord. Do it daily!

3. What was Adam's unrepentant response to God in Genesis 3:12? What was Eve's from verse 13? What does Paul tell us in 1 Timothy 2:14? In your opinion, who was the guiltier party?

4. Consequences follow sin. Similarly, blessings follow obedience. The serpent is not the subject of our study, although God pronounced curses upon him in Genesis 3:13-14. In verse 15, God gave a promise. Read and record Genesis 3:15 below. Locate God's promise and underline it.

5. From Genesis 3:16, note the word *desire*. It doesn't mean what you might think. *Desire* in this sense means *to usurp your husband's authority and seek to rule over him*. That's a sin. The relational battle of the sexes began in the garden. If you are married, God has given headship to your husband and not to you. We sin when we desire or covet what God has not ordained for us. Take a moment and prayerfully consider your submission to God's plan. If you are out of order, stop, confess and pray. Now is the perfect time to come into agreement with God!

6. God not only created marriage, but He also had a plan for its success. It was to reflect the love and unity of the Trinity as well as Christ's perfect and sacrificial love for His Bride, the Church. In short, marriage was a blessing from God. Read Ephesians 5:22-25. List the key points from each verse. These passages outline aspects of Godly submission as they relate to marriage. If you struggle with submission, you are not alone. Most of us have at one time or another. Practicing God-honoring submission is liberating and brings great joy and freedom, as well as harmony within the home. If you're struggling, trust Him. He will give you the grace to embrace Godly submission.

v. 22

v. 23

v. 24

v. 25

7. Eve was given a rich promise within the curse. "Her seed" in Genesis 3:15, referred to Christ, her descendents, and all those in Him. God would redeem her and give her purpose. Although Eve had fallen, she had not fallen beyond the grace of God. This should give you hope. She would have children and from them, one would crush the head of Satan. God then gave her the grace to believe the promise. Has God given you a promise from scripture? If so, write it down. Ask Him for the grace to believe Romans 8:28. Write the verse below.

8. Adam turned his back on the voice of God. In Genesis 3:17, God said something interesting to Adam about Eve. What was it?

9. Take notice. God initially addressed Adam, not Eve, concerning their sin. Another indication God is serious about headship and family order. God certainly knew what happened, yet He called Adam into account. If you are married, your husband will be held accountable for the state of your marriage. Are you both prayerfully submitted to God's plan? If not, what steps do you plan to take to realign your hearts with God? Remember, disobedience to God is not only sin, it shows a lack of faith. Those of great faith obey God. They trust Him fearlessly and obediently, leaving the results to Him. If you are single, the same applies to you. You are called to submit to Christ, in all things.

Epilogue.

God was faithful, just as He promised. Although sin had entered the delightful garden, bringing chaos and disharmony into God's original plan, He restored order. He pronounced consequences to their sinful disobedience and moved them forward. God never leaves us where we are. He is continually at work to redeem us and put us back on track. As a consequence, Adam and Eve had to leave the garden, and could never return, but God never left them. Their union did produce children, and although Cain killed Abel, God redeemed it, by giving Eve another son, Seth. God was faithful to His promise, and from this line, Christ came. So even in the beginning, we can see God had a plan to save us from ourselves. What an awesome God we serve!

Meditation
Acts 5:29 But Peter and the other apostles answered and said: "We ought to obey God rather than men."

Notes – Eve: Mother Of All Living

Sarah

Sarah: Believing The Promise

As a missionary, I've been moved by God many times. I can relate to Sarah. I have said goodbye to friends and family, repeatedly, as God called us to new cities or countries to accomplish His plan and purposes. At times, our foreign service required lengthy separation from family and friends for several years. Was it fearful? Not as much as you might think. It was quite thrilling to have a new adventure and challenges with every call. Bear in mind; God accomplished this. He gave me a missionary heart as well as the call and passion for placing His word and discipleship of others before my personal preferences, pleasures, and pursuits. I could never have walked this path apart from deep faith and fellowship with Jesus. Only God can make a missionary heart. Is it in your future? Only He knows for sure. But if it is, He will prepare you, equip you, and provide everything. As we studied last week, where God guides, He provides! Remember, if it is God's call for you, you will have all you need.

I smile as I write those words because as a child I didn't like spending the night away from home. Isn't it just like God to do the most radical and unexpected thing? You might well imagine not many little girls have confessed, "When I grow up, I want to be a missionary!" It was never in my heart or mind until God revealed it. God does amazing things in and through us when He saves us. Here's another example. Not long after my salvation, I would catch myself saying or thinking curious things - things very much unlike me. That is the me I'd always known. These things would astonish me so much I'd ponder their origin. You see, I was the most selfish of women before I was born of God's Spirit. I was the quintessential 80's girl! It was indeed all about me! That's part of the reason this has been such a terrific journey. As God would have it, my focus is now on others and not myself. It's become about God's plan and purposes and not my own. And that my friends, is an extraordinary miracle! God accomplishes unfathomable things when He saves us by His grace and for His glory.

Remember, from the time God envisioned you in His mind, and fashioned you (yāṣar), He had a plan and purpose for you. He saw the total number of your days before there was one. Psalm 139:16. At the appointed time you had a natural birth over which you had no control, and if you're saved, your rebirth occurred at His appointed time as well. At the very moment it suited God's plan and purposes you collided with the Holy God - the Great I AM - the Creator of heaven and earth! One minute you were without His Spirit or witness of His presence, and the next moment you were filled with Him. Your entire life and destiny changed in an instant. This reality leads us to the point of Sarah's story. God enabled her to be on board with Abraham. He had a plan to move them to a particular location so they could testify of Him. They were to be His witness to a dying world of lost people. Idol worshippers and pagans were living in the land! If you're saved, you're also called to be His witness. Acts 1:8. Incidentally, there are still idol worshippers and pagans living in the land! In fact, they're everywhere!

God Moves Us.

God has moved me, and He moved Sarah. It is unlikely, however, God will call you to the foreign mission field if you have not effectively ministered next door or across the street. God knew what type of wife Sarah was. He knew of her love and faithful devotion to Abraham. We shall see in our study she reverently referred to him as "lord"! If you're married, how many of you call your husband lord? Perhaps some of you don't speak to him at all unless it's absolutely necessary. If that's the case, you won't be the one going - next door, across the street, or across the world. God chooses to use people who are yielded to Him and submitted to His Word. He generally likes to use the ones who are on board with His plan and aligned with His Word. Albeit true, there are some random cases in scripture when God chose to do otherwise. In so doing, you can rest assured, He governed and guided their participation and activity. His plan will not be thwarted. God always wins!

Sarah Was Right For The Job.

God knew Sarah was perfect for the job. She was already an adoring *helper ('ēzer)* for Abraham.

You see, missionary service always begins at home. Even the disciples were called to Jerusalem first! Just in case you don't know, it's the missionary's hardest ground to conquer - the home turf. Having the home field advantage in sports might be a good thing. In ministry, some consider it a disadvantage. Why? Because your family members know you, and they know you well. You have a long history with them. If your salvation occurred later in life, like mine, they remember you before your call and conversion. They have seen the good, the bad, and the regrettable ugly of your life. We can't hide from them! Truth be told, if you can efficiently minister there, you can minister anywhere!

Even Jesus was not received in the town of his youth, Nazareth. You may recall, an angry mob wanted to throw Him off the nearest cliff. You can read this exciting story in Luke 4:16-30. Perhaps you've experienced the same reception among your family members. Why? I believe, sometimes, those who know us best have a difficult time understanding when God saves us, He makes us new creatures IN HIM. The naysayers and critics have a hard time embracing our newfound humility and joy, or passion and faithfulness as authentic. It will take time. Initially, they may be skeptical, mainly if they are not believers, or are not walking faithfully with Jesus. I find it interesting these are the ones who want all the grace God is willing to extend to them, but are unwilling to offer a sliver to you. Perhaps you've found the same to be true.

Regardless of what others might think, as His Spirit takes up residence or abides in us, He transforms us. It's called sanctification. These changes are always for the better and have a divine purpose. You might say He changes us from the inside out! Over time, we have His heart and mind and are useful to His plan and eternal purposes. Then we are prepared to "go with God." I'll sum it up like this. If He desires that you go, He will surely accomplish everything necessary to send you. Just like He did Sarah and me. Until then…

Keep Looking Unto Jesus.

Keep your eyes on Jesus! Being His is the most thrilling journey. He has the whole world in His hands which makes my missionary heart melt. If it's in His hands, it's in His heart and His view. How delicious - that makes it our oyster. He still wants to save the world. "For God so loved the world that He gave His only begotten Son, that whoever believes in Him should not perish but have everlasting life." (John 3:16). There are countless "whoever's" still out there. Many are still waiting to hear the Good News! Being used by Him is my highest honor and privilege. It is an exciting journey from start to finish, wherever you serve! Our fellowship with Jesus is unlimited and so are His plans. He will do everything necessary to save the least and the lost. To that account, Jesus paid it all.

Who Is Sarah?

Her given name is *Sarai* which means *princess*. In her culture, this was not a name given to ordinary folk. It identifies her as a member of a noble or honored family. Tradition holds she was a refined woman of stature, grace, and elegance. She was probably well educated. She came from Ur of the Chaldeans. Historians agree even for Sarah's day it was a thriving center of culture, science, and education.

An Unsurpassed Beauty.

Thankfully, outward beauty is not a prerequisite for those God chooses, calls, and saves. Salvation is ours because we believe not because we're beautiful. Scripture assures us, God looks at the heart. (1 Samuel 16:7.) That's why it's compelling to see Sarah's beauty is expressly recorded in scripture. Apparently, she was a stunning beauty; so gorgeous that her husband fearfully lied about her identity and their relationship, not once, but twice. I must confess, perhaps I have not personally known any woman of such stunning beauty. However, our study will reveal God used her incredible beauty remarkably. I'll give you a hint. He used it to bless their marriage as well as to discipline Abraham. That's right! God used Sarah's beauty to reveal an area of Abraham's life which needed not only exposure, but careful examination and change.

One commentator suggested Sarah holds the distinction of being the only woman who was like fine wine. She got remarkably better with age! I find that astounding! Makes getting older seem a little more exciting, doesn't it? So that you know, I'm talking exceedingly better! Our Sarah was a show stopper, a sight to behold and with every passing year, she got better and better. Sarah was still turning heads at the age of 89. In fact, one day she turned the head of a king. When he beheld her, nothing else satisfied his lustful eye, and King Abimelech had to have her for himself. Believe it or not, with Abraham's blessing, his beautiful wife, and princess, Sarah, was added to the king's harem! How astonishing is that?

Jewish tradition teaches Eve was the most beautiful of all women, and Sarah was a close second. She possessed beauty unequaled in her day. It is no wonder Sarah caught Abraham's eye. Well, that coupled with the fact she was his little sister. That's right, Sarah married her older – handsome, and esteemed half-brother, Abraham. Although he sounds like an excellent catch, how could she marry her brother?

Well for starters, Abraham and Sarah had the same father, Terah, but not the same mother. Remember, this was a place and time in history when having more than one wife was reasonably typical. Therefore, Terah was in good company. Although it appears odd to us, falling in love and marrying a half-sibling was not an oddity either. Many little girls have experienced childhood crushes on their older brothers, but time has moved us well beyond those youthful attractions. Nonetheless, their faithful love would last a lifetime. Abraham was ten years her senior. She most probably knew him well. You might say she grew up right under his watchful eye. They were most likely raised in separate households but lived in the same community. When were they married? We don't know for sure, but scripture references their marriage in Genesis 11:29.

Called By God.

Abraham's call from God was astounding and unprecedented. The community was not acquainted with the God Abraham and Sarah set out to follow. I find it even more astonishing she went with him. Why? Abraham had no idea where he was going, or if, and when they would return.

I would have liked to be present for that discussion, wouldn't you? I imagine that the dialogue went somewhat like this:

Abraham: Sarah get your coat and all the things you might need, we're leaving Ur.

Sarah: Where are we going? And, how long will we be gone?

Abraham: I don't have an answer to either question. But, we are going! We are being called by God to someplace, and I'm not sure where, but I'll know it when we get there. God will guide us.

Sarah: What God? Nanna, the moon God?

Abraham: No, Sarah, "the Lord!"

Sarah: What!!!???? So, let me get this straight. We are leaving the only home we've ever known, and we're going to a place you don't know. And, we are doing so at the request of a God no one's heard of and no one knows?

Abraham: That's right, Sarah, I'll get the camel, you get your coat!

I know it wasn't quite like that, but I do find it interesting to consider what it must have been like to get word from Abraham he'd not only been called by God but called by a God no one knows. Thankfully, when we received our initial call, I knew who had called and where we were headed. Of course, I couldn't conceive everything God would accomplish through our going, but I knew our call was authentic. We had confirmation God was calling us to full-time missionary service.

I also know, generally speaking, women like information. We are just curious that way. There's always much to consider with every move. Will medical exams, shots and traveling documents or passports be required? What about the climate? It helps to know if the climate will be suitable for snow skiing and ice skating or swimming and sunbathing. Little details matter. Skis take up a lot more room in the suitcase than a bikini and flip-flops. Depending upon the duration of the call and its projected outcome, we might want to plan a bon voyage party, meet with the mission's board, and or speak to local churches to raise support and solicit prayer for the journey. Additionally, personal things must be considered too. Saying goodbye to family and friends, boarding the dogs, if need be. Details like interviewing renters to occupy the home in your absence must be talked about and prayed through. If you are traveling by car, it must be serviced, and reservations for overnight stays along the way must be obtained. The bottom line is although scripture doesn't go into detail about it, Abraham and Sarah were living full lives in Ur before their call. They undoubtedly had responsibilities and commitments ongoing up to their spiritual awakening. They were doing life there – every day. Abraham wasn't merely sitting on a stump looking heavenward and waiting on God to speak. No, not at all. Both of them were living life to the fullest and loving one another and others well, right up until one fateful day.

All missionaries had productive lives before answering God's call. We all had much to consider as well as much preparation at the onset. But, the thrill and excitement of saying "yes" to God puts everything in its proper perspective. Nothing, absolutely nothing compares to such a privilege. Knowing God has plans to save lost souls and include you in His work is sobering, indeed.

What could mean more than the salvation of a soul? Incidentally, it's all our work. Some go, and some stay – it's all up to God. Abraham and Sarah were going, we went too, but many others stayed behind and prayed. That's the primary work, and none is more important than that. I know firsthand what it takes to go, in the natural and in the spiritual. I can only imagine what Sarah prayerfully considered as she busily made ready and her heart overflowed with excitement. I know, too, God met her every moment of every day as she prayerfully prepared, trusting the significant tasks to Him. Our most extended service was two years on foreign soil – twice. I know what preparation it required. I can't begin to imagine the preparation for an unending adventure which could last throughout her lifetime! Thrilling indeed!

Answering God's Call.

Fortunately for me, with each call and move, God has provided me the necessary time. That's interesting because some of our relocations occurred within a month or six weeks. Even though I have simplified our story and tempered it with a humorous touch, a call from God is never anything but reverent, somber, and powerful. To receive a new call, as well as confirmation of each call, is thrilling. God has always handled every detail. Nothing was ever left to chance; nothing was left unconsidered or unimportant. If it mattered to me, it mattered to God, and thankfully, He had it figured out. My job was to submit to God, pray fervently, follow my husband's lead, and make wise choices which aligned my heart and plans with God's Word by His grace and for His glory, for the benefit of the gospel! The key was the heart and cross in the middle of our love triangle which is headed by God. We looked at this last week. Asking for the mind of Christ and recalling God's overarching plan for humanity, which is the salvation of the lost, was paramount. It has always been His plan and purpose to save the lost. It has been our call and primary focus from the beginning, sharing the love of God and His life-changing Word among the least and the lost. Loving others and desiring they come to saving faith has always been our focus – that and their discipleship. Thanks to God, with each move, foreign or domestic, every detail was handled by our most gracious Lord. Remember, where He guides, He provides!

The Journey Begins.

In Genesis 12, we find the couple's life-changing call was to a place they did not know. In fact, they had no idea where they were headed. Nor, did they understand all the benefits of why they were going. It happened that one day Abraham heard the voice of God, and from that moment forward everything changed. Let's review Abraham's initial call:

> "Now the Lord had said to Abram:
> "Get out of your country,
> From your family,
> And from your father's house,
> To a land that I will show you.
> I will make you a great nation;
> I will bless you,
> And make your name great;
> And you shall be a blessing.
> I will bless those who bless you,

And I will curse him who curses you
And in you, all the families of the earth shall be blessed." (Genesis 12:1-3).

It's incredible to realize that's all the information they had when God awakened them spiritually and enabled Abraham to hear and respond to His call. The fact that Sarah believed Abraham heard God correctly is even more astounding! It's incredibly amazing. Abraham was 75 years old when he heard the voice of God. Sarah was 65 when she believed it.

Please notice, after all those years, the call is still the same. The same grace of God which enabled you to respond to the Spirit's tug on your heart tugged on theirs. Same God, same Savior - Jesus, same Holy Spirit, same salvation, same grace, and the same faith. It's been the same since the beginning of time. Remember, the old testament believers died in faith looking toward the promise of a coming redeemer and the cross.

Where Is Sarah In God's Redemption Story?

We find Sarah at the beginning of the faith journey. She and Abraham embarked on an unprecedented journey to follow God. Their life story is the beginning record of God's having "a people" who walked by faith. According to God, Abraham's faith is notably the faith which is acceptable. It is the model. Remember, Abraham believed God, and it was credited to him as righteousness. Genesis 15:6. That was it. They indeed were pilgrims in a foreign land who believed God. They never owned any property, that is, until Sarah's death. Then Abraham purchased the cave at Machpelah for her tomb, desiring something more than the traditional desert burial for his beloved bride. In this culture, the graves were frequently opened and poached by carnivorous wildlife leaving nothing behind but white bones. Abraham wasn't having that, not for his princess. It was not only the first real estate transaction in scripture; it is the first mention of someone's grave or tomb. Abraham and Sarah had lived in tents under the stars. It made journeying from place to place easier. Hebrews 11:10 comes to mind. "… for he [Abraham] waited for the city which has foundations, whose builder and maker is God."

So, the couple moved about as God instructed because they were following His call. Abraham knew this was not his home and Sarah knew it too. Therefore, they were delighted to be wherever God said and went as He instructed. Their simple three-fold plan was as follows: (1) God spoke, and they listened. (2) God promised, and they believed. (3) God commanded, and they obeyed. They were quite a team. Not just Abraham is listed among those of noteworthy faith in Hebrews 11. Sarah is listed there as well. In fact, she and Rahab are the only women who made the inspired list. Our memory verse for this week comes from Hebrews 11. The verse says, "By faith Sarah herself received strength to conceive seed, and was delivered of a child when she was past age, because she judged Him faithful who had promised" (Hebrews 11:11). What amazing faith! I hope you will remember this verse forever. When there was no other way but for God to work a miracle, Sarah believed God. She had tremendous faith, and God proved Himself faithful. The time may come in your life when a situation can only be faced with big faith. I want a remarkable faith like that, don't you? I believe we can certainly have it. Biblical faith is living and active faith that's obedient to God's word despite the circumstances or consequences. Faith like this delights and pleases the Lord Jesus. The author of Hebrews says, "But without faith it is impossible to please Him, for he who comes to God must believe that He is, and that He is a rewarder of those who diligently seek Him" (Hebrews 11:6).

A Pagan Lifestyle.

It's interesting God chose Abraham and Sarah for such a journey. They were living a pagan lifestyle in a heathen land and worshipping other Gods, according to the book of Joshua. Let's take a quick look.

And Joshua said to all the people, "Thus says the Lord God of Israel: 'Your fathers, including Terah, the father of Abraham and the father of Nahor, dwelt on the other side of the River in old times; and they served other gods. Then I took your father Abraham from the other side of the River, led him throughout all the land of Canaan, and multiplied his descendants and gave him Isaac…" (Joshua 24:2-3).

Before God changed his heart, Abraham was lost. Nonetheless, God wanted them for the job. Why? Because it's always God who does the choosing. Notice in Joshua 24:3, God says, "I took your father Abraham…" God did it. Abraham didn't! Sarah didn't! We can't create ministry within ourselves. Only God can do this. When God chose them, He chose well. When He chose us, all of us, it was not by mistake either. I can assure you, there is nothing good in any of us apart from Christ. For whatever reason, God chose to use Abraham to reveal Himself to humanity and to bring forth the nation Israel, and ultimately Jesus. From the barren womb of a princess, Kings would come. Most notably, the King of all kings - Jesus Christ our Lord.

Incidentally, by birth, Abraham and Sarah were gentiles. Isn't it interesting to discover Abraham is the source of all Judiasm? Scripture does not identify him as "Abraham the Hebrew," until Genesis 14:13. There were no Jews before Abraham and Sarah. Not only are they the source of all Christianity (those called and chosen who believed and were saved by grace through faith), but they were also the source and fountainhead of all Judaism as well. Incidentally, the word *Hebrew* means *immigrant*. Indeed, they were immigrants or foreigners in a foreign land.

What Did Sarah Get Right?

Lots of things, I believe. Sarah loved her husband tremendously. She honored and respected him. Sarah not only believed him, she believed in him. Although most of us would have doubted or resisted, when it counted most, Sarah trusted her husband had indeed received a word from God. She submitted appropriately, even when things might have appeared questionable. She had colossal faith. I can tell you as a married woman, having colossal faith is an automatic boost to your husband's faith. When you believe big, it encourages their faith. Not only your husband's faith, but the faith of your whole family. If you have kids and grandkids, their faith is strengthened and nurtured when yours is immovable.

Sarah was faithful, and she was willing to submit to her husband in a way which honored God. In fact, she played a huge role in the overall success of their story. She honored God with her whole life, and when Isaac was finally born, she was not only a protective mother but loving and devoted as well. She showed proper respect to Abraham, even "calling him lord." She just didn't talk about being a respectful wife and honoring her husband; she did it. If you're married, you might want to make a note of this because at the end of our story this will be an important fact to remember. Sarah talked the talk and walked the walk. And, by the way, when we live accordingly, people notice. She walked humbly before our God and lived a life of grace, love, and honor toward Abraham. Peter reminds Christian women they can become "children" or "daughters of Sarah," when they live as God intends. Peter says, "…as Sarah obeyed Abraham, calling him lord, whose daughters you are if you do good and are not afraid with any terror." (1 Peter 3:6). Peter assures Christian women need never fear when they are devoted to the Lord Jesus and submitted to their husbands. You might want to read that again. What a promise! Whatever occurs, we can face it without fear and with the certainty of knowing a loving God is in control. He is ordering our steps. He is for us and not against us.

A Wonderful Example.

Sarah is an excellent example for us to follow. She was the real deal. Not only was she a marvelous *helper ('ēzer)* for Abraham, and the perfect mother for Isaac, she was a beauty through and through. Let's talk about that for a moment. Her inner beauty equaled or surpassed her outward appearance. Authentic beauty comes from a life lived for God, and it reflects the love, peace, and absolute joy of being His. We've all encountered women who radiated with indescribable beauty and joy. To make my point, we'll call them "show-stoppers." You know who I'm referencing. Women who changed the room's overall atmosphere and chemistry the minute they walked in. You just couldn't miss their presence, even if they never spoke a word. They brought with them something unusual and undefinable, yet not mystic or phony. They were not flashy or vulgar or dressed any more fashionable than others. Nonetheless, everyone was drawn to them. Their secret? What is seen and recognized by others as beauty is the reflection of their love for God, their peace with God, and Christ's glory and radiance as it shines through them - from the inside out. I believe Sarah had this! That's the attraction, and it's why we're drawn to them. I think it's precisely what made Sarah so overwhelmingly drop dead gorgeous at 89 years young. It's this beauty – a genuine and authentic beauty - a Godly beauty that's worth mentioning. This beauty never fades, never wears out, and is never unfashionable. Authentic beauty always comes from a life lived for God, and it's meant to last and endure a lifetime. Yes, Sarah had this, and perhaps you do too. If not, I believe it can be yours, too, for the asking!

Lastly, Sarah was linked to Abraham by marriage, but she was a devoted believer and faithful follower in her own right. We will never get to heaven on our husbands' backs. Our walk is just that - our walk. From what I can see, she delighted to do the will of God. She was eager to leave it all behind to follow God. Being a missionary wife, I can attest to this. Over the years, my husband would have had great difficulty accomplishing all the tasks God placed before him if I had not been on board. What a tragic event it would have been if I insisted on plotting our steps instead of submitting to my husband and God. There is nothing more beautiful than a life yielded to God. For me, the promises of all that lie ahead were just too exciting to miss. Sarah must have felt like that too. She had great faith, indeed.

What Did She Get Wrong?

She had great faith, that is - until she didn't. She got tired of waiting on God. One day her faith wavered, and she made a miserable, unfortunate mistake – an embarrassing mistake. As a woman, wife, and mother I know she regretted it deeply many times. Perhaps, from the moment she uttered her thoughts. How we wait for the promises of God is very important. I'll say it again. The manner in which we trust and wait patiently for God's promises truly matters! Are you waiting on a promise from God? I suspect you might be. Who knows? Your answer could come at any minute. Sometimes they come almost instantly, and at other times I have had to wait and wait. In fact, I am still waiting on some promises from God. Unfortunately, we don't make good waiters for the most part. We want everything now. We are a society fueled by instant gratification, self-aggrandizement, and immediate results. We're most definitely the do-it-all, have-it-all society and we're not willing to wait in a way that trusts and honors God.

Generally speaking, most people wait with poise and grace for about two weeks. Then we lose it, as all hope passes. That's when we begin to despair, complain, grumble, and doubt. Not all of us, but most of us. Sarah waited ten years after the initial promise concerning a child, and then her faith wavered. Then she gave her beloved Abraham up - for a little while, or so she thought. Honestly, she gave up a part of Abraham which could never be regained or replaced. In so doing, she opened up his heart so the name, whispers, and touch of another woman might claim part of it. That's right, Sarah gave Abraham to Hagar, her Egyptian servant girl to lie with him. Right under her nose, and with her blessing, Abraham held another woman in his arms and made love to her. My heart aches as I type those words… glory be, Sarah gave the love of her life into the arms of another woman. Day four of our study guide will expand her plan and its painful outcome.

In Sarah's defense, the promise of a child was never given to her directly. She waited 24 long years for the confirmation from God her womb would hold Abraham's seed and bring forth the nation of Israel. It finally occurred through her name change. See Genesis 17:15-16. Up until then she lived faithfully, but in the shadow of some uncertainty. Whose womb would it be? God could use anyone He chose. Her womb certainly hadn't worked well. With that thought in mind, she knew ultimately Abraham would give himself to another. What I haven't shared with you about her name is the root word meaning. *Sar* means *chieftainess and implies captain or commander, someone in control.* After 10 long years of waiting, Sarah decided if the love of her life were to give himself to another, it would be someone of her choosing. Here we see a princess in control. I suspect this decision didn't come quickly or easily. Perhaps she agonized over her decision for quite some time. Most assuredly, she didn't just rush in. Nonetheless, she gave her maidservant, Hagar, to Abraham to engage in sexual intercourse for the express purpose of conceiving a child. If you're wondering how could she or why would she? You're not alone. I dare say, countless women have wondered the same things. Perhaps down deep, Hagar wondered too! Maybe it was damage control! If Hagar were the one, Sarah would remain in control and have power, or so she thought. Why? Because Hagar belonged to Sarah, and it was her prerogative. Since she owned Hagar, any offspring of Hagar's would be credited to Sarah's account. In other words, the baby would be Sarah's. Hagar was the first surrogate mother of record. Quite ingenious actually. Regrettably, she overlooked the most important thing. She got ahead of God who had always proved Himself faithful. When this is our practice, we always suffer consequences. For Sarah, the painful consequences would last a lifetime!

It's fascinating, but this was real life drama we can hardly believe. I am certain barren Sarah had second thoughts about this immediately. And, wonder of wonders; as it would happen, Hagar conceived quickly. Wouldn't you just know it? Ultimately, Abraham marries her, and now he has two wives. One he loves desperately, yet she is still barren. The other, Sarah's folly, is glowing and growing right before her eyes. Sarah will blame Abraham for all of it. What a twisty turn we have! Wife number two, the younger and newer model, is not the love of his life, nor is she the one God chose for Abraham.

Nevertheless, she's got Abraham's seed, and Sarah doesn't. I imagine in the camp of Abraham and company - things were tense. I'm not the overly jealous type. I trust my husband completely, but if another woman were cozying up to him, it would certainly get my attention. I shudder to think what Sarah honestly thought when all was said and done. Our study guide will look at a scriptural account of the highs and lows of Sarah's decision as well as the painful results.

We find many life lessons and some rich theology in Sarah's story. It will be good for us to study the things which go wrong when we get ahead of God or better yet when we ignore Him altogether. Next week, we will be considering Hagar, because there are two sides to every story. That lesson is called Hagar: A Woman Of Flight, and it will explore what it was like to be the second wife of Abraham. I'll let you in on a little secret; the ending is a thriller. You won't want to miss this.

How Did God's Love Redeem It All?

God redeemed Sarah through the birth of her son, Isaac. Finally, after twenty-five long years, Sarah would hear the word "mama." On that day, her identity would change forever. She was no longer just Abraham's wife and a woman of faith; she was a mother. At long last! God had not taken anything from her. In fact, He had elevated her status, because now she was a player in God's story of creation and redemption. Every time she held little Isaac in her arms, she must have realized she was caressing a miracle. It paints such a beautiful picture of God's faithfulness that we can recognize. The name Isaac means, laughter. Sarah was 90 years old and Abraham 100, when Isaac was born. Let's review the words of Sarah, "God has made me laugh, and all who hear will laugh with me." (Genesis 21:6). Isaac brought joy into the tent of Abraham and Sarah. On the spiritual side, the wait was not without purpose. What was God up to and why? Day five of study guide will help us navigate God's Word to find these answers.

Nothing Surprises God.

Remember, there are no surprises in God's economy. Sarah's folly did not surprise God! Nothing happens in the life of a believer which has not first run through His loving hands. So, today if you are struggling in some measure, look up. The Lord Jesus has got it. He is in control of your life. All of it! Do you believe that? Sarah did, apart from one not so minor disaster and its painful results. Overall, she was faithful. We know this because the Bible tells us so in Hebrews 11. God has judged her faithful, and His inspired word has commemorated her as such by including her name among the faithful for eternity. That should encourage us and give us hope. Whatever happens, whatever mistakes we've made, whatever pain we've suffered or created, God's redeeming love can and will prevail.

Remember, even Sarah's folly was not too much for God. Trust Him, He will triumph. God always wins, and He is more than capable of handling your indiscretions as well. Moreover, He is willing. Relax, take a deep breath, God's eye is on you, and He will see you through. He has plans for your success. You will finish strong! Remember, our faithful God is redeeming us every day and will do so until He calls us home. On that, you can rely!

Be blessed this week as you study Sarah: Believing The Promise.

Next week, Hagar: A Woman Of Flight.

Sarah's story unfolds in Genesis 11 – 23.

Sarah: Believing The Promise

Day One: Who Is Sarah?

Memory Verse: Hebrews 11:11 By faith Sarah herself also received strength to conceive seed, and she bore a child when she was the past age, because she judged Him faithful who had promised.

1. There is a lot in a name, particularly in the Bible. Most often, the very character or nature of the person is embedded in the meaning of the name itself. *Sarai*, her given name, means *my princess*. Her name was fitting since her family of origin was an honored family hailing from Ur of the Chaldeans. Incidentally, this was Abraham's family origin as well. Her name was changed by God from Sarai to Sarah. How unique! Think about it: Sarah is the only woman in the Bible whose name was changed by God. Review Genesis 17:15-16. What is the new name's meaning? What is the spiritual significance of the new name?

2. How magnificent, yet ironic is this? At the appointed time, after 24 years of waiting, Sarah would be transformed through God's word (name change) from a barren woman to the mother of the Jewish nation. God cannot lie. Her name change was her guarantee. Read Genesis 17:17. No wonder Abraham laughed in awe and amazement. What astonishing work has God done in your life which still causes you to laugh in amazement?

3. God accomplishes much when we are waiting. Sarah waited a long time for this promise. In the wait, what do you think God accomplished in Sarah which prepared her for this great honor and spiritual challenge? Possibly more patience, trust, contentment, humility, a more profound faith, deeper intimacy through prayer, or an incredible testimony in the end, for His glory, etc.? Please share your insight.

4. What promises are you waiting on from God? What is He revealing to you while you wait?

5. The same God loves each of us. The same Jesus saves us, and we believe the same gospel through the same means of grace by faith. However, our individual walks are unique. Sarah was on a fantastic faith journey, and it led her to Canaan. God changed her name, and she received a verbal blessing, generally reserved for male patriarchs. Genesis 17:16. What about your faith journey? List three personal successes or failures that highlight your faith journey and God's redeeming love.

1.

2.

3.

Women of the Bible and God's Redeeming Love

6. According to scripture, Sarah has noteworthy faith. Her name appears in the Hall of Faith in Hebrews 11. Only she and Rahab made this impressive list. The last section of this week's memory verse identifies what placed her there. "Because she judged Him faithful that had promised." That is huge, and the spiritual implications are tremendous. What does this verse tell you about faith and how God views it? Has your faith passed a trial? If so, share.

7. "But without faith it is impossible to please Him, for he who comes to God must believe that He is, and that He is a rewarder of those who diligently seek Him." (Hebrews 11:6). Look at the verse. God rewards those who seek Him. If we search for Him, we will surely find Him. When we find Him, we have all we need. He is our treasure, our reward, and our "pearl of great price." Our Lord Jesus is the crown jewel of heaven, and when we have Him, we have everything: Jesus! Do you seek Him? How has God personally rewarded you for seeking Him?

8. Sarah's faith was challenged while she waited twenty-four years on the child of promise. According to Hebrews 11:11, her faith did not fail. James assures us trials are coming our way because they are unavoidable. So too, our faith will be challenged. He also assures us that this testing will produce pleasing by-products. Prayerfully read James 1:2-4. What will your tested faith produce? What is the meaning of perfect and complete, lacking nothing in James 1:4?

Meditation
Hebrews 11:1 Now faith is the substance of things hoped for, the evidence of things not seen.

Sarah: Believing The Promise

Day Two: Where Is Sarah In God's Redemption Story?

Memory Verse: Hebrews 11:11 By faith Sarah herself also received strength to conceive seed, and she bore a child when she was the past age, because she judged Him faithful who had promised.

1. I love Sarah's story because she models what all believers are invited to do. Give it all up, abandon self, and free-fall with God. Believers should be in love with Him and live for Him. We see this repeatedly commanded in scripture. Mark 12:30-31 states the command. List the five things believers are commanded to do.

1.

2.

3.

4.

5.

2. Sarah's life models Mark 12:30. For the most part, it appears from scripture her life honored God as she walked humbly before Him. Mark 12:31, however, is another matter. She didn't love her neighbor as herself, as we shall see in day four. Her dealings with Hagar were not very loving. Next week's lesson takes us into the trenches with Hagar, as we endeavor to see things from her perspective. Read Mark 12:31 again and answer the following questions:

    a. What is the meaning of loving your neighbor as yourself?

    b. As believers, how is this accomplished?

    c. Who is your neighbor?

3. Sarah and Abraham were the original recipients of the means of grace by which believers lived by faith. It was the purpose of their journey. Through them, God would reveal Himself. Through them, the nation of Israel would be born - a people separated or consecrated unto God - faithful followers. They were to be the children of God - the Israelites. Although imperfect and worldly at times, they were chosen to be the recipients of God's electing love. To accomplish His plan, at the appointed time, and when it pleased God, He awakened Abraham and Sarah spiritually. By grace through faith, they were enabled to respond to God's unique call, and their faith journey began. It's the same with us. Where did your faith journey begin? What is its purpose, and where has it taken you?

4. Their role in God's redemption story highlights saving faith, God's amazing love, and His plan to redeem humanity. Abraham was justified and declared righteous because of his faith. Read Hebrews 10:38 and record the verse. What does it mean to you?

5. God made a covenant with Abraham. That's fabulous news for us. It is irrevocable; it will never change. The fact is, the promise endures through a covenant-keeping God who is always faithful to His pledge. God cannot lie. What a comfort; He who calls you is faithful! Read Genesis 12:1-3. List all of the "I will" promises of God.

1.

2.

3.

4.

5.

6.

7.

8.

6. Wouldn't you know these amazing promises were conditional. There was a qualifier in Genesis 12:1. Do you see it? What was required of Abraham (and Sarah) to receive the blessings?

7. Abraham heard, "Get out of from your country…" A verbal commitment would not be enough. To activate the promises, Abraham had to move forward, leave, journey, etc. He had to go! This required faith on Abraham's part. What would it prove?

8. There are many scriptures concerning faith in the Bible. What is your favorite faith verse? Why? How has it strengthened your faith along the way?

Anne Nicholson

9. Abraham (and Sarah) traveled from north to south building altars along the way. Read and review Genesis 12:1-9. Where were the two altars built and what did they represent? List the verses.

10. Abraham (and Sarah) were emboldened to build altars in the face of the enemy. Everywhere they turned, pagans occupied the land. The pair really were immigrants in a foreign land. Nonetheless, Abraham had a mind to worship and glorify His God, Yahweh, the true and living God. Their collective hearts said, "We will worship our God, no matter what!" The onlookers must have been astounded by their actions. Have you built a spiritual altar (have you worshiped) in the face of the enemy and a worldly culture? What were the results? How were you received?

Meditation
Psalm 30:1 I will extol thee, O Lord, for you have lifted me up...

Sarah: Believing The Promise

Day Three: What Did Sarah Get Right?

Memory Verse: Hebrews 11:11 By faith Sarah herself also received strength to conceive seed, and she bore a child when she was the past age, because she judged Him faithful who had promised.

There are many things Sarah did right. We see many stories of her faithfulness in Genesis. The bottom line is she submitted and followed Abraham in a way that honored God. Incidentally, this was not because her hope was wrapped up in Abraham. If it had been, she would have failed miserably. When our focus is on people instead of the Lord Jesus and Him alone, we never get it right. People will fail us, hurt us, and disappoint us. It's not always intentional. Nonetheless, we are sinners, all of us, and sometimes our behavior is less than admirable. The painful results affect others, sometimes those we love best. Today's lesson is about great love, a great lie, and a wife's gracious loyalty.

1. Trials frequently follow triumphs, so the famine came to Israel. It was a literal famine with a very significant spiritual purpose. Famines, whether literal or spiritual, reveal to us the reality of our faith. God already knows the truth, but He wants us to know it too. He uses crises such as this to show us. When disasters come, we discover the measure of our faith. The depth or strength of our faith is revealed. How do you respond when trials or tragedies arise?

By Standing firm _____ Failing miserably _____. (check one)

Read Genesis 12:10-13. Answer the following questions:

2. The famine was severe in the land. Who directed Abraham to go to Egypt? Whose authority was he operating under?

3. Previously, Abraham moved by faith. At whose instruction? Record the identifying verse below.

4. In your opinion, was Abraham's move to Egypt a move of faith? Yes or no? Based on God's definition of faith in Hebrews 11:1, and the words of Paul in 2 Corinthians 5:7, does this move meet God's criteria? Why or why not?

5. a. What was Abraham's concern in Genesis 12:11-12?

v 11

v. 12

b. What did he instruct His wife to do?

v. 13

6. Previously Abraham was moved by faith. What moves him now? _____

Based on scripture, this is a sin. Fret and fear are the devil's twins. They trouble us causing us to make decisions without a scriptural foundation. Beware of the devil's discouraging tactics.

Read Genesis 12:14-16. Answer the following questions:

7. In your own words, briefly describe the important points to Genesis 12:14-16.

v. 14

v. 15

v. 16

8. Bible scholars suggest Genesis 12:16 pinpoints Hagar's introduction into the story of Abraham and Sarah, although scripture is silent on the matter. Reading verse 16, among other things, Abraham received "male and female servants." Despite Abraham's sin, God ultimately blessed them in Genesis 12:16. Who treated Abraham well? Why do you think this occurred?

9. The Lord intervened with the house of Pharaoh. What happened? Be specific. The Lord did this because of whom? Genesis 12:17. The risk to Sarah was great. To protect her purity, the Lord intervened. God had big plans for her and Abraham that involved a child of promise. At this point, although she is unaware of God's plans, God was not. It would never do for Pharaoh to violate God's plan.

10. God protects His interests, and those He partners with to accomplish His will. This thought should give you comfort. God knows the plans He has for you as well. Remember, nothing, absolutely nothing, can thwart God's plan. He will succeed. Write the words to Jeremiah 29:11 below. Next, using a descriptive word or two, clarify how this verse encourages your faith.

Read Genesis 12:17-20. Answer the following question:

11. Pharaoh is very angry and calls Abraham's motives into question. Abraham has blown his witness in Egypt. God has used a pagan ruler to discipline His servant verbally. How humbling! Sarah is safe, and even though it is never appropriate to lie, the couple appears richly blessed. God used this fiasco to increase the riches and wealth of his servant. Abraham was wrong, but he was still God's man. God had not changed his mind just because Abraham messed up, prompting Sarah to lie. He also kept Sarah safe in Abraham's blunder. Through it all, God had not withheld great blessings from the patriarch. When was your last noteworthy mistake? How did God protect you?

A Great Love.

Sarah loved Abraham and submitted, even though she did not know what would happen. Her submission showed great trust in him, but more so, her faith in God. It also showed her wisdom to protect the "Father of a nation." At this point, Abraham was still capable of producing offspring. The man's age is not nearly as critical as the woman's. Her thoughts were utterly selfless. Even if something happened to Sarah, God could use Abraham to produce an heir through marriage to someone else. Amazing! God blessed them because of her loyalty and submission. She never uttered a sound to endanger Abraham. After God, he was the great love of her life. Her actions were impressive indeed. But, the grandest love of all was demonstrated through God's dealings with the couple and His abundant blessings even when Abraham got off track.

A Great Lie.

Having received God's call, previously Abraham was moved by faith - Genesis 12:1-9. Fear has prompted his most recent move. Tragically, that same fear prompted the man of God to lie, destroying his testimony as an honorable man of God - that is, at least in Egypt. Fear also compelled him to have his wife lie about her identity, placing her in great danger. Overall, the lie was selfish and could have cost him his beloved princess. Apparently, Abraham is a slow learner. This entire episode will repeat itself in Genesis 20.

Gracious Loyalty.

Sarah was loyal to Abraham, and her submission was honoring to him and God. She passed the test with poise and grace. In this instance, she proved to be worthier of respect, honor, and position than her husband, Abraham. Nonetheless, Sarah wholeheartedly loved and adored Abraham through thick and thin. Enough so to reverently refer to him as "Lord." Genesis 18:12 and 1 Peter 3:6.

Meditation
1 Corinthians 1:9 God is faithful, by whom you were called into
the fellowship of His Son, Jesus Christ our Lord

Sarah: Believing The Promise

Day Four: What Did Sarah Get Wrong?

Memory Verse: Hebrews 11:11 By faith Sarah herself also received strength to conceive seed, and she bore a child when she was the past age, because she judged Him faithful who had promised.

In today's lesson, Sarah will make a choice - a significant one. Even today, we are enduring the painful consequences of her decision. Bible scholars suggest this decision was the beginning of the Arab-Israeli conflict. Consequently, there will be no peace in Israel until the Prince of Peace returns. As you prayerfully work through today's lesson, ask yourself two questions: (1) When is it okay to take matters into my own hands? (2) Is my faith strong enough to carry me in a God-honoring fashion, even when things don't turn out the way I had planned?

1. Read Genesis 16:1-2. After ten years of waiting, Sarah's patience wears thin. It appears her faith has weakened. What was the issue? Who seems to be in charge? What specific words within the verse cause you to form this opinion?

2. "And Abram heeded the voice of Sarai." (Genesis 16:2). What was he thinking? What was the motivation behind his response?

3. In Genesis 16:2, whom does Sarai (Sarah) openly blame for her situation? Record the identifying phrase.

4. Answer these two questions as honestly as possible. (1) Have you ever blamed God when things did not go according to your plan or turned out contrary to your thinking? (2) Where was God in the midst of the outcome?

(1)

(2)

5. What happened to renew your strength or encourage your faith? Please share. For the benefit of others, if possible, provide a verse to describe your victory over the enemy's ploy in this situation.

6. "Please" in Genesis 16:2 embodies urgency and implies an outcome or a cause. The Hebrew word *nā'* generally means - *I pray, I beg you, I urge you, etc*. The cause or outcome was to produce "a feeling of happiness and satisfaction." Essentially, Sarah said to her husband, "Please do this for me so that I may be happy and satisfied." (Genesis 16:2). The implication?

Abraham's cooperation and performance would produce satisfactory or favorable results. The desired outcome? The birth of a child. Sarah implies Abraham's participation and performance would facilitate her pleasure and satisfaction. Poor Abram! What was a loving husband to do?

Question: In your opinion was this manipulation? Why or why not? What does the bible say about manipulation – i.e., to control, exploit, maneuver, misrepresent or falsify? Cite a verse to support your thoughts.

7. From the nature of this request, you know things can't turn out well. I am confident, the moment Hagar and Abraham entered the tent, Sarah had second thoughts. What do you think God thought of this plan? Was it sinful? Why or why not? Give a verse to support your position.

Women of the Bible and God's Redeeming Love

8. Thinking biblically, who was at fault, Sarah or Abraham? What about Hagar? Was she merely an innocent party in Sarah's twisted and selfish plan?

9. What does the bible teach about adultery? List your scriptural references.

10. According to Genesis 16:1, Hagar was a slave, a maidservant. Tragically, she was mistreated and manipulated at the hands of her mistress and master. In essence, you are a slave, too; a bondservant of the Lord Jesus. Thanks to God, He is our righteous King, whose actions are always holy and just. To be His bondservant means you have allowed Him to help Himself to the ownership of your life. You are no longer calling the shots. That requires faith. Write the definition of faith from Hebrews 11:1 below. Then, in your own words, describe what it means to you to be a bondservant of Christ.

Hebrews 11:1

To be a bondservant of Christ means:

Biblical faith is confident obedience to God's word, despite the circumstances or consequences. The world says, "I'll believe it when I see it." According to Hebrews 11:1, Christians say, "We believe and know we will see it!"

Meditation
Hebrews 10:38 Now the just shall live by faith

Sarah: Believing The Promise

Day Five: How Did God's Love Redeem It All?

Memory Verse: Hebrews 11:11 By faith Sarah herself also received strength to conceive seed, and she bore a child when she was the past age, because she judged Him faithful who had promised.

In Hebrews 11:11, notice the effort was not upon Sarah, but wholly upon God! God has the final word in all of our lives, and His redeeming love covers all sin, all emptiness, all longing, all hurt, all heartache. Including anything the enemy can throw our way! What a faithful God we serve!

1. After waiting 25 years, when Sarah was 90 years old, the child of promise was born. Isaac burst onto the scene and brought laughter into the tent of Abraham and Sarah. Let's look back to the enhanced revelation of the covenant promise to Abraham. Read Genesis 17:17-19. What is Abraham's question in v. 17? What was God's promise (both parts) from v. 19?

v. 17

v. 19

2. Look at the promise concerning Isaac. "I will establish My covenant with him for an everlasting covenant, and with his descendants after him." Using a dictionary write the meaning of "covenant." Does this covenant give you hope? Yes or No?

Women of the Bible and God's Redeeming Love

3. Read Genesis 17:21. After 24 long years, God provides a date for the promise. Identify the time.

4. Read Genesis 18:14 and write the verse. What do these words mean to you?

5. Is there an impossibility in your life? Whatever is going on in your life is not too hard for the Lord. In one or two words, define the impossible situation or circumstance you are facing. Next, praise and thank God, in advance for His resolution!

6. God is faithful! Reading Genesis 21:2, identify the time of Isaac's arrival. Write the verse and underline the time.

7. What did Sarah say in Genesis 21:6? Can you relate to the joy and redemption Sarah must have felt? If so, please share.

8. Sarah waited 25 years to hold the child of promise. When Isaac was born, within an instant, many years of longing, pain, speculation, and humiliation were settled. His birth attended and satisfied many spiritual matters, but went beyond that. His birth captivated Sarah's heart and satisfied her soul. When she held him close, her heart could say, "My love is complete, my God is faithful." Little Isaac healed all the deep wounds in Sarah. Wounds so deep, even Abraham could not attend them. God had given her the deep desire to partner with Him in His creation story. Finally, and at long last, it was accomplished! Don't you know as Isaac grew and matured, he was a "blessed" reminder of God's redeeming love? Do you see both the personal and spiritual redemption in this story? If so, what are they?

Personal:

Spiritual:

9. Nothing stops the fulfillment of God's purposes. He brings about His sovereign plan, often in spite of us, not because of us. Let's take a closer look at the reoccurring "sister-wife" lie between Abraham and Sarah. Read Genesis 12:13 and Genesis 20:12-13. Answer the following questions:

    a. In your opinion, did Abraham lie?

    b. Did Sarah lie?

c. When, if ever, is it appropriate to lie?

d. Provide scripture to support your thoughts.

Epilogue.

Sarah is referenced in scripture as a woman found faithful. She is held out as an example for us to emulate by both Peter and Paul, as well as the writer of Hebrews. She was a woman who genuinely loved and trusted God. Her great love for God empowered her to love her husband well, and serve as the matriarch of the people of Israel.

Meditation
1 Peter 3:6 "…as Sarah obeyed Abraham, calling him lord,
whose daughters you are if you do good and are not afraid with any terror."

Notes - Sarah: Believing The Promise

Hagar

Hagar: A Woman Of Flight

Hagar was a woman on the run, that is, from time to time. I feel for her. I've been a runner myself. In fact, before my conversion, I was quite a runner. I was given to flight often and, sometimes, shamefully, the results were not pretty. Apart from Jesus and salvation, I was a mess, and at times my life was messy. Do you know messy? I can't describe it any other way. Sometimes the circumstances were created by me. There were times when I proved to be my own worst enemy. There were also times when I was the victim. Whatever the case, I could relate to Hagar. Chances are you might too. If not personally, I'll just bet that you know a Hagar or have encountered one such as she.

I can say without exception, Hagar is perhaps one of the most fascinating women in the Bible. Women of all ages were captivated by her story when we initially studied this material. Many confessed they didn't know much about her life. Others said they had never considered what she might have thought when Sarah hatched a scheme involving her in such an intimate way. You see, this week's lesson will examine the Abraham and Sarah folly from Hagar's viewpoint. Have you ever stopped to consider what it might have been like to be her? She was in an awkward spot. She was in the middle of a difficult situation. I must admit, when I wrote the study I was mad at Sarah and Abraham for a few days. Yes, I get it - they were the chosen, but Hagar had no way out. Or did she? As we work through scripture, you'll have the opportunity to form your own opinion. So that you know, your discovery might ruffle your feathers a bit. But remember, we are on a journey to discover who God is and how He deals with us in our frail humanity. And that was Hagar, young, vulnerable, and very, very human.

Guess what? God loved her - desperately. When she fled, He pursued her. His love found her and embraced her. She had a divine visitation, not once, but twice. Have you ever had a divine encounter? Has God spoken audibly to you? Of course, I've heard Him speak through scripture, but He has never appeared to me in the way He did Hagar. To my astonishment, He never appeared to Sarah, either. But alas, both of Hagar's encounters were personal, intentional, and thrilling!

Let me welcome you to Hagar's world. If you've ever made a mistake, fled the scene, or have been used and hurt deeply - this story is for you. I am confident it will speak directly to your heart. I know it did mine! It is my pleasure to introduce you to Hagar, a woman of flight.

God So Loved The World.

As you study, keep the promise of John 3:16 in the back of your mind. The verse says, "For God so loved the world that He gave His only begotten Son, that whoever believes in Him should not perish but have everlasting life." The way I read the verse, that's everybody! In fact, it would be all those the Spirit "so moves" to call upon the name of the Lord - Jesus!

Remembering Paul's encouraging words from Romans, "For whoever calls on the name of the LORD shall be saved." (Romans 10:13).

James tells us Abraham was God's friend. Those inspired words are found in James 2:23. As we learned last week, Abraham was God's representative upon the earth, and Sarah was his female counterpart. They were handpicked by God to bear His image and live by faith within a pagan world. They were to testify of Him. But, guess what? They were people too. Same humanity invaded them that invades us. Same inadequacies, same sin nature - all of it. As His image bearers, we look like God, sometimes, and sometimes not so much. The backdrop of this story was challenging for me to grasp. I had to hold these words close to my heart and fervently pray so I could teach them. To that end, I lived deep in Hagar's story for many days. Everything I ever wanted to know about Hagar - and then some - is found within this study.

The Heart Knows.

Deep within my heart I know God loves us, all of us, and He is good. I know this! I know it academically, I can see it in His word, and I know it in my spirit. I can comprehend this, but I struggled to understand the depth of God's love for Hagar and His plan for her life. I'll admit, I had some teary-eyed moments writing this lesson. She is so much like us in many ways. The one difference between Hagar and us could be that she was bound in servitude to Sarah. We're not slaves; nonetheless, we can be bound as well. Not in literal slavery, but in sin.

Sin binds and restricts us, it weakens us, and tragically it separates us from God. Unless and until we are free from the sins which bind us, we will continue to suffer its many consequences. Similarly, until Hagar fled, she continued to endure the painful consequences of being linked in servitude to Sarah, and all it involved. All is not lost, however, not even for Hagar. At the end of our study, she receives the promise of liberty! We have that too. It's available to you for the asking. Jesus has come to save us and set us free. He is waiting and willing to free us from all sin and reconcile us to God. When He sets us free, we can be truly free. The words of Jesus, "Therefore if the Son makes you free, you are free indeed." (John 8:36).

Who Is Hagar?

The first thing we will notice about Hagar's life is how tightly it's wound with Sarah's. When we find her, she's faithfully serving Sarah and journeying right along with her and Abraham. You might say the trio and others traveling with them were on a journey of faith - they were following God.

The name Hagar is an Egyptian name, from an Arabic root word meaning "flight." Other translations of the word are *fugitive, wanderer*. The word's meaning speaks of fleeing or running from the scene, as in escaping. As our story unfolds, you will recognize the evidence of this embedded characteristic within her name. In general, biblical names reflect the nature or character traits of their owner. Hagar's name is no exception.

Hagar was the second wife of Abraham. She is the mother of Ishmael, Abraham's firstborn son. Not the son God promised, nonetheless a son. Fathers naturally delight in the birth of a child, but for a Jewish father to have a son, it's everything! Not to discount daughters in the least, but everything including the inheritance passed from father to son. They desired and needed heirs to carry on the family name, traditions, and trades or livelihood. Sons were also their social security and provision in old age, so their futures depended on it. Therefore, Abraham needed a son! Our story will reveal Abraham found delight in little Ishmael much to Sarah's chagrin and disgust. Ishmael proved to be a hotbed of conflict in the lives of Abraham and wives one and two - Sarah, a princess, and Hagar, her slave.

Where Is Hagar In God's Redemption Story?

As we begin to study Genesis 16, about ten years have passed since Abraham and Sarah answered God's call. We examined their unprecedented call and life-changing departure from Ur last week. As you may recall, they abandoned life as they knew it, leaving everything including family and friends to be on mission with God. Abraham and Sarah were to get out of their country, away from their family, and their father's house to a land God would show them. (Genesis 12:1.) Their going initiated all the promised blessings, and most notably, "… And in you, all the families of the earth shall be blessed." (Genesis 12:3). To an otherwise pagan world, they were to be the living and true testimony, declaring "our God, Yahweh, lives, and reigns." They were found faithful. That's important for us because in Abraham, saving faith was identified, noted, and credited to him as righteousness. (Genesis 15:6.) His faith is the faith by which all faith is judged. Through their daily lives - in word, action, and deed, the Lord - Yahweh, the God of all - was to be seen and glorified. You might say before Sarah got ahead of God the couple existed harmoniously in a love triangle with Him.

As far as we can determine, Hagar's been moving from place to place and serving Sarah well. For the most part, the couple has been found faithful, except for a detour to Egypt which was humiliating and costly. In fact, Jewish tradition suggests this is where they acquired Hagar. Some Bible scholars believe all the treasures and gifts Abraham received in Egypt were an endowment from Pharaoh to secure his union with Sarah. In Genesis 12, we see Pharaoh intended to have Sarah for himself. To guarantee their union, he rewarded Abraham richly.

"So it was, when Abram came into Egypt, that the Egyptians saw the woman, that she was very beautiful. The princes of Pharaoh also saw her and commended her to Pharaoh. And the woman was taken to Pharaoh's house. He treated Abram well for her sake. He had sheep, oxen, male donkeys, male and female servants, female donkeys, and camels." (Genesis 12:14–16).

Do you see the transaction or exchange of sorts? For Sarah's sake, a lusting and smitten Pharaoh bestowed many gifts on Abraham.

The Hand Of God.

This true story reads much like a soap opera or a movie made for television. Without any warning, Hagar will find herself in the midst of a crisis. As astonishing as this story is, it did not surprise God. How could it be? A faithful Abraham would heed his wife's recommendation and invitation to sleep or lay with her maid for the express purpose of conceiving a child. When I read this story many years ago, I had to go back and reread it. I couldn't believe my eyes. In fact, it still astounds me. The good news is, God does redeem all of our mistakes. He reconciles the whole of our lives, not just bits, and pieces. These incredible records of faithful people in the Bible who made terrible choices should give us hope. They were real people just like us who messed up and made mistakes. The focus is not on their errors and mistakes or the painful consequences. Instead, it's God's redemptive work in and through their lives, in spite of them.

Through it all, God was building character within the patriarchs, notably Abraham. He was working patience, trust, and obedience in His servants. In life, we come to many crossroads or places which demand a choice or decision. In this week's study, we find our sojourners at such a place - a place requiring godly discernment. Each of them is facing a dilemma and an important decision. Sadly, they will make a wrong move. The tragedy of this decision is the devastation it unleashed into the world as a result. We never sin in a vacuum. Our sin affects those around us. The consequences ripple outward from the source and touch all those in its path. These painful effects have proved perpetual, and the lasting consequences endure. Since Abraham heeded Sarah's lousy advice, lay with her maidservant, and conceived a son of the flesh - one of their own making - the painful consequences have endured.

Pushing Against Grace.

When Abraham heeded his wife's advice instead of waiting for the promise of God, they pushed against His grace. As a result, their lives got harder and more complicated. Did they not consider the possible repercussions their cunning plan might produce - for them or us? Of course not! Sarah wanted her way, and she meant to have it. Abraham loved Sarah and wanted to satisfy his wife and fulfill her dream. Culturally, what Sarah asked was not out of the ordinary. It was quite the norm. But, we must remember, this couple was supposed to be different. They had faith! They were handpicked or consecrated and set apart by God for a unique purpose. Do you remember their call and the mission? They were to witness or testify to a pagan world their God, the Lord - Yahweh, lived and reigned. They were to glorify Him and testify of Him at all times, in all places, and to all people. They were to walk by faith and not by sight. They were to trust God and wait on Him. Is that not our call as well? We will examine this in our study guide.

God Is Serious About Sin.

Jealousy, envy, violence, abuse, pride, ridicule, and mistrust were unleashed when they took matters into their own hands. Almost immediately their harmony and peace were threatened. It is our job to obey God, trust Him, and do the next right thing. We must not rush in. Make a note. All sin operates outside God's defined boundaries, and the discipline can be severe. Let's stop a moment to define sin. According to Dr. Wayne Grudem, sin is "any failure to conform to the moral law of God in act, attitude, or nature." [1]

God is serious about sin. In love, He has drawn a line in the sand. He has defined the boundaries in His word. It's our job to know what it says. For our good, protection, and well-being - spiritual and otherwise, it's always best to come into agreement with God. It means we agree with God's Word. Jesus said in essence, if you love me, you'll obey me. His exact words, "If you love me, keep my commandments." (John 15:14). People of great faith obey God!

What Was In Her Heart?

We will never know what Hagar felt, or thought as she lay in Abraham's arms. Nonetheless, she did it! At Sarah's insistence, she lay with Abraham. The scene is almost too unthinkable because Sarah planned it, insisted upon it, and begged Abraham to follow through. In fact, it appears she all but threw a fit to have her way. In Hebrew, her insistence went beyond a mere suggestion. She insisted, "her very happiness was linked to the fruitful outcome of her request." We examined this last week. Sarah begged and pleaded with Abraham, "Please [nā'] go in to my maid." (Genesis 16:2).

Abraham wanted to bring his wife happiness and satisfaction – He loved her. So, they did it! As inconceivable as it might seem. At Sarah's insistence, and with her approval, Abraham made love to another woman. Not just another woman, but one who was deeply intertwined in their lives. She was no longer merely connected through the master-slave relationship. Through no plan of her own, Hagar had occupied an intimate place of no return. Abraham had held the slave of his princess in his arms and loved her.

What was Abraham thinking? What was Hagar thinking? Did Hagar hope to elevate her status? Was she in love with Abraham? Or, was she fearful? Would there ever be a life for her other than servitude? Remember, God was in control. He is sovereign over all creation. The good news is that includes us, and it undoubtedly included them. Only God can make something beautiful from our ashes. He is our Redeemer! Thankfully, He is in the business of redeeming the whole of our lives, including the ugly. Even when things appear ugly or hopeless, Paul assures us, "And we know that all things work together for good to those who love God, to those who are the called according to His purpose." (Romans 8:28).

---

[1] Grudem, W. A. (2004). <u>Systematic theology: an introduction to biblical doctrine</u> (p. 490). Leicester, England; Grand Rapids, MI: Inter-Varsity Press; Zondervan Pub. House.

Anne Nicholson

What Did Hagar Get Right?

We can sum this up in a few words. Hagar submitted! As jaw-dropping as it may seem, Hagar did what was required. Not only did she submit, but twice, in extreme circumstances, Hagar prevailed through obedience. In the midst of it all, she has an incredible visitation. She is attended physically and spiritually in the most unexpected way. And, when we least expect it, she does the most remarkable thing of all. She comes into agreement with God! She displays grace and humility which far exceeds her mistress Sarah's. There is much more to Hagar than we might imagine. When it's all said and done, she proves to be a woman of real substance and character. She obeyed God even though she could not see the benefit of what was being required and regardless of the outcome. Sound familiar? Sounds a bit like walking by faith and not by sight, doesn't it? Could it be Hagar, too, had faith?

Be forewarned. Our study will not debate the moral implications of Hagar's fornication with Abraham. Remember, we are on a journey to discover how God's love redeemed the women of the Bible because, mercifully, God never changes. He is the same yesterday, today, and forever. His dealings with them will give us a clue how He will deal with us. Women are still women, and God is still God! When we know God better, we stand a better chance of knowing who He has lovingly created us to become. After all, we are women made in His image.

What Did Hagar Get Wrong?

The right and wrong of Hagar's life are commingled and hard to separate. Let's review some passages from Genesis 16.

Hagar had an adulterous encounter with Abraham. Once the pregnancy was a reality, Hagar despised her mistress. "And when she saw that she had conceived, her mistress became *despised* in her eyes." (Genesis 16:4).

In verse 4, *"despise"* in Hebrew is *qālal.* In the Piel verb tense it implies, *"her mistress lost status in her estimation."* The implication. Hagar had respect for Sarah - that is, until she didn't. Once pregnant, pride set in and Hagar viewed Sarah as "inferior, inadequate, less than herself" because of her barrenness. She could do for Abraham something Sarah had never accomplished. I find this most interesting. It would seem Hagar's been dealt a new hand. Now the tables were turned, and she feels superior to her mistress, Sarah. Fascinating! I love a story with a twist, and now, at least in Hagar's mind, the tables have turned. From that fateful night, they've been rubbing along together with their sin hanging over their heads. How did they face one another? What did they say? It surely boggles my mind. Nonetheless, nurturing Abraham's seed, Hagar's glowing and growing right under Sarah's nose! Can you imagine the tension in the camp of Abraham?

It's interesting to note, Hagar despised her mistress because before her pregnancy I could see no scriptural evidence of Sarah's abuse or mistreatment of Hagar. But, scripture affirms once pregnant, Hagar taunted her barren mistress in a mean-spirited way. She flaunted her pregnancy. I don't even want to imagine what that might mean. Hagar's behavior enraged Sarah, further magnifying her inadequacy and barrenness, her emptiness and longing. Hagar's conduct heaped anguish upon grief and added insult to injury. Sarah's heart was broken. The moment it was apparent Hagar was with child, Sarah blamed Abraham. As in, "How could you!!??? Look what you've done! You wronged me." Genesis 16:5-6 reveals an exchange of harsh words between the patriarchal couple.

Our study guide will examine the original language to discover something pretty amazing about the word "*wrong.*" In the original language, the word is "*hamas.*" Do you recognize the word? Its Hebrew origin began with Abraham. It's too astonishing for words. To this day, whenever a Jew hears the word, hamas, they recall its painful origin - Father Abraham. Bittersweet, indeed!

The results? Tempers flare, things escalate, and in a moment of fury, Sarah struck Hagar, her pregnant slave. The original language says it got physical. Genesis 16:6 discloses, "…Sarai dealt harshly" with Hagar. In Hebrew, *"dealt harshly"* is one word, *ānâ,* meaning *rigorously, roughly, painfully.* That's the implied meaning, but the word means *afflict, oppress, humble.* Sarah planned to humble Hagar through a few good beatings! Sarah struck a pregnant woman! Perish the thought. How horrible is this? Nonetheless, it was an abusive scene! There was a cat fight in the hen house! What's going on with Abraham and company? What was poor Abraham to do?

In this scenario, Hagar proved painfully - literally and spiritually - not to be the answer to the problem. Imagine that! Sarah and Abraham got ahead of God. As a result, they all suffered. To this very day, we're still suffering from their botched plan to help God out. You will cover this in our study guide.

The results were bone chilling. Sarah struck a pregnant woman. The very remedy Sarah begged Abraham to perform proved to be no remedy at all. The verse reads in part, "Please go in to my maid…" (Genesis 16:2). The verse could well read, "please sleep, lay, or have sex with my maid." It's ironic, in this verse the Hebrew word for 'please' is *na,* and the meaning is to *cause to feel happy and satisfied.* As you can see, the word implies this act would bring Sarah joy and satisfaction. Low and behold, Abraham satisfied his wife! Gives a whole new dimension to "Yes, dear." He did as she "pleased." He aimed to "please," but guess what? It had the opposite effect! It tormented her. Instead of bringing her joy, it brought her heartache and anguish. We think we know what we need and go after it, but God knows so much better what's best. If we can wait upon Him and walk with Him our journey is so much easier; it's always better! The best plan is always to come into agreement with God as quickly as possible.

Anne Nicholson

How Did God's Love Redeem It All?

Well for starters, God gave Hagar a promise. Face to face, Hagar had two visitations from God. Now, think about this. On the one hand, we have Sarah, this wealthy princess with undeniable good looks. In fact, she's such a beauty some scholars believe her outward appearance was unrivaled by anyone of her time. Jewish tradition holds Eve was the most remarkable beauty God ever created and Sarah was a close second. We could sum it up by saying Sarah was a 12 on a scale of 1 to 10. We can add to her remarkable beauty, her privileged family standing, and her most upright position as Abraham's wife. As his wife, she was called to be the matriarch of the entire Jewish nation. However, she never saw God. She never had a theophany. Remember, a theophany is a visible manifestation to humankind of God. It simply means God, in whatever form He pleases manifests Himself to a person. Sarah merely heard an angel of the Lord address Abraham, and only once! But, God never spoke to her directly, nor did He appear to her.

What was Sarah's reaction when she heard the Lord say to her husband she would have a son? The verse says, And He said, "I will certainly return to you according to the time of life, and behold, Sarah, your wife shall have a son." (Genesis 18:10). Sarah was listening in the tent door, and she laughed to herself, thinking this a ridiculous impossibility. She was called into account about her faulty thinking and misconception about God's purpose and divine power. (Genesis 18:13.) Nonetheless, her faith is noteworthy. Remember, she made the inspired list of Hebrews 11. That should encourage us. God's word says Sarah is faithful, even after such a misstep! But, she never had a visitation from God. On the other hand, Hagar, her slave, had two. That's right, Hagar had two! Her second theophany unfolds in Genesis 21:17-18.

For clarity, Sarah was not visited by the Lord in Genesis 21:1. The verse reads, "And the Lord visited Sarah as He had said, and the Lord did for Sarah as He had spoken." Notice the words, *"the Lord visited..."* Upon examination of the original language, we discover the Hebrew word *pāqad* (from the root word *pqd*) is translated *"visited." Visited* in this verse means something other than we might think. It does not mean visited in its general sense. In the Old Testament, this word often meant *mustered or mustering or gathering of troops for battle*. In this context, God musters the needed resources of heaven to give Sarah a child in old age. Along those lines, in its qal verb tense, the word can mean: *care for, come to aid, watch over, i.e., help someone in a manner that shows concern and help in a difficult circumstance*. Note in some contexts this may be a reward or recompense.[2]

Rather than visit in person, God supernaturally attended to the needs at hand. We see *visit* takes the same meaning near the end of Joseph's life in Genesis 50. Joseph's faith is noteworthy. The verse says: And Joseph said to his brethren, "I am dying; but God will surely *visit* you, and bring you out of this land to the land of which He swore to Abraham, to Isaac, and to Jacob."

---

[2] Swanson, J. (1997). *Dictionary of Biblical Languages with Semantic Domains : Hebrew (Old Testament)* (electronic ed.). Oak Harbor: Logos Research Systems, Inc.

(Genesis 50:24). Notice Joseph's words of comfort to his brothers. He was persuaded God would surely *visit* them and come to their aid, but it would be in the spiritual sense. Joseph knew God's divine visitation would come through a supernatural work from heaven. Same word - same meaning.

God Loves The Outcast.

There is good news for all of us in this. God loves the outcast. God loved Hagar's unborn son. How thrilling - God loved Ishmael. Remember, no baby happens apart from the hand of God. You might think otherwise, but scripture is clear on it. We examined this in our study of Eve. Ultimately, none of this surprised God. As you study this week, you will discover the first time Hagar fled to the desert it was to escape Sarah's brutality. The second time, she doesn't run, she is thrown out of the camp by the one she had looked to for provision and protection – Abraham. The very one to whom she had surrendered her entire life and body. Abraham, the only one who had gathered her close, held her in his arms and loved her.

Did she love Abraham? I suspect she possibly did. After all, she was his second wife. Abraham had been her provider and protector for more than ten years. She was carrying his child. The amazing thing is at the time Hagar flees Sarah's brutality, Abraham's most imminent hope of a child, a descendant - an heir - is carried with her. For the seed of Abraham is tucked securely in her womb. But, true to her name – when she fled, Hagar was a woman on the run.

It's interesting to note, too, at Sarah's insistence and with her consent, Abraham married Hagar. (Genesis 16:3.) However, God never recognized or sanctioned this marriage. We find this tidbit in God's first divine encounter with Hagar: And He said, "Hagar, Sarai's maid, where have you come from, and where are you going?" (Genesis 16:8). Notice from the passage: 1) Hagar is addressed as "Sarai's maid," instead of Abraham's wife, and 2) God calls her by name. Neither Abraham or Sarah have done so in scripture. On the other hand, the God of all comfort, the Great I AM addresses Hagar directly, calling her by name. Interestingly, He will do it again in Genesis 21:17. How unbelievably thrilling! Then, God permits this Egyptian slave girl to give Him a name. Hagar holds the distinction of being the only person, ever - male or female to name God. What an honor and privilege for Hagar. God announced all other revelations of "the names of God" in scripture Himself. There in the desert, under the hot middle eastern sun, the most unlikely thing occurred. Hagar met with God and gave Him a name.

A Happy Ending After All.

Genesis 25:1 reveals after Sarah's death and burial, Abraham took a new wife. A woman named Keturah. Jewish rabbis are of the opinion Hagar and Keturah were one in the same. However, scripture does not confirm this. Instead, it is silent on Keturah's identity. Down through the generations, however, Rabbis, historians, and traditionalists have reconciled their belief as follows:

After being emancipated from Abraham, Hagar resumed her Egyptian lifestyle, resettled in the south, and raised her son to maturity. We can verify she resettled in the south, and scripture confirms she acquired a wife for Ishmael from the south – from Egypt. (Genesis 21:21.) Rabbis speculate Abraham's power, wealth and notoriety prompted Hagar to change her name to Keturah to protect her privacy. Who would want to be identified as the ex-wife of the wealthiest man in the region? But, two questions remain. 1) Who united Keturah with Abraham? And, 2) How did she end up marrying Abraham? For our clue, let's look briefly at a passage from the homiletic teachings of the Torah:

"Three years after Sarah's death, Abraham remarries Hagar - Keturah. The reconciliation is now complete--indeed it is Sarah's son, Isaac, who brings Hagar back for her marriage with his father."

So the question remains: Could Hagar and Keturah be one in the same? Just before Isaac marries Rebekah, he returns from Beer Lahoi Roi. According to Genesis 24:62, "he [Isaac] dwelt in the South." Isaac was living in a region on the Palestine-Egypt border, approximately 25 miles NW of Kadesh-Barnea.[3] Guess who else resided in the area? According to Jewish tradition, Isaac discovered Hagar living in Beer Lahoi Roi. Once emancipated from Abraham and Sarah, Hagar returned to the place where she named God. She returned to an area of comfort and peace, love, and acceptance. Why Beer Lahoi Roi? In this place Hagar: 1) encountered God, 2) was attended by God, 3) found peace with God, and 4) named God. How could she ever forget what happened in Beer Lahoi Roi? Naturally, once free, she would be drawn there. She returned to a place where she mattered to God, a place where she found dignity. In Beer Lahoi Roi, Hagar's brokenness collided with the love of God. Jewish tradition confirms it would be inappropriate for Abraham to marry again until Isaac took a bride. But once Isaac married, Abraham could do as he pleased.

After a reasonable time of mourning (about three years) it was time for Abraham to move forward. Ultimately, he takes a bride named Keturah. (Genesis 25:1.) Their union was blessed, and she gave Abraham six more sons. They are the forefathers or ancestors of the Arab people of Southern and Eastern Palestine. Isaac remained there. Scripture records he resided in Beer Lahoi Roi after Abraham's death. (Genesis 25:11.)

Before Abraham died, six sons were born with Keturah. (Genesis 25:2.) These six sons, plus Ishmael, confirm the covenant and prophetic words. Abraham would be "the father of nations." That's all the Jews, and all the Gentiles – everybody (including all the Arab people) came from the seed of Abraham. It fulfills God's promise from Abraham's initial call. He indeed is the Father of Nations. That's why he's called Father Abraham; often referred to as the Father of Faith. He's the spiritual father of everyone who calls upon the name Jesus Christ, the Son of God, for salvation.

---

[3] MacArthur, J. F., Jr. (2006). The MacArthur study Bible: New American Standard Bible. (Ge 24:62). Nashville, TN: Thomas Nelson Publishers

One Last Look.

Before we turn to our study guide, I want to point out one interesting thing about Hagar and her courage. She had done all the Angel of the Lord commanded. We see from scripture: The Angel of the Lord said to her, "Return to your mistress, and submit yourself under her hand." (Genesis 16:9). It must have been an awful command to hear, until she heard the promise of Genesis 16:10-12. Our study guide will navigate these fantastic verses. What did she hear? Essentially this. "Hagar, if you return, Ishmael will be a free man." What mother wouldn't do that? Hagar picked her pregnant self up and went back home. Hagar returned to her mistress. But, I want you to know she was not the same woman - not by a long shot. Things would be different, at least in Hagar's mind. She went back strengthened by the hand of heaven. Hagar had newfound peace and courage. With every step she took, she knew she had been with God. Hagar knew she mattered to God. She would return to be Sarah's slave and remain faithful until she is banished from the camp by Abraham in Genesis 21. While she served her mistress, Hagar's heart confidently counted down the days knowing her son would be free! Hagar believed the promise of God.

A careful review of Genesis 16:10-12 reveals a conditional provision within God's promise. Notice from the passage Hagar had to return to Sarah to activate the promise. Sound familiar? Abraham was given a provisional promise in Genesis 12:1-9. He had to go. He had to "get out from his father's house" and follow God to receive the blessing and be a blessing. Hagar had to return to her mistress Sarah to free Ishmael. From all appearances, she might still be a slave, but she was a slave who had been with God. That's always a game changer, isn't it? And, no one could ever take that from her. Hagar had seen God - El Roi, "The-God-Who-Sees," and given Him a name. (Genesis 16:13.) Astounding! Remember, this week as you study, the God who saw Hagar is the God who sees you.

He Knows You!

Right this moment He sees you and knows everything about you. He recognizes your struggles as well as your joys and accomplishments. He knows all you need, even the innermost secrets of your heart. El Roi, The-God-Who-Sees - sees you! I hope that revelation gives you comfort and peace as you dig into Hagar's life. She was delighted, God came for her, loved her and put her back on track. Rejoice! God's got His eye on you, and He loves you completely, insecurities, warts, and all. You are His masterpiece and the apple of His eye. He will never leave you or forsake you.

Do I believe Keturah was Hagar? The romantic side of me would like to think so. I hope Jewish tradition has it right because I am an incurable romantic and I love a good ending! No one loves a love story better than me. That's why I love the Bible so very much. It's the very best love story ever written - from start to finish!

Be blessed this week as you study Hagar: A Woman Of Flight.

Next week, Rebekah: A Bride For Isaac.

Hagar's story unfolds in Genesis 16; 21:9-17; 25:12. She is referenced in Galatians 4:24-25

Hagar: A Woman Of Flight

Day One: Who Is Hagar?

Memory Verse: Genesis 16:8 And He said "Hagar, Sarai's maid, where have you come from, and where are you going?" She said, "I am fleeing from the presence of my mistress Sarai."

We don't sin in a vacuum – it touches the lives of those around us because it has a ripple effect. This week's lesson invites us into the trenches with Hagar, an Egyptian slave girl whose life was radically changed because of her masters' sin and the consequences. God views every sin the same. To God, sin is always sin! It never morphs into something other than an offense against Him. *Sin* basically means *to have a different opinion, about any topic, that is contrary to God's.* Anything that is in direct opposition to what God has said through His word = sin. Webster's dictionary defines sin as *"transgression against divine law."* That's it in a nutshell. When we sin, although it can begin small, it can end like a flood, taking many casualties in its wake. The story of Hagar is an example of the effects of sin. It's been more than 4,000 years since these events occurred, but we're still living in the wake of the consequences of sin.

Read Genesis 16:1-2. Answer the following questions:

1. In these verses, we find the first scriptural record of Hagar. We see from verse 1, Hagar belonged to Sarah. Last week's lesson linked Hagar to the couple through a substantial acquisition from the Egyptian Pharaoh. Through the course of events which involved a lie to Pharaoh, and its exposure, the couple was blessed with many gifts, among other things, slaves, both male and female. (Genesis 12:16.) Most Bible scholars speculate this is where Hagar entered their life. As part of an endowment given Abraham for Pharaoh's impending union with Sarah. Nonetheless, today's lesson will reveal some things which appear to be blessings prove to be otherwise. God uses all things to shape Christ-like character in us. Read James 1:17. Who gives the perfect gifts and from where do they come? Write the verse.

2. Read Hebrews 11:11. This was our memory verse for last week. How does this verse describe Sarah? Is this description evidenced in Genesis 16:1-2? Explain.

3. Read Esphesians 6:5-9. What instruction does Paul give slaves in verses 5-8? What instruction does Paul give masters in verse 9? List the important points from each verse below.

v. 5

v. 6

v. 7

v. 8

v. 9

Read Genesis 16:3-4. Answer the following questions.

4. It appears Hagar's fate is sealed. Was Hagar bound by the decisions of Sarah and Abraham? Why?

Who is Hagar? In reality, she was a female Egyptian slave who belonged to Sarah and Abraham. She was Sarah's attendant. Her life was not her own. She had no rights, no standing, no money, no property, or privileges. She had no future or hope apart from them. She was in a foreign land and was duty-bound to a life of servitude unless Abraham had a mind to set her free. That's who Hagar was. However, this is not how God saw her. She was His image bearer. She was also Sarah's closest companion next to Abraham. That is, until her destiny placed her, naked, in a tent in the arms of her mistress Sarah's husband. That would be Abraham.

5. Believers are called to walk with God and wait upon God. Both actions require faith. Sarah and Abraham are listed among those of noteworthy faith in Hebrews 11. In your opinion was Sarah walking with God and waiting upon God? In light of Genesis 16:3, was Abraham?

6. As customary, barren women of this culture could solicit the use of their slave as a surrogate. The idea? Since the slave belonged to her master, the baby would be her master's as well. Let's review Genesis 30:1-24 for another perspective. What did Rachel do? What did Leah do? According to the law, whose children were these?

Rachel -

Anne Nicholson

Leah -

According to the law -

7. Read the first phrase of Genesis 16:4. As was the custom for slaves, Hagar submitted to her masters' request. Her submission was two-fold. First, with her heart to Sarah's plan, and next with her body to Abraham. In light of her position as Sarah's maidservant, she performed faithfully in this scenario. Put yourself in her place for a moment. How do you think she was feeling in this situation? How might you feel?

8. Walking by faith and not by sight means trusting God and not scheming. It's interesting to note, Sarah was scheming. What, if anything, does the Bible say about plotting and scheming? What does it say about getting ahead of God? Record a verse to share.

9. What about Hagar, did she scheme? Or, was she a victim? What does Jesus say about our attitude toward those who mistreat us? Record a verse to share.

10. Hagar was duty-bound. The entirety of her life was wrapped up in Sarah and Abraham. She was the real sufferer. She bore Sarah's sin, and Abraham's, literally, a son born of the flesh. A son of bitterness, resentment, and loathing. A son of their own making, which was bitter fruit, indeed. In giving Hagar to Abraham, Sarah unleashed evil like the world had never seen. Their actions ignited a rivalry that's fueled by hatred. Like a curse, this hatred perpetually feeds itself, generation after generation. Its insatiable fury still rages because it's raw, bitter, and passionate. Oceans of blood have been shed on both sides, but the hostility and resentment have not been satisfied. There is not enough human blood to accomplish or satisfy. But the blood of Jesus - it's enough, it's sufficient. It's perfect! How does the Savior's blood reconcile humanity's colossal mess of hatred and brokenness? Record the words of John 3:16 below and pray their promise. Only the Prince of Peace, Jesus - our soon and coming King, can satisfy the twisted and evil hearts of men.

Meditation

Isaiah 40:31 But those who wait on the Lord shall renew their strength; They shall mount up with wings like eagles, They shall run and not be weary, They shall walk and not faint.

Hagar: A Woman Of Flight

Day Two: Where Is Hagar In God's Redemption Story?

Memory Verse: Genesis 16:8 And He said, "Hagar, Sarai's maid, where have you come from, and where are you going?" She said, "I am fleeing from the presence of my mistress Sarai."

Fertility issues are never easy. The thing we need to remember is God is in control. Unfortunately, that does not bring relief to some women, Sarah was one of those. Enough was enough! Even though God was with them and she knew Abraham was on a mission with God, her heart still ached. She wanted and needed a child to love, to hold, and nurture. She had been waiting all her life to be a mother. Since they were in a childless marriage, not a loveless marriage, mind you, it occurred to her to appeal to her husband's heart to solicit support. So, one fateful day, she hatched a plan. To accomplish it, however, she needed Abraham not only to agree but to participate. Hagar, too. But that was a non-issue. After all, Hagar was her slave. She would do as instructed - or else! So, where was Hagar in God's redemption story? In the midst of a scheme conceived by Sarah. A selfish scheme which got ahead of God. About thirteen years or so, it seems.

1. Waiting for the promises of God can be difficult, even for someone who has a history of faithfully following God. Since Sarah took matters into her own hands, we can safely assume she believed God's delayed response to her barrenness was most certainly a *no*. Read Proverbs 3:5-6. Instead, how should believers respond? What do these verses ensure God will do?

1.

2.

3.

4.

2. "So he went into Hagar, and she conceived." (Genesis 16:4). Too late to turn back now. It was a done deal. What was the outcome? For the answer, read and record the last sentence of verse 4.

3. The word *despise* in verse 4 has a different meaning than the English text conveys. Hagar had a loss of esteem or a lesser opinion of her mistress once her pregnancy was confirmed. The original definition implies she viewed Sarah as "of little account" because she could do for Abraham something his "princess" could not. Read Romans 12:3. From this passage, what does God's word suggest about self exaltation and pride?

4. Read Genesis 16:3-4 and Genesis 3:6. We find some prideful similarities in these verses - both, at the hands of women. What was taken, given, and/or received in these verses?

Genesis 3:6 -

Genesis 16:3-4 -

Where is Hagar in God's redemption story? In the middle of willful disobedience to God's plan.

5. Then Sarai said to Abram, "My wrong be upon you!" (Genesis 16:5). The word *"wrong"* in Hebrew is *"hamas."* It means *pertaining to malicious lies (liars) and betrayal; sometimes used of physical violence.* Ishmael, born from the seed of Abraham is the root from which the Arab-Israeli conflict springs! Ishmael grew to become the father of 12 sons who birthed the Arab nation. And, it all occurred because Abraham and Sarah got ahead of God. A couple living by faith and not by sight were to wait on God and walk with God. But, when she could wait no longer, Sarah took matters into her own hands and gave her husband into the caressing hands of another. Tragically, her plan backfired. Glory be, what we think will satisfy often doesn't. Instead of joy and satisfaction, it brought despair, indeed! The consequences were tremendous and still are. Consider the biblical meaning of consequences to sin. Are God's consequences always justified? Yes or no? If possible, record a verse to support your thoughts.

About Hamas.

Are you unfamiliar with the word, *ḥāmās,* and it's biblical implications? Although this is a simple explanation, it will adequately satisfy our purposes within this study. Traditionally, Hamas is recognized and identified as an international terrorist organization by the European Union, Canada, Israel, Egypt, Japan, and the United States. The proper name Hamas is an acronym for the name of an Islamic terrorist organization built on malicious lies, betrayal and physical violence, often resulting in terrorist activity. From the text before us, the Hebrew word *ḥāmās* means *violence, wronged.* I find it interesting, every time a Jew hears the name Hamas – or the word *ḥāmās*, he is aware of its biblical origin when Sarah blamed Abraham for her self-inflicted poor decision and permanent consequences. In its Old Testament usage, the word is commonly connected to sinful violence (of man), rather than natural catastrophes or weather-related disasters, etc.

6. Sarah confessed, "I gave my maid into your embrace…" (Genesis 16:5). The Hebrew word *embrace* is *ḥêq* meaning *lap, bosom, i.e., an area of the body between the waist and arm* (Ge 16:5; Nu 11:12; Ru 4:16; 2Sa 12:3; 1Ki 3:20; Pr 5:20; 6:27), note: this is the area where one embraces and cuddles as an act of love and warmth; [4] Apparently, when speaking these words for the first time, Sarah gets a visual of Hagar in Abraham's arms. What she saw in her mind's eye was unthinkable! I'm not sure what Sarah thought her recommendation might look like,

---

[4] Swanson, J. (1997). <u>Dictionary of Biblical Languages with Semantic Domains : Hebrew (Old Testament)</u> (electronic ed.). Oak Harbor: Logos Research Systems, Inc.

but the reality now overwhelmed her! Maybe she never considered these moments of passion or pleasure – but this was it! Her Abraham holding, caressing and loving another woman. It was simply too much! When Sarah pictured the intimacy they enjoyed - at her expense - she is hurt and furious. Never mind she had insisted upon it. Now, she plays the victim. How typical and utterly human. Her joyful scheme had become her worst nightmare. Her Abraham had been intimate with another woman, and it was of her own making. Is Sarah's anger justifiable? Why or why not? From a biblical perspective, what is justifiable, valid, or legitimate anger and when is it appropriate? (Ex. Jesus experienced justifiable anger when He cleansed the Temple in Jerusalem by beating the money changers. See Matthew 21:12-13.)

Meditation
John 14:15 If you love Me, keep my commandments.

Hagar: Woman Of Flight

Day Three: Hagar's Submission - What Happened First?

Memory Verse: Genesis 16:8 And He said "Hagar, Sarai's maid, where have you come from, and where are you going?" She said, "I am fleeing from the presence of my mistress Sarai."

In many ways, Hagar was a victim. Slaves lived under the authority of their master - regardless. That authority wavered somewhere between just and unjust because people are flawed and sinful, and the surrounding culture was heathen. Apart from God's law ruling and reigning in the hearts of men, there is no authentic justice. All slaves were duty-bound to perform at the pleasure of their master. The rules applied to Hagar. Sarah had made a big request, indeed. But, it appears from Ephesians 6:5-9, Hagar had no options. Keep in mind, however, believers with slaves were to treat them with fairness. In turn, slaves were to submit to their masters *"as to Christ."* The golden rule comes to mind. Out of Christian charity, we are to treat all others the way we would like to be treated. Matthew 7:12, says it all. "Therefore, whatever you want men to do to you, do also to them, for this is the Law and the Prophets.*"* That goes hand in hand with the greatest commandment and the second like it. "And you shall love the Lord your God with all your heart, with all your soul, with all your mind, and with all your strength. This is the first commandment. And the second, like it, is this: 'You shall love your neighbor as yourself.' There is no other commandment greater than these." (Mark 12:30-31).

1. Under the master/slave relationship, Hagar submitted to the most bizarre request. As required, Hagar complied with Sarah's request. Considering Sarah's plan, what woman in her right mind would give the love of her life into the arms of another woman? One who was desperate. Using a dictionary, write a definition for desperate/desperation.

    desperate/desperation -

2. What does God's word say about placing our trust in Him? Does it apply to all circumstances and consequences of our life? (1) Record your favorite trust verse to share. (2) When, if ever, has this verse prevented you from taking the wrong course of action?

3. Read Genesis 2:24, 1 Corinthians 6:18, and Hebrews 13:4. In light of these verses, although a surrogate was customary in this culture, what does God recommend? Why?

4. Read Romans 8:28 and 2 Timothy 1:9. God is always bringing about His purposes. His plan will prevail. How are verses like these (and other similar verses) encouraging you presently? How have they encouraged you previously?

5. In your opinion, what does their open adulterous activity convey about their trust in God? What does it say about their faith in light of Hebrews 11:8-11?

6. There is heartache, strife, and conflict in the camp of Abraham. He finds himself caught in the middle of a hot mess proposed by Sarah. Ultimately, she places all the blame and responsibility squarely upon Abraham. She accuses him of doing wrong, (ḥāmās), from the root word meaning *to wrong, do violence to, treat violently*. Remember, all this occurred through Sarah's attempt to help God out and build a family through their own devices.

Although she is the architect of the plan of unpleasant events, she demands vindication and justice. Read Proverbs 30:21, 23. What does it say about a servant who displaces her mistress?

7. What is Abraham to do? Apparently, he doesn't know, so he does nothing. He is passive. How disappointing. He quiets his jealous wife's tongue, but at the expense of Hagar. Genesis 16:6 says, So Abram said to Sarai, "Indeed your maid is in your hand; do to her as you please." Abraham chooses to do nothing and places Hagar in Sarah's angry, jealous hands. In your opinion, has Abraham made another poor decision? Why? Provide scriptural instruction which would have served the situation better for all concerned.

In her jealousy, Sarah turns her rage from Abraham to Hagar, making life very difficult for Hagar. We read from scripture: So Abram said to Sarai, "Indeed your maid is in your hand; do to her as you please." And when Sarai **dealt harshly** with her, she fled from her presence. Genesis 16:6 (NKJV). (Emphasis added).

To convey its original meaning, other Bible editors have chosen the words, *"mistreated, dealt hardly, and treated her harshly,"* to describe the assault. All the transliterations come from the verb *'ānā*, meaning to *"afflict, oppress, humble."* To fully grasp the force of Sarah's rage, we must not overlook the primary meaning of the root word in this event. It means *"to force, or try to force submission, and to punish or inflict pain upon."* Bible scholars have concluded the verb is used to describe what one does to his enemy. It identifies the discomfort Sarah willfully inflicted upon Hagar. From all translations, it's apparent. In her anger, Sarah inflicted physical pain upon Hagar; possibly through a few good beatings! Suffice it to say; this was not Sarah's finest hour. Understandably, Hagar flees.

8. Hagar's need to escape is two-fold. First, to escape the wrath of Sarah and, second, the deafening silence of Abraham. It's possible his silence was equally as painful, if not more so, causing more heartache and humiliation than Sarah's physical assault. Abraham's passive demeanor is shameful. There is no scriptural evidence he ever came to Hagar's defense. Quite the contrary. He gave Hagar into the hands of Sarah. Shamefully, with sealed lips, Abraham turned a blind eye. As a result, we discover the meaning of Hagar's name in her actions. In your opinion, did she have another option? What would you have done?

9. When we hatch a plan to bring about our desired end, it never works. God will never allow His children to sin - successfully. In other words, we will not get away with floating our boat forever. Eventually, His great love runs it aground! Thanks to God, we are not left in our sin. Can you share a time when you hatched a plan to bring about your desired end? What were the results?

Meditation
1 John 4:8 . . .for God is love

Hagar: Woman Of Flight

Day Four: Hagar's Submission - What Happened Next?

Memory Verse: Genesis 16:8 And He said "Hagar, Sarai's maid, where have you come from, and where are you going?" She said, "I am fleeing from the presence of my mistress Sarai."

At the beginning of today's lesson, we find three adults and one unborn child commingled through sin. What a colossal mess! They've connected alright. They're bound by many sins, including adultery, hatred, and anger. Of course, at the root of it all, we find pride and self. That's always the case with sin. It thrives and abounds when we love and worship the "creature, or the created rather than our Creator." When had this occurred? It happened when Sarah took her eyes of God and placed them on herself; and when she failed to worship and recall the goodness of God and His faithful keeping throughout the years. Simply stated, it occurred when Sarah was unable to trust. That's when Sarah: 1) thought she knew more than God; 2) wanted what God had not given her – yet; and 3) took matters into her own hands. That pretty much sums it up.

Now the trio exists in an unpleasant situation, and it's rapidly deteriorating. It's volatile, turbulent, and unpredictable. Glory be! Sarah struck a pregnant woman, and Abraham turned a blind eye. The patriarchal couple had failed to trust God in a way that honors Him. "But God" had a plan. He always does, even in our failures. As Hagar fled Abraham's passive neglect and Sarah's physical abuse, she encountered "the Angel of the Lord." Unbeknownst to her, she was not alone. Hagar had run, but not beyond the reach of a loving God.

1. When Hagar fled, she carried Abraham's seed with her. Eventually, she stopped to rest by a spring on the road to Shur. Hagar was homeward bound. After ten years of servitude, she was now a slave on the run - a fugitive. "But God" had a plan. Read Genesis 16:7-8. Hagar could run, but she could not escape the watchful eye of God. What does this tell you about God?

Women of the Bible and God's Redeeming Love

2. The God of comfort is always near. God has left us many promises in scripture. One of great comfort is found in the book of Hebrews. God has pledged: "I will never leave you nor forsake you" (Hebrews 13:5). Although Hagar has wandered far beyond the protection of Abraham, she could never wander beyond the protection of God. How does this verse encourage you in your present circumstances?

3. Hagar has been called out by God. Review Genesis 16:7-12. Note the words, "the Angel of the Lord found her..." (Genesis 16:7). Hagar was not lost! *Found* in this passage means something altogether different. The Angel of the Lord has come to her aid. Hagar has a theophany in which she receives a prophetic promise of personal blessing from God. How very rare and special. This is the first encounter with "the Angel of the Lord" in the Bible. He is generally identified as our Lord Jesus Christ. Look closely a the statements made by the one appearing. It must be God, because the Angel promises only what God can accomplish. How comforting! The Son of God was not too busy to reveal His love and mercy to an outcast servant girl on the run. What does scripture assure us about God's love in Psalm 9:9? Record the verse below. In your opinion, is God's love evidenced in Genesis 16:7-8?

4. The omniscient God knows Hagar's name, but more than that. He intimately cares for her. God could never forget Hagar. With tenderness, with purpose, and with care, He calls her name. Unlike Sarah and Abraham, who never uttered her name in scripture. To them, she was a mere slave, a possession. Albeit true, Hagar was a slave and a foreigner, but to God, Hagar was so much more. She was His image bearer. She was loved, cherished, and called forth by God with divine purpose. Reread that sentence. You are just as significant to God, today - right here and right now. Regardless! How special is this? God afforded great privilege to a hopeless, helpless, and homeless slave girl - a fugitive on the run. He came for her. God found Hagar! He is near, always, but most certainly in times of despair. He is there for you! How do you think Hagar felt when she heard the Angel of the Lord call her name? Read Psalm 46:1. What does it mean to you? Record the verse below.

5. Hagar responded truthfully to the Angel of the Lord but fails to say where she's headed. At that moment, she's a woman without hope; she sees no future. Have you ever felt like you were a woman without hope? How did God rescue you? If possible, record a verse to convey your thoughts.

6. Read Genesis 16:9. What did the Angel of the Lord tell Hagar to do? Why do you suppose He makes this request? Surely if The Angel asks this - it is good! In your opinion, what, if any, good could come from this?

7. Review Genesis 16:7-16. Hagar is commanded: "Return and submit yourself under her hand." (Genesis 16:9). Our definition of *submit* means to *voluntarily place oneself under the authority of another.* Hagar knew what this meant. *Return* from this passage is an imperative in Hebrew - it was a command! Don't you know these words shook Hagar to the core? Remember, having a conversation with the Angel of the Lord did not change her identity; Hagar was still a slave, and she would remain a slave. Only Abraham could release her from a life of servitude. However, she hears and receives the conditional promise God makes concerning her unborn child. Do you see it in the passage? (See Genesis 16:12). Through Hagar's return and submission, a significant event will occur - Ishmael's emancipation. What good news! To activate the promise, Hagar would go back. Her submission and obedient response will speak volumes! What message will it send to Sarah and Abraham? And others?

8. Let's take another look. Reread Genesis 16:10-11. What does the Angel of the Lord promise in verse 10? What does the Angel reveal and require in verse 11?

v. 10

v. 11

9. For closer examination, read and review Genesis 16:12. What four things are outlined?

1.

2.

3.

4.

10. Note the prophecy and promises revealed in Genesis 16:12. Hagar's son would be the beginning of a people God would multiply so greatly they could not be counted? Who are they? Has God kept His word?

11. Ishmael's name is significant. It means God heard. *El = God; yisma = hears; yišmāʿēʾl.*

The name commemorates the Lord who heard Hagar's affliction. God heard her misery. What was Hagar's affliction?

Meditation
Psalm 119:90a Your faithfulness endures to all generations

Hagar: Woman Of Flight

Day Five: How Did God's Love Redeem It All?

Memory Verse: Genesis 16:8 And He said "Hagar, Sarai's maid, where have you come from, and where are you going?" She said, "I am fleeing from the presence of my mistress Sarai."

Hagar gave God a name. She holds the distinction of being the only person, male or female to name God. Through the name, Hagar confirms the Lord both *hears and sees* her sorrow by appropriately naming Him, "You-Are-The-God-Who-Sees." (Genesis 16:13). You are El-Roi - *'attâ 'ēl rŏ'î,* its meaning, *"a God of seeing"* or *"the God who sees me."* The Amplified Bible translation expands the verse to read as follows: Then she called the name of the Lord who spoke to her, "You are God Who Sees"; for she said, "Have I not even here [in the wilderness] remained alive after seeing Him [who sees me with understanding and compassion]?" **(Genesis 16:13) (AMP).** Notice the Amplified translation reveals God's watchful eye is upon us. But more so, it exposes the depth of the Lord's tender care for us. What a marvelous gift in scripture. A runaway slave has memorialized God's understanding and compassionate care for us through this divine encounter. There is undoubtedly more to Hagar than meets the eye!

1. Read Genesis 16:13-14. Our Lord sees and knows each of us intimately. Record a sentence or two sharing your thoughts concerning Hagar's divine encounter. Is it comforting to know God sees you in all times and all places? Why or why not?

2. The reality is riveting. The Angel of the Lord not only reveals Hagar's pregnancy, but her disdain and hatred for her mistress Sarah as well. Hagar is busted! Don't you hate it when that happens – when our hearts are exposed? Hagar knew full well when He saw her misery, the depth of her heart was revealed, including its hardness. Hagar experiences an

unfamiliar amazing grace. Grace which overlooks our imperfections, including thoughts or social standing and loves us still.

Do you think God's grace and mercy helped her to have the courage to return to Sarah and Abraham? Why or why not?

We know God is omniscient, all knowing and all seeing. Nothing escapes Him. That means He knows what we will do before we do it. He foreknew all the days of your life before the first one according to the psalmist David who wrote: "Your eyes saw my substance, being yet unformed. And in Your book they all were written, The days fashioned for me, When as yet there were none of them." (Psalm 139:16).

3. Within these mortal bodies, we coexist with thoughts of good and evil and do both good and bad. That's a sobering thought, and Paul knew it all too well. Prayerfully read Romans 7:13-25. Will this knowledge guide you into praying more and acting out less? Why or why not? Allow *"The God Who Sees"* to search your heart. You are invited to share.

4. In our text, *"The God Who Sees,"* gave Hagar a promise. He desires to speak to you as well. Ask the Lord Jesus to reveal His plans for this season of your life. Ask for guidance, wisdom, direction, and reassurance. Are you perhaps waiting for the fruit of God's promises? Don't despair, don't grow weary in the wait, and don't run ahead as Sarah did. When and if we do, it never works in our favor. To guide your prayers, read the following verses and pray God confirms His promises in your heart. Pray and meditate on these passages. They are some of God's most beloved promises in the Bible. (Listed alphabetically).

Isaiah 40:29-31; Jeremiah 29:11; John 3:16; John 14:27, Matthew 11:28-29; Philippians 4:19; Proverbs 1:33; Romans 6:23; Romans 8:37-39; Romans 10:9.

If the *"God Who Sees You"* gives or has given you a scriptural promise, record it below.

5. According to Genesis 16:16, Abraham was 86 years old when Ishmael was born. His ever-increasing age heightens the improbability of another child, naturally. "But God" has a plan. The age issue will make the miracle birth of Isaac even more magnified, for the glory of God. Although the Angel of the Lord had given Hagar a command to name her son, she didn't do it. Read Genesis 16:15. What happened? Who gave him a name?

6. In Genesis 21, we find the long-awaited arrival of Isaac, the child of promise. Read Genesis 21:8-9. Give a brief summary of what occurred at the celebration where Isaac was weaned.

v. 8

v. 9

Anne Nicholson

7. From Genesis 21:10, Sarah expressed concern, what was it? What was Abraham's displeasure in Genesis 21:11?

Sarah's concern v. 10:

Abraham's displeasure v. 11:

8. God has an amazing plan. How does He soothe Abraham? What does God require of Abraham? Read Genesis 21:12-13 and list the three major points God makes to Abraham.

1.

2.

3.

9. Read Genesis 21:14-17. Abraham obeyed God. Notice the words, "So she sat opposite him and lifted her voice and wept." (Genesis 21:16). Seems as if Hagar has been in this spot before, spiritually and physically. To whose voice does God respond in verse 17?

Women of the Bible and God's Redeeming Love

10. Read Genesis 21:17-21. Another theophany! The Angel of God visits Hagar again. How astounding! What does He ask, assure, and instruct in verses 17 & 18?

v. 17

v. 18

11. Observe the spiritual and natural satisfaction found in "the water" of Genesis 21:19. We cannot live without water. Our Lord Jesus is the spiritual water; He is the living water. In this instance, the revelation of water is a useful metaphor, highlighting the sustainable provision of God. Who revealed the water to Hagar?

12. Record the first six words of Genesis 21:20. These words of comfort affirm no one is beyond the reach of God.

Meditation
Romans 10:13 For whosoever shall call upon the name of the Lord shall be saved.

Let's Ponder.

Did Hagar believe? Scripture is silent on the topic; however, Genesis 16:13 begins, *"Then..."* When was then? First and foremost, *"Then..."* was after Hagar's amazing theophany with the Angel whom she recognized as God. You may recall, the event occurred when Hagar fled from Sarah's abusive treatment and God *found* her by a spring of water in the wilderness. (See Genesis 16:6). Hagar was on the run, but her spiritual journey began the moment God called her by name. (See Genesis 16:8). Most assuredly, being identified by God got Hagar's attention. Remember, neither Sarah or Abraham ever called her by name. The *"Then"* of v. 13 also occurred after God acknowledged her pregnancy. (See Genesis 16:11). In so doing, He shared various details about her pregnancy. The details included forecasting the infant's sex and giving him a name. Next, He spoke a prophetic promise concerning Ishmael's life and explained how Hagar's return and submission would spare her son a life of servitude. Ultimately, *"Then..."* was after Hagar's life was touched by God. You could say, for Hagar, everything changed in an instant. That was the instant Hagar, a woman of flight, was made whole. It all happened when her sad and lonely heart collided with the love of God.

A Rare Encounter.

This rare encounter, a visitation of the pre-incarnate Christ, most certainly got Hagar's attention. Undoubtedly, His astounding presence was riveting enough to apprehend her wholly - mind, body, spirit, and soul. His work is always complete; it is never lacking.

A Rare Occurrence.

God named her unborn child. The name Ishmael is the first of three names in the Bible given by God during pregnancies. Gabriel, who identified himself as the one *"who stands in the presence of God,"* later named both John the Baptist and Jesus while they grew and flourished within the security of their respective mothers' wombs. We will look at these events in our study of Mary, the Virgin Mother.

An Unprecedented Privilege.

When all of this was said and done – lastly, and *"Then..."* Hagar named God. Was all this enough for her to come to faith? I believe it was because she gave God a name that contains the name *"God"* within it. She named Him, *El* (God) *Roi, "The God Who Sees."* Remember, we have been chosen, called to faith, and believed apart from divine visitation, unlike Hagar who looked deep into God's face and lived. After naming Him, she humbly asked: "Have I also here seen Him who sees me?" (Genesis 16:13).

According to Jewish tradition, within the act of naming God, Hagar came to faith. Rabbinic teachings confirm and support that position. They teach Hagar was awakened spiritually and came to faith in the God of Abraham at His appearing. The results? She gave Him a name – a rare unprecedented privilege, indeed. Hagar not only saw God and lived, but she is also the only human being to name God - ever! As we conclude our study of Hagar, prayerfully read Romans 10:13. Do you believe Hagar had saving faith?

Notes - Hagar: A Woman Of Flight

Rebekah

Rebekah: A Bride For Isaac

When I consider all the women in the Bible, Rebekah stands out. She ranks high on the chart of those to whom I can relate. I'll confess, I see bits and pieces of myself in all of them, but I have a particular affinity for Rebekah. A verse in her romantic story pierced my heart and changed my perspective. You might say, it aligned me with God. The last verse of Genesis 24 pulls back the curtain and invites us into Isaac and Rebekah's life at the very beginning. Here we find the scriptural account of their marriage ceremony and its tender consummation. It was the beginning of their lifetime of devotion, love, and faithfulness. The passage says, "Then Isaac brought her into his mother Sarah's tent; and he took Rebekah and she became his wife, and he loved her. So Isaac was comforted after his mother's death." (Genesis 24:67). Unlike other men of this time, including his father, Isaac never took another lover. He had no other wives or concubines. Rebekah would be the love of his life for all of his life. After God, she was his one and only.

I'm sure you must be thinking, "That's a curious verse to choose!" But you shall see as the lesson progresses how this was such profound news to me. I'll just bet it will be news to you as well. It was a nugget and blessing which changed my heart and redefined my marriage in a time when I needed desperately to hear God's voice! In fact, it is one of my favorite passages in the entire Bible. When I feel that I am out of sorts or out of order, whichever the case might be, that verse, coupled with this one, "Is anything too hard for the Lord?" (Genesis 18:14) set me to rights every time! You see, at the root of both passages, there's an underlying thread of submission. It might be hard to see on the surface, but we'll unpack that and so much more in our exciting study.

Who Is Rebekah?

Simply stated, she was Abraham's grandniece or great niece. She was the granddaughter of Abraham's brother, Nahor. In Genesis 24:10, we learn Rebekah hails from the town of Nahor, in the region of Mesopotamia which is nestled between the Tigris and Euphrates Rivers. That would be roughly the area of modern-day Iraq and southeastern Syria. The town was settled and named by Rebekah's grandfather, Nahor - Abraham's older brother. That's important to note because later in our study, we will discover Abraham has big plans for a relative's daughter. He has determined since it's crucial Isaac marry and marry soon, his bride must come from the right family. In other words, Abraham was fully persuaded Isaac's bride must come from their family tree.

The first mention of Rebekah in scripture is Genesis 22:20-24. Reading from verse 23, "And Bethuel begot Rebekah. These eight Milcah bore to Nahor, Abraham's brother." The Rebekah identified in this passage is our Rebekah.

In biblical times, large families were quite the norm. Although Abraham and Sarah had some fertility issues, it appears from Genesis 22:20-24 his brother, Nahor didn't. As you can see, in all, twelve sons were born of Nahor and his wife Milcah and concubine, Reumah. From these twelve, the family tree grew quite large. Take note. Issac and Rebekah adorn the same family tree - both occupying "second cousin" branches. Most of us have not married cousins, but as we learned in our study of Sarah, marrying a first or second cousin or a half-sibling was a relatively common occurrence during biblical times. As we move forward, the pair will undoubtedly prove to be more than merely "kissing cousins." Ultimately, their devoted love will span a lifetime.

We find Rebekah's birth and familial ties referenced again. The verse reads in part, "Rebekah, who was born to Bethuel, son of Milcah, the wife of Nahor, Abraham's brother…" (Genesis 24:15). Scripture does not provide us with a lot of information about Rebekah's family. It is interesting to note although her father is identified, Rebekah's mother is not. She is mentioned briefly in the company of Eliezer, but her name is not revealed. On the contrary, her brother, Laban, is named and identified in Genesis 24:29. Later in Genesis, he will reappear and play a huge role in shaping Rebekah's son, Jacob's future. Namely, concerning the selection of Jacob's wives. Their dramatic story of romance, deceit, and betrayal unfolds in Genesis 29 – 31.

Scripture tells us Rebekah was not only pure, but she was also beautiful. Although outward beauty does not guarantee a good wife or the perfect match, her beauty would be a bonus for Isaac. The verse reads, "Now the young woman was very beautiful to behold, a virgin; no man had known her." (Genesis 24:16).

She has other outstanding qualities as well, most notably a servant's heart. That will make her an excellent match for Isaac. Remember, his bride will have the esteemed privilege and responsibility of co-leading the nation of Israel. As a couple, they will have big shoes to fill because Abraham and Sarah have led God's people well. Her servant's heart is a tremendous asset. It will prove beneficial because to effectively lead others - it's a must. We'll examine this in our study guide. It will not take long to discover she goes far above and beyond what would typically be expected to aid a stranger she encounters at the well.

Day three of our study guide will examine her other exceptional qualities, like giving attention to detail, taking the initiative, steadfast determination, and follow-through. She was a take-charge kind of gal. She sees a task and jumps right in with a remedy. You might say she is a problem-solver of sorts. Which can be a good thing, and it will prove to be such - that is, until it isn't.

Where Is Rebekah In God's Redemption Story?

Sarah died. The circumstances surrounding her death are not revealed in scripture, but we do know Abraham's wife - the mother of Isaac, has died. At the age of 127, she drew her last breath and was buried in a cave at Machpelah. So that you know, the cave Abraham purchased to bury his beloved Sarah was the first real estate transaction in the Bible. Abraham lived in the promised land for 62 years without owning anything permanent until he purchased the family tomb. So, who's buried there? Three patriarchal couples: Abraham and Sarah; Isaac and Rebekah; Jacob and Leah.

You may be wondering what does this have to do with Rebekah? Just this. Abraham was willing to place his beloved wife's body in the cave in Machpelah - in Canaan - because he believed according to God's covenant promise, Canaan would be his and his descendants, and Isaac was next in line. God had promised it, and Abraham believed it. By the way, Abraham's faith is noteworthy. It is accounted to him for righteousness. The measure of his faith is recorded in Genesis 15:6; Romans 4:3; Galatians 3:6; as well as James 2:23, which adds Abraham was also called God's friend. How thrilling! So, too, with us. We believe, and we are justified by faith just like Abraham. That is the foundation of our faith. We believe God.

Abraham never owned a piece of dirt up until this time. It's essential to our story because this will hugely impact Rebekah's life. She will live with Isaac after the pattern established by her in-laws. They would live by faith and follow God. God never said, "Abraham, I'm calling you out, I've made you wealthy, go buy a big house and live comfy the remaining days of your life." God never allowed him to purchase anything permanent until the appointed time. This world was not their home; they were merely passing through.

Abraham and Sarah were looking for a different kind of city. They were nomads, living in tents. They were moving from place to place, as God ordained. To the pagan world, their lives were to clearly testify, *our God lives and reigns.* We find a description in the book of Hebrews. "By faith he dwelt in the land of promise as in a foreign country, dwelling in tents with Isaac and Jacob, the heirs with him of the same promise; for he waited for the city which has foundations, whose builder and maker is God." (Hebrews 11:9-10).

Isaac could not accomplish God's plan alone. To be successful, he needed a wife, but not just any wife. Abraham was of the firm opinion Isaac must marry a woman of the family, his family - the family of faith - rather than taking a pagan wife as Ishmael had done. (Genesis 21:21.) After a respectable time of mourning Sarah's death - about three years - Abraham starts thinking about the state of Isaac's singleness and comes up with a plan to send Eliezer to find a suitable bride for his heir. Even though Isaac would appear much too old to need parental assistance in securing a bride, it was protocol. Parents were actively involved in the selection of spouses for their children. You may be thinking perish the thought, but it's true. Additionally, since pagans occupied the surrounding land, and to avoid another inappropriate match, Abraham would intervene.

He knew just the man for the job. He commissioned and sent *"the oldest servant of his house"* to find a bride for Isaac. (Genesis 24:2-4.) Although the servant's name isn't stated in these passages, he is identified by Abraham as Eliezer of Damascus in Genesis 15:1-2. Eliezer received detailed instructions from Abraham and pledged an oath to do as Abraham instructed. It was agreed, if *"the woman"* would not return with him, Eliezer would be released from his oath. (Genesis 24:8.) In short, he was to take ten camels along with many gifts and treasures for an endowment and travel back to Mesopotamia. It was not a short excursion. It was about a two-weeks journey covering 500 miles, each way. Isaac was not to make the trip. It was most important according to Abraham his son not accompany Eliezer on the journey. As instructed, Abraham's faithful servant soon departed at his master's pleasure without delay.

When he reached his destination of Nahor, he knelt and prayed. Eliezer set a fleece before God to know his journey was a success. (Genesis 24:12-14.) It was near evening when God placed Eliezer in the right spot - at the right time to encounter Rebekah. Low and behold, she would appear leading all the other town's women to the well for water. As God would have it, she will successfully fulfill every detail of Eliezer's fleece. Check, check, check! Success. She will offer Eliezer a drink and then go far above and beyond what would be customary by not only providing him a drink of fresh water but offering to water all his camels to their fill. A servant indeed! A thirsty camel can drink up to thirty gallons of water and scripture reveals they drank until they finished. Which means until they were satisfied and stopped drinking! Genesis 24:22. Can you imagine the time, strength, and ingenuity this required? Rebekah worked cheerfully and with precision - until the job was accomplished! A considerable feat; and all for the benefit of a stranger and his thirsty beasts! Rebekah was about to be handpicked, called out, and identified by God as the one - the one for Isaac. Together, they and their descendants would birth the nation of Israel.

Doing The Next Right Thing.

When Eliezer found her, Rebekah was doing the next right thing. I am sure to her it appeared to be just another ordinary day. It was, however, an extraordinary day indeed! As stated above, Rebekah went out to the well one evening as was her daily routine, and while performing this mundane task of collecting water, she collided with her destiny. Talk about being in the right place at the right time. She was found doing the next right thing, serving her family, and in the process, she stepped into her destiny.

When it pleased God and fulfilled His plan and purposes, she was called to become the wife of Abraham's physical and spiritual heir. Rebekah was called to marry his son Isaac, the child of promise! She was a young girl with an extraordinary call on her life. But what's even more fascinating than her call was her ability to trust this was God's plan for her life. In the process, she will overrule her family's objections and attempts to delay her decision. She will handle it all with maturity and grace. Once the matter is settled in her heart, she hastens to do the will of God and never looks back. There is no record in scripture that she ever saw her birth family again. She had been raised up and prepared by God for this high call.

So, Rebekah's journey began that very evening, and what a ride. Less than 48 hours after her encounter with Eliezer at the well, she would embark on a journey. The adventure of a lifetime. Young Rebekah would travel more than 500 miles, on a camel, to marry a man she had never seen. Do you find that fascinating? I do. Fascinating and thrilling. Their story is known as one of the great romances of the Bible. Come with me as we step into Rebekah's world. You're invited to a wedding!

What Did Rebekah Get Right?

She believed the servant, Eliezer, and went! She stepped out of her world and into the promises of God because she believed. But, this didn't just happen. She was being prepared for this moment all her life. Do you think, as she was being raised up for this unique purpose, she knew it? No, of course not. She just got up each day and lived a faithful life, doing the next right thing and leaving the results to God.

What a concept, what a plan. As believers, our plan should be to have no plan. Why? Because, He has a plan - the Master's plan. If we have a program or agenda, generally speaking, I can guarantee it differs from God's. His focus is directed outward - toward others, and it's our natural inclination to think of ourselves first. When we come to faith, however, things begin to change. Ever so subtly, over time our focus evolves. We start to think about others more and ourselves less! What they might need and desire becomes more urgent or critical than we thought possible. We begin to love like Jesus and live for Jesus, even within our marriages. If you're married, you know what I'm saying. A good marriage is Christ-centered, with each mate attempting to out-serve the other. I once heard a pastor say we should endeavor to "out-kind" our mates. That sums it up nicely. To put someone else's needs and preferences above your own is akin to sacrificial love. Love like that reflects Christ's love and is pleasing to God. It requires great faith, significant faith to love in this fashion. You shall see, Rebekah has it. If you don't have it, pray for it. It can be yours for the asking.

God Is Preparing You Today For Tomorrow.

Rebekah's preparation took a lifetime - so, too, with us! God's work in and through us never ends, and it will continue until He calls us home. You are being prepared today for tomorrow. Do we know what tomorrow will bring? No, but we know God's at work, and we can trust He loves us, because He lived to die for us. Additionally, the Bible tells us so! We can also believe God has good things planned for us. (Jeremiah 29:11.) We can understand "all things work together for good to those who love God, to those who are called according to His purpose." (Romans 8:28). If you're wondering how it works in real time, let's look at a few examples.

While we were serving on the foreign mission field, or on the streets of Atlanta, or teaching in homeless shelters, or serving food to the homeless, God was at work molding and shaping our lives. Teaching us slowly about Him and His great love for humanity. He enabled us to love others, even those most of you might deem unloveable or untouchable. He was preparing us each day for the next day. What was my part? To get up each day prepared to accomplish the task at hand, merely to do the next right thing, and keep my eyes on Jesus. Sometimes it was as simple as making two hundred sandwiches and providing lunch, a cold drink, a kind word, and prayer. Other days were different and required other acts of love and service. Here's another example.

I knew seminary was most certainly God's open door. How so? They awarded us scholarships. Subsequently, knowing we are to glorify God in all things, with thankful hearts, I wasn't about to waste a minute of that time. Was it difficult? At times, yes. Did I know what would happen when we graduated? Of course not. But, when you're walking by faith and not by sight, you obediently follow, you walk through open doors, regardless the difficulty or challenge, or the fact you can't see the immediate benefits or the future. That's faith. Did I ever consider I would teach in a Bible college and write curriculum and retreats, this book, or any book? Of course not. It was never in my mind, actually in the natural scheme of things, it would have been the furthest thing I could consider. I mean truly. But God did it. Knowing how flawed and frail I feel most of the time, I'm still surprised He uses me at all. I've said before, "I still feel much like a diamond in the rough!"

The Journey.

Our missionary life necessitated travel and moving from place to place. It meant not putting down deep roots because I knew at any given time God could move us forward. I learned early in our marriage and ministry God is not stagnant. He is always on the move. As a result, people and places were subject to change. As God ordained, they would fade in and out of our lives. I heard a marvelous sermon once about the "ministry of goodbye," and I have that - I think. Although I'll admit, I've had some teary-eyed goodbyes to move forward and "go with God." It has become more comfortable to let go as the years' pass. I store memories of laughter and tears in my heart, carry them with me, and often pray for those left. I can let go without regret, and that is a blessing. It's a God thing! I cling to people and things loosely because it appears that's His plan for me.

If you have never been moved or relocated by God, and can't imagine what it's like to start over again and again, I understand. As I write these words, I have peace in my heart. Because of Him we've seen His glory on the faces of people in other parts of the world. It's His world, and within it, His remnant remains! We have connected with these and left the Lord's handprint and blessing upon their lives by His grace and for His glory. Every place and every person along the journey has been part of God's plan. Nothing escapes Him. There is no happenstance in God's economy. Even unpleasant things, momentarily have been part of His plan, and they have purpose. This life on earth is short, and He has much to accomplish through His chosen vessels, including you!

Going With God.

God has given us good news. He's in control! You don't need to worry each day about having a plan because He's got one. Can you trust that? Rebekah did. And she went! I can assure you she never said, "When I grow up I want to leave my family and never, ever return." But she did. I never said, "When I grow up I want to be a missionary and move from place to place without owning a home of my own." But, I went too! Following God's call has been the best blessing of my life. It was also the best blessing of Rebekah's life. And just so you know, if you're saved, you're on the same journey. You may not move, today or tomorrow. You may not move or relocate, ever. If not, bloom where you're planted by His grace and for His glory. He will equip you to do just that. God equips those He calls wherever you serve. He will give you what you need when you need it. God will enable you to accomplish the work He had prepared for you before the foundation of the world - just as He did Rebekah. Yield to Him, obey His word, seek His face, and enjoy His fellowship. He desires to use you, to lead, and guide you!

Marriage Was In Her Heart.

Do you think Rebekah wanted to be married? Of course, she did - all girls desire this. When we were missionaries in Jerusalem, I queried many young girls, both Jews, and Arabs about their future desires. Guess what they all wanted to be? The bride. They wanted above everything else to be chosen as the bride. I don't recall one saying she wanted to be a pilot or an architect or even a physician, for that matter. Our yearning for marriage comes from God. Reading the curse placed on Eve after she bit the apple gives us our clue. "Your desire shall be for your husband." (Genesis 3:16). There you have it. God has already placed within us, a desire for marriage. A longing to love and be loved is in us. A desire to be affirmed as women; the whole package, it's in us. That would include the pleasurable elements of marriage as well, but it's much more than that. We have a desire to rule over our husbands. We looked at this in our study of Eve. That's what the word, *"desire,"* means from Genesis 3:16.

Throughout this week, our examination of Rebekah's life will prove, for the most part, she conducted herself well. She honors her husband well, except for an unfortunate episode involving her children. We'll touch on that in just a moment. Nonetheless, she was a fascinating woman who loved her husband. She understood his needs, both spiritual and physical. As a young woman, God had given her great wisdom and maturity to fulfill her destiny. What was it? To be the wife Isaac needed to accomplish or fulfill his purpose and destiny. She got God's program; she understood being a *helper - ʽēzer*. It's a marvelous thing when we agree with God. When we do, we have peace; contentment and a sense of fulfillment. There's a special and unique excitement, internally, that's very satisfying when you are following obediently. As my husband says, "As you do so, you see the miracles of God." That's how God does it. To be in harmony with God is why we were created - to know God and enjoy Him forever.

Anne Nicholson

What Did Rebekah Get Wrong?

She got ahead of God. You do realize, don't you, that's where most of us mess up. It's a little more involved; however, pride and impatience were the underlying issues. Waiting and trusting God is a difficult challenge. God had given her a promise concerning her favorite son, but she didn't believe He could or would fulfill the promise - apart from her help. She decided she would help God out a little. Many years ago, I got ahead of God. The results were not nearly as painful as Rebekah's; I was lucky, actually favored. But in the end, my husband asked, "Thought you'd help God out a little, did you? How's it working for you?" It's humiliating and painful when we just don't let God be God. Either He is God, or you have made yourself God. Those are the only possibilities. Settle the matter today, in your heart, once and for all. Let the redeemed of the Lord say so, and then live accordingly! We will be looking at the high price Rebekah paid for her mistake on day four of the study guide. It's a powerful lesson for all of us. The very thing she was trying to accomplish left her empty, lonely and heartbroken. She would remember the painful results of her mistake all the remaining days of her life.

By the way, what occurred did not surprise God. None of it. He knew before she hatched a plan what it would be and when she would hatch it. He knew it before she knew it. He is never surprised. His sovereignty and omniscience cover everything that will happen or has happened since "In the beginning God…" (Genesis 1:1). He does, however, allow us to make choices, for we have free will. Sometimes we get it right and sometimes we don't. You will see yourself in her story. Every time I study women of the Bible, I see myself in both the good and the bad of their lives. We are all the same. Since the beginning of time, and women are still women.

How Did God's Love Redeem It All?

As we study Rebekah's life, hopefully, you will take stock of your own. It is unique, and only God knows all it involves. Do you trust God enough to follow? I mean follow with abandon? Can you, today, stop planning? Can you yield to His plan and determine in your heart to move forward without a plan? If you can, hold on to your hat. Rebekah journeyed 500 miles across the desert to be united with Isaac. After weeks, she looked out upon the horizon to inquire about a man walking in the field toward them. The verse says: Then Rebekah lifted her eyes, and when she saw Isaac she dismounted from her camel; for she had said to the servant, "Who is this man walking in the field to meet us?" The servant said, "It is my master." So she took a veil and covered herself. And the servant told Isaac all the things that he had done. Then Isaac brought her into his mother Sarah's tent; and he took Rebekah and she became his wife, and he loved her. So Isaac was comforted after his mother's death. (Genesis 24:64-67).

Do you think she knew the man in the field was Isaac? Did her heart leap when she realized who it was? What was she thinking in the moment? And what was he doing out there? He was praying, most likely. Isaac was a devout man of prayer. You will see that in our study. From the very beginning, she would have seen his unique heart and passion for God. I know it must have thrilled her and encouraged her faith. Nothing excites me more than a man after God - that's why I love my husband so very much. His hunger and thirst for God have led us on a great journey. Honestly, I would not be writing this apart from God's perfect plan and my husband's understanding that having no plan is the better plan. I recall from years ago, someone asked him? "So, what's the plan?" And he proudly answered, "I plan to have no plan." Upon hearing his words, I was stupefied. At the time, I'll have to admit - I thought he was flat-out crazy. It scared me. How could a grown man, an educated man, have no plan? It was counter-cultural, indeed. It went against all I'd ever known. No one lived like this. I thought, "Is he dreaming?" I can see it now and understand. He's not crazy at all, merely favored. After a type and pattern of Abraham, he's walking by faith and not by sight, and looking "…for a city which has foundations, whose builder and maker is God."

The Verse That Changed My Heart.

I shared at the beginning of our study a biblical understanding of Genesis 24:67 changed my life - our lives by redefining our marriage. It altered my thoughts and ideas concerning marriage because it realigned me with God's purposes. You see, there is nothing in Genesis 24:67 about me. It was not about Rebekah either. It was all about Isaac, for his sake, and for his benefit. We looked at God's foundational plan for marriage in our study of Eve. Through her thrilling story, we identified God's purpose in creating women - for man's sake - for their benefit - to complete them. We are to be about helping them become the men God created them to be. Apart from us, they are incomplete - always. Isaac was comforted; Isaac was comforted. Those words sunk deep into my heart. I was flooded with emotion. Rebekah traveled no less than two weeks to fulfill her God-given destiny, her purpose. When she arrived, she promptly dismounted and veiled her face, as was the custom before marriage. In so doing, in essence, Rebekah said, "I honor you, I respect you, and I submit to you. I give myself freely to you… Take me; I am yours." Immediately they were married and consummated their happy union. And, Isaac was comforted.

Consider this if you will. After two long weeks of travel, regardless of the season, it would have been an arduous journey. Nonetheless, from the moment Rebekah saw Isaac, she stepped into her call - to be his bride - his helper or helpmate, his helpmeet – his *ēzer* - his completion. What we must realize is being this unleashes more blessings than we could imagine. Don't believe me? Put it to the test. "Wives, submit to your own husbands, as to the Lord." (Ephesians 5:22). Practice unconditional, unreserved love and affection for your husband and see what happens. Give yourself to him frequently, in fact, Paul says daily. Dote on him, encourage him, love him, and pray for him. It's a blessing and privilege to be a wife - his wife, whoever your husband is. God has put you together. You can aid its blessedness! You can make it better – far better than it is. It is a high and holy call from God to become a wife. Cherish your call! Rejoice, you were made for this. Through your complete love for him, you can reach a place deep within him which can't be accessed through any other means. It's a place only God could create and only your God-ordained love for him can satisfy. Trust me when I tell you your unreserved love for him can and will break through the most hardened walls and barriers. It can heal wounds and deep hurts as well. How do I know? Isaac was comforted. Isaac was comforted. I've lived it – am living it, and I see it in God's word.

Let's look at the word *comfort* a bit closer. Rebekah had compassion from the heart. She embraced Isaac, but not just physically. She gave her whole heart tenderly to him. Rebekah consoled him, commiserated with him, supported him, reassured him, and cheered him. Generally speaking, she elevated him – the total man – mind, body, spirit, and soul by loving and accepting him so freely. By understanding his grief, meeting him there, and embracing it with him. In essence, wise well beyond her years, Rebekah said: "I see you, I feel you, I understand your sorrow, and I embrace all that you are – I accept you just as you are. I'm yours to have and to hold for a lifetime, and I will comfort you! Isaac, I'm here for you!" That's it, in a nutshell - I believe! It's as if the hands of heaven - God - held Isaac in the moment. Rebekah's comfort set the tone for their entire marriage. If she could love him this freely upon just meeting him, it was undoubtedly a divine work of God!

Yes, Rebekah was on a mission from God, and she got it - all of it. She loved Isaac, and he was comforted! Rebekah knew it was not about her. Instead, it was about Isaac, and for his benefit. Submission may appear complicated or too challenging on the surface, but through the process, we are blessed more than words can express. If you want to be loved, deeply loved, and cherished this side of heaven, submit to your husband as to the Lord. And, then watch as God redefines your marriage. Embracing Godly submission has liberated me, more than anything else – ever. It has freed me to love my husband just as he is. I respect him, just as he is – warts and all. He is far from perfect, as we all are. Nonetheless, my unconditional love and respect for him is an expression of God's love. And, it thrills him.

I can never make my husband into a better man, that's not my job! But, I can love him, unreservedly, without criticism or nagging, and watch God move the mountains of his heart as I submit to God's plan. It's a real victory for me in the end. How so? As I gladly submit, according to God's plan, Jimmy's God-given authority is unthreatened, and he is free to keep his focus on Jesus and the kingdom, not me, or my drama. Unencumbered by the battle of the sexes, God can work in him and through him. The results? God makes him a better man every day! That is, the man God planned before the foundation of the world.

A Lifetime Of Love.

I want you to show you something that's pretty amazing. Let's examine one more passage before we turn to the study guide. "Now it came to pass, when he had been there a long time, that Abimelech king of the Philistines looked through a window, and saw, and there was Isaac, showing endearment to Rebekah his wife." (Genesis 26:8). In Hebrew, *showing endearment* basically means *Isaac was making a pass at Rebekah*. King Abimelech catches Isaac in the midst of making sexual overtures - petting and such with Rebekah. In the original language, a sexual connotation is implied. Quoting from *The Theological Wordbook of The Old Testament*, "Isaac was sporting with Rebekah his wife" - Gen 26:8; RSV "fondling", NIV "caressing;" ICC, *Genesis*, p. 364, "to exchange conjugal caresses"[5] Our study guide will navigate these exciting passages on day five of the study.

From the text, we see Isaac unashamedly making public overtures towards his bride many years after their honeymoon. You must understand, generally speaking, Jews are very private and reserved people. Isaac's public caresses were a rare occurrence. Even if he felt like touching her in such a forward, romantic way, generally speaking, Jewish men are much more reserved, much more reverent and respectful of their wives. In fact, when we lived in Jerusalem, I don't recall ever seeing a Jewish man touch his wife in public and we lived among them for two full years. It's important also to note, Isaac and Rebekah are not courting young lovers. Their sons are grown and gone. They were out of the house. My point is this. Many years have passed – yet, Isaac can't resist her. He is still head over heels in love with Rebekah. I want to be loved like that! Don't you?

Honestly, my husband and I have a marvelous marriage, and we are romantically in love – still. Nonetheless, I find it fascinating, Rebekah got it! She was on board with God's plan. She gave herself wholly to Isaac, and it enabled him to be the man God called him to be. That's worth repeating. Ladies, we can never make our husbands better men - only God can. But, He can and will use you to influence your husband and profoundly reach him through your love. Through you, he will feel God's love and respond, and vice versa. Isaac was comforted and satisfied at a time when the loss of his mother still ached raw in his heart. But Rebekah loved him, and he was comforted – his heart was cheered. Guess what? She was comforted too! That was the plan! She had been prepared by God to be Isaac's helper from before the foundation of the world. And, Rebekah would love and comfort Isaac faithfully, until the very end.

One more thought. Who was the man Isaac, whom Rebekah loved, married, and adored? Although he was prayerful, obedient, respectful, trustful, dutiful, and submitted to God, he still messed up. Yes, that's right. Abraham's heir apparent was a marvelous patriarch, but he was human just like the rest of us. Same weaknesses, same inhibitions, same sin nature. Isaac lied out of fear, just like his father, about his wife's true identity. Glory be, he told Abimelech, king of the Philistines Rebekah was his sister! It's another excellent story, suffice it to say, the apple doesn't fall far from the tree. It never does! This story unfolds in Genesis 26.

For me, the real joy of Rebekah's story was exposing the depth of their lasting love. It was also identifying how much God wants to love our husbands through us. Through our reassuring words, submitted hearts, touch, and tender caresses! Ladies, our husbands need us. They are lost and incomplete without us. It is my prayer we will come into agreement with God, except our high calls, and love our husbands in a way that pleases God. I believe it's our call. It's also

---

[5] Payne, J. B. (1999). 1905 צָחַק. R. L. Harris, G. L. Archer Jr., & B. K. Waltke (Eds.), *Theological Wordbook of the Old Testament* (electronic ed., p. 763). Chicago: Moody Press.

the challenge before us. Every natural inclination will push against it, but God can strengthen you to embrace and practice Godly submission, and reap its benefits. Rebekah did! Enjoy the study. It's an adventure of steadfast love which endures a lifetime.

Be blessed this week as you study Rebekah: A Bride For Isaac

Next week - Miriam: Sister Of Moses

Rebekah's story unfolds in Genesis 24 – 49; she is referenced by Paul in Romans 9:10

Rebekah: A Bride For Isaac

Day One: Who Is Rebekah?

Memory verse: Genesis 24:67 Then Isaac brought her into his mother Sarah's tent; and he took Rebekah and she became his wife, and he loved her. So Isaac was comforted after his mother's death.

During this week's study, we will navigate several chapters of the book of Genesis. Our journey will examine passages which pertain to Rebekah's relationship with God and its outward flow to others. That will be of particular importance, as we endeavor to learn of her call, obedience, and submission to God. In light of this, her marriage will take center stage; it will be the backdrop for our entire study. Remember, she was handpicked, called, and chosen by God for a specific purpose - to belong to God first, and then to be a wife. She would not be an ordinary wife; she was called to love and submit to a man who would shoulder significant responsibility for the spiritual well-being of a nation. Abraham had been an excellent leader. Being married to his heir would be challenging, but God would see them through. Together, they will lead the nation of Israel's next generation of faith into the future. We know nothing happens apart from God's sovereignty. When the passing of the torch occurs, it will be at precisely the time God appointed.

1. Read Genesis 24:24. Nahor is Rebekah's grandfather, Abraham's older brother. Why is this significant in light of Genesis 24:3-4? Be specific.

2. Read Genesis 24:1-4. Once before, we saw Abraham move by fear and not by faith. This occurred when he journeyed down to Egypt to avoid the famine. (Genesis 12.) In your opinion, what is guiding Abraham's decision to secure a wife for Isaac? Is this faith, fear, or perhaps standard procedure? Explain.

3. Read Genesis 24:15-16. What is revealed about Rebekah? Compile a list. Hint: leader, servant, and hospitableness are implied from the verses. Can you see where they are implied? If so, make note and add them to your list.

4. Genesis 24:16 speaks of Rebekah's outward beauty. Her beauty would be a blessing for Isaac, indeed. But, what does 1 Peter 3:3-4 tell us about real beauty? Record verse 4 below and explain its meaning.

5. Rebekah didn't just wake up one day ready to be Isaac's wife. God had been at work, equipping and preparing her from childhood. Read Hebrews 13:20-21. How do these verses encourage you, in light of God's call on your life?

6. Rebekah was not looking for God or His call upon her life when it occurred. What was she doing when God's servant apprehended her? Read John 15:16. What were you doing when God called you? How have you responded?

7. Abraham anticipated God. In Genesis 18:1-2, he positioned himself facing outward in the doorway of the tent, in anticipation of a move of God. God did not disappoint. What encouragement! Do you ever anticipate God? Do you practice His presence and are you open and listening for His still small voice? Read Isaiah 55:6 and Matthew 7:7-8. How do these verses bring you hope?

8. In response to God's call, Abraham's was compelled to move forward with God. See Genesis 12:1-9. Only God can make a missionary heart. Like Abraham, Rebekah was being invited into the inner circle of service. Believers are encouraged to abandon everything for the benefit of the gospel. However, for some, the evidence of a new life is not apparent. Rebekah's new life would involve a heart change, a mind change, a physical change, and a relocation. Not to mention the joy of a husband! Rebekah was all in. Everything about her world was about to change. Read and pray the words of Luke 9:23. Record the verse below.

Luke 9:23

9. The words of Jesus in Luke 9:23 were straightforward. Notice who Jesus is addressing, *them all*. That would be the multitudes, (as the Arabic version renders it) who were called unto Him along with His disciples. A parallel verse is found in Mark 8. "When He had called the people to Himself, with His disciples also, He said to them…" (Mark 8:35). Jesus' words would undoubtedly pierce hearts and bring the "calls or spiritual awakenings" of those listening

to remembrance. Let's review Jesus' words: Then He said to them all, "If anyone desires to come after Me, let him deny himself, and take up his cross daily, and follow Me." (Luke 9:23). These words apply to us, we too, are called. *Deny* in this verse speaks of *dying to the desires of the flesh and worldly pursuits and pleasures - to kill the desire.* That's accomplished as we admit like Paul, there is nothing good within us, apart from Christ. Agreeing with God prepares us to yield to His spirit and put our worldly spirit to the sword. It's a daily practice, just like practicing His presence. Have you denied yourself? Do you do it daily? Yes or no? What are the results?

Meditation
Deuteronomy 31:8 And the Lord, He is the One who goes before you. He will be with you, He will not leave you nor forsake you; do not fear nor be dismayed."

Rebekah: A Bride For Isaac

Day Two: Where Is Rebekah In God's Redemption Story?
Rebekah's Preparation

Memory verse: Genesis 24:67 Then Isaac brought her into his mother Sarah's tent; and he took Rebekah and she became his wife, and he loved her. So Isaac was comforted after his mother's death.

Abraham's focus now turns to Isaac and his state of singleness. Recalling God's covenant promise, Abraham is energized and approaches his burden of responsibility with newfound interest. His thoughtful plan will alter lives for eternity – his, Isaac's, and most assuredly, Rebekah's.

On what appears to be an ordinary day, an unassuming young girl comes to the well for water and collides with her destiny. Unbeknownst to her, God's servant, Eliezer, prayerfully awaits her appearing. He is a man on a mission and will not be denied. Although unnamed in our text, he is identified in scripture as Abraham's eldest or chief servant. (See Genesis 15:1; Genesis 24:2). As we shall discover, he is an excellent model for Christian service. He does God's work, God way! Take note. He approaches his challenging assignment with soberness, attention to detail, single-mindedness, and careful planning. With everything sufficiently undergirded in prayer, he moves forward knowing the success of his journey rests squarely upon God.

1. Read Genesis 23:19. Describe what happened.

2. Why do you think Abraham's attention turned to Isaac's singleness so suddenly? What do you think prompted his decision?

Anne Nicholson

3. Read Genesis 24:1-11. Describe the servant. Who traveled with him? Be specific and record your verse of reference.

4. It's all in the name. As we've discussed previously, biblical names have significant meaning. Often the definition or essence of the name is embedded within the character of the name bearer. A literal translation for Eliezer is as follows: *ĕl'ĭ ē'zər* of Hebrew origin meaning, *my God is my help or God is help.* We've seen *ezer* before; it means *helper.* The last syllable of Eliezer is the same word which identified not only Eve's purpose, but all wives. (Genesis 2.) The words and meaning are one in the same. Considering the mission before him, why do you believe this is a fitting name for Eliezer?

5. Good help is hard to find, but Abraham had a gem in his servant Eliezer. Although he is unnamed in Genesis 24, he is identified in Genesis 15:2. Eliezer and his traveling companions would journey several weeks before they reached their destination some 500 miles away. Reading Genesis 24:3-9 record the verse(s) which reflect the faithful servant's actions.

    a. Accepted the challenge -

    b. Examined the alternatives -

    c. Promised to follow instructions -

Women of the Bible and God's Redeeming Love

6. Read Genesis 24:10-21. Notice in verse 12, the first thing Eliezer did was pray. Why and on whose behalf? Why was this important? Record Genesis 24:12 below.

7. Review Genesis 24:10-21. Eliezer's steps model leadership. Record the verse where the specific action has occurred. Notice Eliezer's attention to detail. These steps provide an excellent guide for all leaders.

    a. Devised a plan.

    b. Submitted the plan to God.

    c. Prayed for guidance and leading.

    d. Committed human effort to the plan, but left room for God.

    e. Waited.

    f. Watched carefully.

Anne Nicholson

8. Who was really in charge? Record your favorite verse to share about the sovereignty of God.

9. Review Genesis 24:17-20. Rebekah reveals her servant's heart. Eliezer had not prayed for a woman with incredible looks or great wealth. Instead, he had asked God to show him a woman with a heart and attitude of service. Read Matthew 23:11-12 to gain Jesus' perspective on leadership. In light of Jesus' words, why do you think these qualities were necessary for the wife of Isaac?

10. Read Genesis 24:18-21. List five significant facts below.

1.

2.

3.

4.

5.

11. Rebekah was whose daughter? Was Eliezer successful? Record the news of Genesis 24:24.

12. After giving Rebekah the nose ring and bracelets, Eliezer did something significant in Genesis 24:26. What did he do? What did this represent? Record the words of the verse below.

A Servant's Heart.

Rebekah has a servant's heart. A camel can drink up to 30 gallons of water to refresh and refuel after a long journey. Ten could consume up to 300 gallons to drink their fill. Rebekah watered the camels until they finished drinking. See Genesis 24:19 below. Notice at the end of a long day, late into the evening, Rebekah was still serving. Serving was definitely in her heart. Only God can make a genuine servant; it was in her nature. What joy, Rebekah had passed the camel-test!

Meditation
Genesis 24:19 …"I will draw water for your camels also, until they have finished drinking."

Rebekah: A Bride For Isaac

Day Three: What Did Rebekah Get Right?
Rebekah's Blessed Submission

Memory verse: Genesis 24:67 Then Isaac brought her into his mother Sarah's tent; and he took Rebekah and she became his wife, and he loved her. So Isaac was comforted after his mother's death.

Rebekah went! She followed in the footsteps of her great-uncle Abraham. It was in the blood! Only God can shape a missionary heart, and hers was abandoned to His purposes. She was willing to leave it all behind to be in the perfect and pleasing will of God. Rebekah was facing an arduous journey; some 500 miles would be traveled before she met her Isaac. With her heart, her mind, her soul, and her strength, Rebekah said yes to God. How thrilling to discover and know your purpose! She had been molded and shaped by the hands of the Master, and she knew it. God can and will prepare us to accomplish His plan! At long last, Rebekah was ready. Today, we will examine the results of God's preparatory work in His chosen servant.

1. Read and review Genesis 24:15-25. After God's preparatory work was accomplished, and at the appointed time, Rebekah joined His redemption story. His sovereignty had led her to the well at the perfect time. God's timing is always excellent. Below is a partial list of attributes which made her a suitable mate for Isaac. For each attribute record a verse which, in your opinion, best represents that characteristic in action. Note: There may be multiple answers for each attribute - list one to share.

    Servant - _____

    Leader - _____

    Hospitableness - _____

    Compassion - _____

Beauty -_____

Purity -_____

Initiative -_____

Commitment -_____

2. Rebekah had passed the camel-test! What did Eliezer say and do in Genesis 24:26-27? Where is his focus?

3. Read Genesis 24:28-31. These verses reveal something significant about Laban's character. What is it? Incidentally, this character weakness will recur. Thinking forward, can you identify the person whom it will impact in Genesis 29? What is the connection to Rebekah?

Anne Nicholson

4. Eliezer had not lost sight of his mission. Read Genesis 24:33. What does he refuse? Identify who occupies his thoughts and conversation. He is a trustworthy servant indeed.

5. Read Genesis 24:34-35. What three things were appealing to Laban? Be specific.

1.

2.

3.

6. Eliezer's name is not mentioned in this chapter. His focus is solely his master and his master's work! Thinking biblically, who does his character-type reflect? Is there a particular verse to support your answer?

7. Read Genesis 24:34-49. Eliezer testifies about his encounter at the well with Rebekah. God's faithfulness highlights his testimony. Notice in verse 48, Eliezer calls for a decision. What is he seeking, and on whose behalf?

8. Read Genesis 24:50-53. What is Eliezer doing in verse 53? What was accomplished?

9. Read Genesis 24:54-67. Following debate and negotiation, they summons Rebekah. After all, she is the one called and chosen. Notice her poise and confidence. She had purposed in her heart to follow God! From this point forward, no turning back! Document her moment of decision by recording verse 58 below.

Throughout this chapter, Eliezer has called people to a place of decision. Is that not what the Holy Spirit does? What a beautiful picture of His work in our lives. First Bethuel and Laban in verses 50-56, and now, Rebekah in verse 58.

Epilogue.

Rebekah had drunk the cup of betrothal. Her life was no longer her own. Their marriage would be consummated upon their meeting. Read Genesis 24:67. Rebekah gave herself to a man she did not know because it was God's plan. It was her destiny. She is walking by faith and not by sight. She loved him well, as we see in the verse, *"Isaac was comforted."* From the Hebrew, *comforted* means *consoled with compassion*. Rebekah comforted Isaac with her whole being. She engaged or connected with him spiritually and naturally. Rebekah didn't hold back, but gave from the depths of her whole heart. Simply stated, she invested in Isaac. Through this, Isaac was restored to life. It was not about Rebekah at all. It never was! Their union was for the benefit of Isaac, although it would be a blessing for her as well. She was his *ezer*, his *help*. God had sent help - a suitable or comparable helper to Isaac. He was a blessed man, indeed.

King Solomon spoke of wives as follows: "He who finds a wife finds a good thing, And obtains favor from the Lord." (Proverbs 18:22). As His daughters and believing wives, this is the challenge before us. We must remember, it's not about us and never has been. Paul shared these instructive words of wisdom with the church of Corinth, "Nor was man created for woman, but woman for the man. (1 Corinthians 11:9). Ladies, rejoice and be blessed in your call – you were made for this.

Meditation
Genesis 24:58 "…And she said, "I will go.'

Rebekah: A Bride For Isaac

Day Four: What Did Rebekah Get Wrong? - Rebekah's Deception

Memory verse: Genesis 24:67 Then Isaac brought her into his mother Sarah's tent; and he took Rebekah and she became his wife, and he loved her. So Isaac was comforted after his mother's death.

Finally, after twenty years of marriage, twin boys are expected. As we shall discover, Rebekah's pregnancy was volatile. So much so, at one point, she inquired of the Lord to determine the reason for such turmoil in her womb. Read Genesis 25:22-23. The boys were already striving against one another. They were at war within the womb. The Lord reported the older would serve the younger. A conflict which began in the womb would hinder their relationship for most of their lives.

Today's lesson will examine the big mistake of Rebekah's life. Unfortunately, it centered around her children. The outcome would be irreversible. The events were rooted in lack of faith. Rebekah got ahead of God. Haven't we all? Her actions were sinful. She would live the rest of her life enduring the heartbreak of her own making.

1. As with Isaac's parents, conceiving children proved to be more challenging than expected. However, Isaac had a different approach to the problem. What did Isaac do in Genesis 25:21? What does this tell you about Isaac? Why was this the better plan?

2. Thinking biblically, what purposes do you think were being served in the delay? Record a verse to support your thoughts.

3. Describe the events and particulars surrounding the twins' births in Genesis 25:24-26.

v. 24

v. 25

v. 26

4. Read Genesis 25:27-28. List the highlights concerning the twins as they grew.

v. 27

v. 28

5. Review Genesis 25:27-28. Do you think Rebekah's overwhelming love for Jacob and Isaac's competing love for Esau may have fueled the twins' conflict and hostility? Why or why not?

A thorough reading of Genesis 27:1-46 and Genesis 28:1-10 are recommended to grasp the full story of Rebekah's deception and failure to honor her husband. The remainder of today's lesson will be limited to: (1) the reason Rebekah got ahead of God, (2) the deception of Isaac, and (3) what happened to Jacob?

6. Read Genesis 27:1-5. Old and blind, Isaac has in his mind to grant the birthright blessing. He desires to bestow the blessing on his favorite son, Esau, even though he knows God had given Rebekah a promise concerning Jacob before the twins were born.

a. How did Rebekah know this?

b. What does she decide to do?

7. Based on her plan, has Rebekah also lost sight of God's promise concerning Jacob? Read Genesis 25:23. What was the promise? In your opinion, what has happened to Rebekah?

8. Select a verse to share from Genesis 27 that highlights Rebekah's spiritual and/or moral failure.

141

Jacob followed his mother's plan, although he was hesitant. Ironically, Jacob's name means deceiver. How fitting. He will continue in this posture throughout his life until he is painfully deceived by his uncle Laban, while in pursuit of securing his wife, Rachel. Being on the receiving end of deception stung far worse than deceiving or cheating others; it certainly got Jacob's attention. Thankfully, God never leaves us as He finds us. We'll fast forward just a bit. In Genesis 32, God finally wrestled the "need to deceive" right of out Jacob and changed his name to Israel. In one night's time, Jacob was permanently transformed. The difference? Now, Jacob was governed by God, rather than self. An expanded definition of the name Israel: *He will be a prince with God; prince with God; contender of God; he strives with God; soldier of God; God will rule; God ruled man; ruling with God; one that prevails with God.*[6] Moving forward, Jacob delighted to do the will of God. At long last, the struggle ended. Jacob became Israel, God-ruled - the patriarchal leader God had planned from before the foundation of the world.

9. Rebekah has an agenda fueled by a lack of faith. Review Genesis 27:5-17 and answer the following questions:

> a. Jacob had a decision to make. It always comes down to choices! If he obeyed his mother, he deceived his father. If he ignored his mother's request, he disobeyed her command. He was in a dilemma, indeed. In your opinion, did Jacob have a choice?

> b. What should he do?

> c. Who would take responsibility for the plan?

> d. Ultimately who was in control?

---

[6] Smith, S., & Cornwall, J. (1998). In <u>The exhaustive dictionary of Bible names</u> (p. 114). North Brunswick, NJ: Bridge-Logos.

10. The results were devastating. Esau is furious and plans to kill Jacob. Read Genesis 27:42-45. What does Rebekah advise Jacob to do?

11. Note Rebekah's attempt to divert Isaac's attention in Genesis 27:46. What does Rebekah say?

12. Read Genesis 28:1-5. Notice Jacob is blessed and charged by Isaac. What does this mean?

Epilogue.

Jacob escapes Esau by fleeing to Rebekah's brother, Laban. Ironically, there is no record in scripture of a reunion between Rebekah and Jacob. They were separated for the remainder of her life. How tragic, she got ahead of God, and it cost her the favored son. Esau took a bride in Genesis 28. Scripture records, "So Esau went to Ishmael and took Mahalath the daughter of Ishmael, Abraham's son…. to be his wife in addition to the wives he had." (Genesis 28:9). Poor Esau, he hoped that this would bring pleasure to his father, but in reality, he increased his displeasure by adding a wife from a family which God had rejected.

Meditation
Exodus 20:12 Honor your father and your mother…

Rebekah: A Bride For Isaac

Day Five: How Did God's Love Redeem It All?

Memory verse: Genesis 24:67 Then Isaac brought her into his mother Sarah's tent; and he took Rebekah and she became his wife, and he loved her. So Isaac was comforted after his mother's death.

Rebekah finished strong. In spite of the fiasco with the twins, she and Isaac shared a long, loving life together, and God was in the center of it all. Today's lesson will highlight a pretty amazing account of his infatuation and desire for his wife. I want to call attention to this because, in spite of everything, she knew how to love and comfort her husband, and he adored her. She was indeed a wife who was loved well.

1. Read Genesis 24:67. It's been our memory verse all week. Reread the last phrase of the verse and record it below. Rebekah's understanding of the marital relationship is rooted in this verse. Who was *comforted* in this verse?

2. Read Paul's words from 1 Corinthians 11:9. What do they tell us? What do the words mean to you?

3. Read Genesis 26:1. Who ordered the famine? What did it prompt Isaac to do? The apple doesn't fall far from the tree. It appears God is at work in the life of Isaac. Does this verse seem familiar? Where have you read similar words before?

4. Read Genesis 26:2-5 and highlight the important information from each verse.

v.2

v.3

v.4

v.5

5. Read Genesis 26:6-9. According to verse 6, Isaac was obedient and dwelt in the land. However, his obedience was coupled with deceit. In your own words, describe what occurred in each verse.

v. 6

v. 7

v. 8

v. 9

6. Although Abraham was blessed in his seeming deceit, Isaac receives a harsh reprimand. Read Genesis 26:9-10. What was Isaac's defense in verse 9? Was he justified in his fear and actions?

7. Even though King Abimelech was furious, God's powerful hand was at work to preserve His chosen seed. Which verse reveal's God's soverign protection over Isaac? Review Genesis 26:6-10 to find the answer. Record the verse below.

8. From the window of the palace, Abimelech, king of the Philistines observed Isaac "showing endearment to Rebekah his wife." (Genesis 26:8). In Hebrew, *showing endearment* is ṣāḥaq meaning to exchange conjugal caresses. Undoubtedly, the king knows this type of familiarity was not a common practice among siblings. Busted! In your opinion, what is happening with Isaac?

Scripture tells us Rebekah was remarkably beautiful. Genesis 24:16. It appears, however, that something far beyond her outward beauty had captivated Isaac's heart. He obviously adored her. Jews are not commonly known for public displays of affection; quite the contrary. They reserve all intimacy for private moments, not public squares. This incident occurred many years after the twins, Jacob and Esau, were grown and gone. At this time, Rebekah would have been well into middle age, and Isaac well into his 60's. They were not courting adolescents. It appears from the original language Isaac adored his wife – entirely! Yes, Rebekah was a lucky woman indeed.

9. When Isaac said, "She is my sister," in Genesis 26:7, what was the spiritual issue? In your opinion, was Isaac loving and protecting his wife well, in the moment? Why or why not?

10. The words of Genesis 28:3-5 are significant. What does Isaac reaffirm for Jacob in these verses? Why is this significant?

Epilogue.

To sum it all up, they were a match made in heaven. Truly! At the appointed time, when it pleased God, and when they were both ready, He united them. God did it! Only God can give us our perfect mate at the ideal time! He introduced and launched His plan for marriage in the garden. Since then, He has been bringing couples together. His plan will be accomplished no matter what. The torch passes, Abraham to Isaac, and Isaac to Jacob, and one day Jacob to Joseph; the seed continues. None of the patriarchs was perfect; nonetheless, God accomplished His plan in and through their lives. And, He will do so with us, those chosen to bear His image. God has no other option. He plans that we succeed! To this very day, Isaac and Rebekah's remains rest together, in the family tomb in Machpelah in Hebron.

Meditation
1 Thessalonians 5:24, He who calls you is faithful, who also will do it.

Notes - Rebekah: A Bride For Isaac

Miriam

Miriam: Sister Of Moses

As we turn to our study of Miriam this week, you will fast discover her story is somewhat different from the others. Albeit true, each woman in the Bible has a different story, Miriam's is unique because it does not end on a high note like those we've studied thus far. Nonetheless, we have much to learn from her life and journey. Like all the others, she's captivating. As you will see, her leadership and God-given gifts played an essential role in God's overall story of redemption - that is, until they didn't.

As I prepared to write this lesson, I pondered about her life as I read and prayed through scripture. Almost immediately three things came to mind: (1) what it means to be or have a big sister, (2) finishing strong, and (3) the legacy we leave. I was also reminded, salvation is entirely God's work. As believers, we are all saved by the same means of grace. Paul said it's a spiritual work. His exact words to the church at Ephesus were: "For by grace you have been saved through faith, and that not of yourselves; it is the gift of God, not of works, lest anyone should boast." (Ephesians 2:8-9).

Incidentally, the saints of the Old Testament had faith too. They believed God when He said a Savior would come. That takes faith. They lived and died in faith looking toward the promise of a coming Savior, a Redeemer - Jesus. As New Testament believers, we await His coming as well - His second coming. This side of Calvary, we look back to the cross and forward to His glorious return. Any way you look at it, it takes faith and faith is still faith. That will never change nor will the means of grace by which faith comes. Let's get a baseline definition of faith directly from scripture: "Now faith is the substance of things hoped for, the evidence of things not seen." (Hebrews 11:1).

Who Is Miriam?

You may not be familiar with her until I tell you who her brothers were. They are both well known, perhaps one better than the other. By birth-order, they were Aaron and Moses. That's the same Moses who God raised up to "set his people free" from 430 years of slavery in Egypt. He was a foreshadow of Jesus - a redeemer and deliverer. He freed God's people from oppressive slavery and death. Moses is an Old Testament foreshadow or preview of Jesus who saved us from the bondage of sin, eternal separation from God, and certain death. We'll take a closer look at this in just a bit. But first, what else can we know about Miriam?

The name Miriam comes from the same root word as Mary and Maria which means *bitterness and rebellion.* Again, we see the very nature of the name-bearer embedded within the name. In her later years, she will succumb to overwhelming jealousy as a result of rebellion rooted in deep bitterness. It's a trace of bitterness that's been building for years. It happens that way, I suppose. It starts small, and if it's not dealt with, it builds and builds until it consumes our hearts and minds. Unattended, it can overtake us and cloud our judgment. Miriam's bitterness will be the source of her undoing. This week's study is about a gifted woman, called by God, who falls from a place of leadership and influence. Some have suggested, perhaps Miriam died of a broken heart. Only God knows for sure. Albeit true, deep regrets will overtake us if we remain unrepentant.

Miriam was born of good stock. She had a rich spiritual heritage coming from the Levitical line of priests. Both of her parents, Amram and Jochebed were descendants of the tribe of Levi. She was the older sister of two of Israel's greatest leaders. She was gifted in her own right and served as their partner in ministry. From scripture, it appears she was very influential, and gifted - called and anointed to teach, lead, and guide millions of Israelites into a place of worship. Miriam was a worshiper. In fact, she was the first worship leader for the free nation of Israel.

All In The Family.

What a gifted family, and what a heritage. I've known families like this. Perhaps you have too. I'm talking about families where everyone seems to have great spiritual insight and unique spiritual gifts. They're excellent teachers, some have an anointing or affinity towards powerful prayer, while others write music, lead worship, and sing and play multiple instruments, etc. In fact, they could successfully fill every leadership post within the church, if need be. Their passion promotes excitement, they invite worship, and they can energize even the most lethargic believers. Each one uniquely gifted and called by God. They know their purpose and efficiently operate within their gifts. When they're engaged in God's work, all you can do is praise Him. There is a common denominator in all of them. It's Jesus, and passionate love for God, and His Spirit – alive and well within. The results? They're united in call and purpose. Everyone is living with a kingdom vision and for a kingdom purpose.

Miriam and her brothers were a family like this. They were each uniquely created, called by God, and gifted for ministry. They were united with a kingdom vision and a kingdom purpose. All of them, including Miriam, until things begin to shift, albeit subtly at first. Like some of us, she started out strong, but wanting to have her way proved to be an issue in the end. That's the original sin, you know. Wanting to be God instead of being ruled by God. God had a plan in place, but she thought she knew better. She wanted her plan instead. Simply stated, Miriam wanted Moses' job! She will push hard, too, to have her way. Not only against Moses' grace, but God's grace as well. Tragically, she will drag her younger brother, Aaron, right along with her.

Incidentally, all sin is rooted in pride. Miriam had lots of pride, or so it seems. In addition to racial pride and national pride, she had ambitious pride to a fault. And, it was all topped off with unhealthy portions of jealousy, envy, and covetousness. By the way, when we want what God has not given us, it's a sin - it's covetous. She had been blessed by God, in her own right and elevated to a place of honor and privilege, but it appears she's still wanting. What God had done was not enough, that is, in her opinion. Ultimately, her bitterness, jealousy, and envy will lead to her demise.

Meddling While Mothering.

Regardless of our attempts to conceal our shortcomings, they always come out. They rise to the surface like sin, and expose us! Miriam's were no exception. Although she never married or had any children, it seems she had a penchant or passion for meddling while mothering. It's possible her unfulfilled maternal instincts led to this unhealthy practice. Her intentions might have been good, or so she thought. At that moment, they may have afforded her some personal satisfaction, possibly quenching an unfulfilled desire to be needed. As the elder sibling, she desired to control her younger brothers. But as we know, with each passing year kids grow older – even Moses. Finally, her attempts to guide his path climax when he is well past 80. Years after he had been called and equipped by God to lead a nation. He surely didn't need her help and guidance, for God alone was his guide. He met with Moses face to face.

Nonetheless, she will meddle one time too many. Not to spoil our study, but ultimately, she will step into a trap of her own making and forever seal her fate. This time, it's meddling, not mothering that's the issue. She will publicly criticize God's anointed and undermine Moses at every turn in an attempt to remove him from his God-given place as Israel's spiritual leader and authority. We'll unpack her pride and other issues shortly. We can rest assured, if we push against God and His plan, He deals with us. Miriam's attempts to usurp God's plan and authority will come at a high price. It will be a hard-learned lesson; a lesson Miriam, her brothers, nor it's witnesses will ever forget.

Called By God.

Now that we've discussed her weakness, we'll examine her strengths. She had many. Our Miriam was a leader in her own right. We see it commemorated by the prophet Micah. This verse references the Israelites who were in bondage under Pharaoh for 430 years. (See Exodus 12:40-41). The verse says, "For I brought you up from the land of Egypt, I redeemed you from the house of bondage; And I sent before you Moses, Aaron, and Miriam." (Micah 6:4). There we see it. According to Micah, Miriam was a contributing member of the leadership team - called, anointed, and established by God.

Scripture also identifies Miriam as a prophetess in Exodus 15:20. She is the first of nine women identified as such in scripture. She was a gifted worship leader as well. After the Israelites cross the Red Sea, they will stand to watch as God's waves roll over Pharaoh and his armies. In celebration, Miriam will lead the nation in an anthem of praise to God! The songs of Moses and Miriam are recorded in Exodus 15:1-21. Bible scholars believe they're the oldest songs ever written and sung. What a celebration it must have been. God's people free from the tyranny of Pharaoh and standing securely on dry ground! The entire troop has witnessed the hand of God move on their behalf. How thrilling! The enemy finished and all of his men. What a moment in history and what teamwork! Moses, the songwriter, and Miriam, the worship leader, shepherd an *a cappella* chorus of 2 million voices to worship and praise the Great I AM - our great God! What a fragrant offering to God.

Think about worship. We have all worshipped many times. You know how thrilling the moment is when everything comes together and you can say with certainty - "My God is in this place!" Not only could they feel it and sense it, but they had also witnessed His deliverance, His power, and majesty with their own eyes! Every heart could say, "My God is in the place - my God is with me!" It appears Miriam had the gift to move people into God's presence through worship. She did what was in her heart; she led them in song. Her heart for worship and spiritual insight was indeed a calling and gift from God. A dreary wilderness and years or wondering faced the children of Israel. Miriam understood they were better equipped to confront whatever lies ahead with a song of praise on the lips and filling their hearts.

Two Million Strong.

To be part of this leadership team was no small feat. For church leaders today, the size of this congregation is staggering. There is a distinct possibility Moses, and his siblings lead the largest congregation of people ever. Under God's guidance, the trio moved a mass of humanity from Egypt to the wilderness of Shur. We know from scripture, 600,000 men were part of the Exodus. The Bible says, "Then the children of Israel journeyed from Rameses to Succoth, about six hundred thousand men on foot, besides children." (Exodus 12:37). Many Bible scholars believe the number referenced pertains to men of fighting age only. With the elders of the nation, the elderly in general, all the women, and all the children, the Israelites' population could have easily topped several million people. There were others too. According to Moses, "A mixed multitude went up with them also, and flocks and herds—a great deal of livestock." (Exodus 12:38). So, we must also consider the foreigners traveling with them who desired to follow the God of Abraham, Isaac, and Jacob, rather than remain in Egypt under the tyranny of Pharaoh. Lest we forget, when Pharaoh let them leave, all of Egypt had seen firsthand the mighty works of God. On behalf of His people and to fulfill His plan and purposes, God had sent ten plagues. Every man, woman, and child in Egypt had seen and witnessed, firsthand, the power of our Great God!

Moses, Aaron, and Miriam had their work cut out for them. The number of souls under their watchful care is almost too staggering to consider. That's what troubled Pharaoh so much in the first place. The prolific Hebrews and their unhandy population explosion. Since in 1875 B.C., 70 entered Egypt with Jacob, and now Moses & company exit 2 million plus strong. Some have suggested this esimate was low. It's been speculated the number was closer to 4 million. Only God knows the exact number. Nonetheless, what Pharaoh most feared had occurred. Nothing could stop the multiplication of millions of Hebrews, not even a shrewd

Pharaoh. When it was all said and done, Pharaoh proved to be no match for Moses and His Almighty God! Remember God always wins!

Where Is Miriam In God's Redemption Story?

Sometimes in stories, we must go backward to move forward, and this is one of those times. In fulfillment of God's promise to Abraham, the Israelites had spent more than 400 years in captivity. (Genesis 15:13-14.) They are suffering under the harsh rule and enslavement of Pharaoh. He was not a fan of the prolific Hebrew nation. A former Pharaoh had been Joseph's friend as well as a friend to the Jews. During a worldwide, catastrophic famine, he had invited them to make Egypt their home, providing them ample fields to shepherd their flocks. As you may recall, Joseph was second in command under his reign. This exciting story unfolds in Genesis 45.

Although things were good for a season, no one lives forever, and the favorable Pharaoh died. His replacement, the new reigning Pharaoh had no affinity toward the Jews. There was no connection. Suffice it to say; he was not a fan. In fact, he had little or no concern for them at all, except how they might benefit him through their labors. Among other things, according to God's plan, the Hebrews were increasing in number daily. According to Exodus 1:19, when Pharaoh inquired about their prolificacy, he was told: "the Hebrew women were healthy, and gave birth with ease." He loathed them and decided to make life as tough for them as possible. So, with evil in his heart, he enslaved them for profit. To fulfill the scriptures, they labored years, generation after generation, under the tyranny of Pharaoh and the hot Egyptian sun. That is until the appointed time when God heard their cries from heaven and intervened, by raising up a redeemer - a deliverer for His people Israel. That would be, Moses, the baby brother of Miriam. We'll see him in a minute floating on the Nile - the river of death. Once again, we'll look back before we move forward. If Moses was to grow up to rescue God's people, it appears he'd need some rescuing himself, first. That would be him, baby Moses, floating down the Nile in a "living ark of the covenant." Here we meet Miriam, a doting older sister of 12, who loved baby Moses with all of her heart.

What Did Miriam Get Right?

Quite a few things. First, at a young age, Miriam played a vital role in his very survival. You might say she was her brother's keeper of sorts. Pharaoh devised an evil plan to engage the Hebrew midwives in a plot to kill all the male babies at birth. But they didn't do it. They couldn't. Why? Overall, because it fulfilled God's plan, but on a personal level, because they feared God and loved life. The midwives were God-fearing, and the Bible tells us God provided homes for the midwives because they feared Him. (Exodus 1:20-21.) They were engaged in the Father's business of bringing life - not destroying it. God blesses our obedience. We see this principle demonstrated over and over again in scripture. When we obey God, there are blessings. God provided because they feared God, not Pharaoh.

Pharaoh's first plan failed, so next, he conceived an idea to have all the male babies thrown into the Nile River and drowned. (Exodus 1:22.) That is where Moses' journey began. Jochebed, his mother, thought otherwise. She decided that the Nile would be his source of life, not death. Mothers generally think their infants are beautiful and special, Jochebed was no exception. She decided since he was such a beautiful child, she'd hide him instead. (Exodus 2:2.) As he grew, she knew she couldn't keep him hidden forever. For all of their sakes, she'd have to act quickly. It had to be now, or perhaps it would never be. So, Jochebed got busy and wove a basket and covered it with "pitch" and placed baby Moses inside. Next, she knelt at the bank of the river Nile and launched his "little ark." Indeed, it floated! Her prayers had been heard. Now, it became a waiting game as the little ark bobbed up and down on the waves. I wonder if Jochebed, a wise Hebrew from the line of priests, recalled the story of Noah and the ark as she wove his little basket? Did she know it would be his deliverance, as it had been Noah's?

Next, young Miriam positioned herself to watch and wait so she could report on Moses' fate. Scripture reveals Miriam's devotion: "And his sister stood afar off, to know what would be done to him." (Exodus 2:4). As God ordained, at the appointed time, Pharaoh's daughter came to the river to bathe and what did she find? To her surprise, a little ark with a baby inside: And when she opened it, she saw the child, and behold, the baby wept. So she had compassion on him, and said, "This is one of the Hebrews' children." (Exodus 2:6). We see from scripture, unlike her father, she had *compassion.* In Hebrew, the word is ḥā·măl which means show mercy on, spare, take pity on, i.e., show kindness to one in an unfavorable, difficult, or dangerous situation, and so help or deliver in some manner, implying in some cases that the one in the distress may deserve the condition.[7]

As God planned, Pharaoh's daughter would rescue Moses. In her compassion, she'd go one step further. She decided to take him home and raise him in the palace. In an instant, God elevated Moses from an abandoned Hebrew floating on the river of death, to a child who would live like a king. He would grow up as one born into favor. Although it's not apparent from the previous scene, Moses was already favored. God's electing love has, once again, handpicked the younger child and elevated him to a place of hope, purpose, and promise. That's an example of God's sovereignty; a beautiful picture of God's redemptive work in action. In it, we see a microcosm of the gospel. Moses was destined for death - but he was plucked from that fate and elevated to royal status.

It is the same with us. His story is our story! We were all doomed, destined for death and eternal separation from God until He determined otherwise. In His infinite love, He chose to save us, and He sent a Redeemer - Jesus. Now we are members of a royal priesthood, sons, and daughters of the King of kings and Lord of lords, the one true and living God! As the redeemed, we rejoice because our identity and eternal destiny have been changed.

---

[7] Swanson, J. (1997). Dictionary of Biblical Languages with Semantic Domains : Hebrew (Old Testament) (electronic ed.). Oak Harbor: Logos Research Systems, Inc.

At the perfect time, God's time, Miriam showed quick wisdom and initiative and came to her brother's aid. Here she is seen serving the greater good, according to God's plan. She cleverly offered to provide a Hebrew nurse to care for the infant. All's well that ends well. Jochebed would be allowed to nurse her infant son! How thrilling is that? Miriam's resourcefulness, love, and concern for Moses shines brightly in this phase of his life. Her usefulness to God is shared in Exodus 2:1-10.

What Did Miriam Get Wrong?

In the end, her resourcefulness works against her. When Moses was a helpless infant, she made a wise decision. Eighty years later the same character traits will cause her great anguish. Right before her eyes, God will call, anoint, and equip "her little Moses" for ministry. And, you know what? God didn't need Miriam's help to accomplish His plan through Moses. Instead, He meets with Moses face to face. (Exodus 33:11; Numbers 12:8.) Insecurity coupled with patriotic passion will grip Miriam as God raises Moses up to lead a nation. Her importance, authority, and dominance over his life will be challenged. It would appear he had been the love of her life and the center of her committed heart, not in a sexual sense, but in a warm, motherly sense from infancy.

Sometimes it's hard for "mothers" to let go, and she will be hesitant to relinquish control. Her frustrations will exacerbate when Moses takes a new bride. She is unwilling to accept the voice of any other women in his head, and she becomes intolerant. The results? Pride issues surface - her national pride and racial pride. Although in error and out of order, she will make it her mission to ensure no one threatens their ministry or her beloved Israel. Jealousy and bitterness also surface fueled by insecurity and fear. Accepting Moses' new bride was asking too much! Of all things, Moses had married an Ethiopian, a Cushite! We read from the book of Numbers: "Then Miriam and Aaron spoke against Moses because of the Ethiopian *[kûšî]* woman whom he had married; for he had married an Ethiopian - a *kûšî* woman. (Numbers 12:1). As you can see from the verse, *kûšî* is translated *Ethiopian or Cushite*.

Truth be told, Moses' choice in a wife was not a threat to the nation of Israel or God's people, nor was it a moral failure. It was none of Miriam's business or Aaron's, but she made it so. Her meddling would surface again. It's interesting to note, however, I couldn't find one thing in scripture to suggest Moses' Ethiopian wife was a poor choice for him. God could have surely prevented it if need be. We already know God met with Moses face to face. If this were an issue, God would have said so or intervened.

National Pride.

Miriam loved Moses, but she was a patriot, first and foremost. In fact, her national pride and love for Israel eclipsed her love for Moses. That's why his marriage to a woman from a pagan culture was unacceptable and intolerable. The country of his new bride did not worship the true and living God. That became the issue. For Miriam, it proved to be the straw that broke the camel's back. Her jealousy spawned rebellion and ignited others - among them, Aaron. Like a firestorm, ultimately, the seeds of bitterness spread quickly, raging out of control. The end is now near. Her most critical offense will be her arrogant and contemptuous posture and disrespectful rejection of Moses as God's anointed leader. It's unthinkable, but Miriam calls God's authority into question.

Let us be forewarned! Bitterness kills and destroys. It will kill and destroy God's work and your ministry because it will destroy you as well as your testimony! It brings everything to a screeching halt! Unrepentant, unconfessed bitterness stops our spiritual growth and renders us useless and ineffective unto God's purposes. May memories of the painful outcome of Miriam's bitterness stop us in our tracks, lest we allow a root of bitterness to grow, and eventually rage out of control. That's what happened to Miriam. One day in the not too distant future, she will be stricken with leprosy, and cast outside the camp, humiliated, crying "unclean, unclean" before a people she once led in worship. She will be clinging to life and stripped of her worshipful leadership. The tragic results? Miriam's prophetic voice will be silenced.

How Did God's Love Redeem It All?

There are consequences to sin, always have been and forever will be. There is no way around it. When we sin against God, He deals with us. Contrary to what you might be thinking, this guarantees God loves us. The author of Hebrews explains, "For whom the Lord loves He chastens, And scourges every son whom He receives." (Hebrews 12:6). Ultimately, God summons Moses, Miriam, and Aaron to the tabernacle of meeting. There, Miriam and Aaron will get a dressing down by God. When He leaves their presence, Miriam will be leprous! Your study guide will help you navigate these exciting passages from Numbers 12:1-16. I am confident neither one of them or Moses ever forgot this encounter with God.

I'm not going to spoil the lesson for you, but God's plan for Miriam never changed. He had placed her in a position of power, honor, and influence, in addition to gifting her with a prophetic voice and anointing her to lead worship. Regretfully, it proved not to be enough – she wanted more. Tragically, it appears she couldn't help herself. As a result, she became prideful, covetous, spread discord, murmured, and complained. It climaxed in her attempt to lead Aaron and others to rebel against Moses, God's anointed.

The take away for us is this. Wanting what God has not ordained for us is a sin. Miriam was not ever called to Moses' position. It was a mantle she was not anointed to carry. God, alone, raises up and takes down leaders. Before the foundation of the world, they are called and chosen, born with purpose and intent, that's the only way. The call from God was not only irrevocable; it was to Moses, not Miriam. I believe as she watched his little "ark of the covenant" bob up and down on the Nile, in her heart she knew Moses was born for greatness. God's plan was already in motion and nothing, not even Pharaoh, could prevent his little ark from salvation.

We Don't Sin In A Vacuum.

Miriam's sin brought millions of people to a screeching halt. That's what sin does. It paralyzes us, and we don't move forward spiritually or naturally. The entire camp of Israelites waited to see Miriam's fate. What did her brothers do? They could have traveled ahead and left her there, but it would have been out of character for both of them. Even though she had pushed hard against Moses and God's plan, and enticed Aaron and others to follow - they still loved her, and they feared for her life! So, they prayed, begging God to restore her. Lest we forget, Moses was an intercessor. He was called by God not only to lead, and teach, but also to pray. With an anguished heart, Moses begged God to spare their beloved sister. God did it! Miriam was restored.

Before you turn to the study guide, I'll like to say a few more words about Miriam. When the Israelites crossed the Red Sea, it was a miracle - an overwhelming, astonishing event. It displayed God's sovereignty in real time. God was ruling and reigning, and they celebrated HIM. It delighted their hearts and encouraged their faith. We've looked briefly at the oldest song known in the history of man – the Song of Moses. It was powerful and electrifying – and when they sang, it was a fantastic *a cappella jubilee*. It was possibly the grandest, most massive and most jubilant chorus of worshipers ever! Think about it. Israel rocked to a tune that glorified Our Great God. Millions of saints united in worship lifted their voices to heaven praising our God! Miriam led the women with tambourines, as they joyfully sang and danced. It must have been a sight to behold. I would have loved to been there. How about you?

I have a secret for you. One day soon, we will sing the Song of Moses and The Song of the Lamb, according to John's inspired words of Revelation 15:1-4. Here's a comparison of the two songs:

The Song of Moses (was sung)	**The Song of the Lamb** (will be sung)
at the Red Sea	at the crystal sea
in triumph over Egypt	in triumph over Babylon
as God brought His people OUT	as God brings His people IN
the first song	the last song
commemorated execution of the foe,	the same to show and confirm:
the expectation of the saints, and	God's faithfulness,
the exaltation of the Lord	God's deliverance of His own
	and judgment of ungodly

(Exploring Revelation, rev.ed. [Chicago: Moody, 1987; reprint, Neptune, N.J.: Loizeaux, 1991], 187)[8]

The entire event will mirror the Israelite's celebration following their miraculous exodus from Egypt. Their triumph in song followed the ten plagues. Our future celebratory anthem will follow plagues as well. When the seven plagues of the seven angels in heaven are complete. At long last, every tongue from every nation will gather on the banks of the glassy sea to praise and worship. United with one heart and one voice, we shall sing the Song of Moses and Song of the Lamb. A foreshadow of this marvelous occasion is found in our study this week. Some scholars have described the scene in Revelation 15 as the New Exodus. How thrilling! What a glorious celebration awaits us!

A Tearful Reunion.

I've thought a lot about the reunion of Miriam and her brothers when her health was restored. I'll just bet it was a tearful scene. They truly loved her and had interceded on her behalf. When Miriam returned, I'm convinced, she had a new walk - one of humanity. She must have finished with love and peace in her heart. The mantle Miriam wrongly coveted was much too heavy for her to carry. Now, she knew it spiritually and naturally. God's mercy would allow her to live her remaining days behind the scenes. Most assuredly, with a heart of gentle worship, Miriam was relieved of the burden of spiritual pride and misguided ambition.

In agreement with God, and at long last, Miriam was free! Free to walk humbly before God and her fellowman – including her loving brothers, Moses and Aaron.

Be blessed this week as you study Miriam: Sister Of Moses.

Next week: Rahab: A Woman On The Wall.

Miriam's story unfolds in Exodus 2 &15 and Numbers 12 & 20.

She is also mentioned in Deuteronomy 24:9; 1 Chronicles 6:3; and Micah 6:4

---

[8] John MacArthur, Revelation 12-22: The MacArthur New Testament Commentary (Chicago, IL: Moody Press, 2000), Rev. 15:3-4.

Miriam: Sister Of Moses

Day One: Who Is Miriam?

Memory Verse: Micah 6:4 For I brought you up from the land of Egypt, I redeemed you from the house of bondage; And I sent before you Moses, Aaron, and Miriam.

I never had an older sister. I was the older sister. Within the family, things like temperaments, personalities, weaknesses, and dispositions are revealed. Let's face it - the family is challenging. I never met anyone from a perfect family, because there are none. I know this because they are made of people, and none of us is perfect. This week we will study about Miriam, sister of Moses and Aaron. Their family was much like ours, flawed and imperfect. But, there was a lot of love there, or so it appears. This trio led the largest congregation of people, ever, because they were called, chosen, and anointed by God.

1. There has been much said and written about birth order. Do you think it's significant? If you have siblings, where are you in the birth order?

2. If you are the oldest sibling, did you assume greater responsibility? Was more expected and/or required of you? If so, how did it make you feel?

3. Who plans the family order? Record a verse below about the sovereignty of God.

Read Exodus 2:1-10. Answer the following questions.

4. In Exodus 2:4, who stood afar off and why?

5. Describe what occurred in Exodus 2:5-6. In your opinion, what made the response of Pharaoh's daughter so significant?

v. 5 -

v. 6 -

6. What does her response reveal to you about her heart? Why is this significant to God? Record a verse to share which expresses your thoughts.

7. Exodus 2:7 reveals some unspoken character traits of Miriam as a young child. What implied traits or qualities are evidenced in Exodus 2:7? Record them below.

8. Who was in control? Is it comforting to see Pharaoh's evil plot could not thwart God's plan concerning Moses and his siblings? Why or why not?

9. One day, many years in the future, Miriam would be called to lead. Please rewrite your answers to question 7 in the space provided below. Indicate by underlining, which character traits or qualities would be necessary for leadership? Explain why.

10. Jesus was an excellent leader. In fact, He had much to say about leadership. How are leaders made? By God or by man? Please record a verse to share in support of your thoughts.

Meditation
Psalm 2:12 …Blessed are all those who put their trust in Him.

Miriam: Sister Of Moses

Day Two: Where Is Miriam In God's Redemption Story?

Memory Verse: Micah 6:4 For I brought you up from the land of Egypt, I redeemed you from the house of bondage; And I sent before you Moses, Aaron, and Miriam.

God had told Abraham his descendants would suffer in slavery for four hundred years. And they did. Now, at long last, they were free. Moses has done the job. Due to their unbelief, however, the newly emancipated would be subject to wilderness wandering for 40 years. They would navigate some 240 square miles of desert, again and again, learning to believe and obey. We must remember, this was more than a desert march. It was more than merely a specific distance to travel. For some, it was a death march. Because of unbelief, they would remain just short of receiving the promises of God, namely "possessing the promised land." Until an entire generation of "unbelieving" Israelites perished in the desert, they could not enter in. Lack of faith had sealed their desert demise. That's where we find Miriam in God's redemption story. Together with Aaron and Moses, she would minister to a stiff-necked, criticizing people - a people who would prove to be slow learners. Some lessons come at a high price, and the wilderness would prove to be a hard training ground. God is serious about unbelief, and this desert detour made His point.

1. God is always at work in His people. Thinking biblically, what do you think He accomplished in the desert wilderness?

2. God is our provider - Jehovah-Jirah. Read Exodus 16:1-8 and briefly describe what happened. From Exodus 16:2, do you think Miriam was among the complainers? Why or why not?

3. In the desert, God formed a covenant with the Israelites, set them apart, tested their faith, and consecrated them in service to Him. Read Exodus 20:1-17. What is this list and what purpose does it serve?

4. Most of us will endure a spiritual wilderness of sorts sometime on our journey of faith. Many describe it as a dry season or season of testing along the way. Prayerfully consider your faith journey – to date, and answer the following questions.

    a. Have you had a wilderness experience? If so, how long did it last?

    b. What did God teach you or reveal to you about Himself?

    c. About yourself?

    d. How did God bring you out?

5. Forty years of wilderness wandering set God's people apart. It forced the Israelites, Miriam included, to confront hunger, fear, and isolation. Through it all God was faithful. List the one thing which stands out in your mind, and why, as you prayerfully read and review Exodus 17:1-7.

6. Let's take a closer look. Review Exodus 17:1-7 and answer the following questions. Notice the pattern - thanklessness, murmuring, and complaining; thankfulness, murmuring, and complaining; thankfulness, murmuring, and complaining, etc., etc. Sound familiar?

    a. From Exodus 17:1, when was "Then…?

    b. From Exodus 17:1-2, what were the people lacking and what did they demand?

    c. From Exodus 17:2, what two things did Moses ask?

    d. From Exodus 17:3, what was their chief complaint?

    e. From Exodus 17:4, what was Moses' response?

f. From Exodus 17:5, what was God's instruction?

g. From Exodus 17:6, what is the promised outcome?

Exodus 17:7 - So he called the name of the place Massah and Meribah, because of the _____ of the children of Israel, and because they _____ the Lord, saying, "_____ _____ _____ _____ _____ _____ _____?"

7. Moses cried out to the Lord over and over again. The entire camp, and Miriam witnessed Moses turn to God in prayer. He was well acquainted with God, the One who could supply all his needs. The Israelites, however, turned to Moses, not God. Where do you go for remedy to life's problems and crises? If not to God, how's it working for you?

8. Read 1 Kings 8:38-40, concerning prayer. From 1 Kings 8:39, what are we to remember about prayer?

9. The wilderness journey was multi-purposed. God was working within the individual hearts of the Israelites. The condition of our hearts has always been crucial to God. In fact, He is more concerned about our hearts than our comfort. Read and record the following heart passages.

Proverbs 4:23 -

Luke 6:45 -

2 Chronicles 16:9 -

Luke 12:34 -

10. We are called to be witnesses. (Acts 1:8.) So were the Israelites. When King Solomon dedicated the Temple, he addressed the Israelites' faithful witness and devotion to God. He concluded the service with a blessing and charge for the people. Read and review 1 Kings 8:57-61. Note that Solomon's blessing included a prayer. Reading from 1 Kings 8:57, "May the Lord our God be with us, as He was with our fathers. May He not leave us nor forsake us, that He may incline our hearts…" To what? How should they respond? List King Solomon's five instructions from 1 Kings 8:58.

1.

2.

3.

4.

5.

Meditation
1 Kings 8:61 "Let your heart therefore be loyal to the Lord our God, to walk in His statutes
and keep His commandments, as at this day."

Miriam: Sister of Moses

Day Three: What Did Miriam Get Right?

Memory Verse: Micah 6:4 For I brought you up from the land of Egypt, I redeemed you from the house of bondage; And I sent before you Moses, Aaron, and Miriam.

1. In Exodus 15:20, Miriam is identified as a prophetess. Although this was rare, Miriam is honored in scripture as the first of such among women. Miriam was also Israel's first worship leader. Using a dictionary, write the definition of a prophet (prophetess) below. What did she do? For whom did she speak?

2. At the inspiration of God, Moses wrote a song. Exodus 15:1-18. It's believed to be the first song ever written. Moving forward, all Israelite hymns would follow this same structure. In other words, they would include the *call to praise, reasons for praise, and a summary of all God had done.* As believers, we are called to praise and worship God. Following that model, write a few sentences highlighting: (1) the reasons for your praise, and (2) a summary of what God has done on your behalf.

1.

2.

3. Miriam was a worship leader. Read Exodus 15:20-21. Miriam sang the Song of Moses and the Song of the Lamb. One day we will sing this song. Read Revelation 15:3-4. What does this mean to you personally when you consider that the first song of the redeemed shall also be our last? We shall sing it throughout eternity! Do you see the completeness of God in this reality?

4. Miriam was called and anointed by God to lead the people of Israel into heartfelt worship. What a privilege. Taking people to the throne of grace and holding them there; this was a most thrilling work. "Worship" is an expression of our reverence and adoration for God. Only the redeemed have this awesome privilege. When we see God correctly, it compels us to worship. Do you have the heart to praise God and worship Him?

5. Read Exodus 14:13. Notice, the Israelites believed the Lord and Moses. Compare that to Exodus 15:24. What happened to their hearts of praise in Exodus 15?

6. Three days earlier the Israelites had celebrated on the banks of the Red Sea after their miraculous escape from Egypt and Pharoah's tyrannous enslavement. Now they murmur and complain. How quickly they forgot they were led to this point by God's pillar of cloud by day and His pillar of fire by night. God was still guiding them, yet the Israelites fell into despair. Looking again at Exodus 15:24, do you think Miriam was included among the grumblers? Why or why not?

7. The people's thirst quenched their adoration for God. When was the last time the concerns of the moment altered your view of God? What does that say about your faith? Share a verse below which encourages your faith. Indicate why this particular verse is significant to you.

8. Read Exodus 15:26. How does God reveal Himself? Write the last sentence of the verse.

About two years into the wilderness wanderings, something changed in Miriam's heart. That was after marvelous works of God like the crossing of the Red Sea, after the jubilant Song of Moses, and after she'd seen God provide water and manna. It was also after the victorious battle over the Amalekites, after the giving of the law at Mt. Sinai, even after she witnessed Moses' divine and radiant glow from being in God's presence. After being part of perhaps the most successful ministry team, ever – Miriam's heart changed. At a time when Moses could have used her help and leadership skills to boost the congregation's morale, she faltered and fell short. She failed him and others, but most significantly herself. Leading a congregation of this size was most definitely an all-hands-on-deck undertaking, and her leadership and direction would have proved invaluable to Moses as well as those Miriam served. We can see, up to now, she has led the Israelite women with poise and grace. But then, she let her pride and envy get the better of her.

9. Moving forward, how might we avoid the trap which caused Miriam's fall? List three scriptural suggestions below. Record a verse of scripture to support each idea.

1.

2.

3.

Meditation
Genesis 22:14 And Abraham called the name of the place, The-Lord-Will-Provide; as it is said to this day, "In the Mount of the Lord it shall be provided."

Miriam: Sister Of Moses

Day Four: What Did Miriam Get Wrong?

Memory Verse: Micah 6:4 For I brought you up from the land of Egypt, I redeemed you from the house of bondage; And I sent before you Moses, Aaron, and Miriam.

Miriam loved her baby brother, Moses. She had rescued him from certain death as an infant, demonstrating initiative and resourcefulness at a crucial time. After his rescue, he was raised in the palace under the watchful eye of Pharaoh's daughter. His little ark of salvation had served him well. He became a palace dweller, while Miriam lived by the grace extended to her mother, Jochebed, Moses' Hebrew nurse. At age forty, Moses murdered an Egyptian for beating a Hebrew slave. Fearing for his life, he retreated into the wilderness. There Moses remained herding sheep for forty years. While there, he also married the eldest daughter of the shepherd-priest in Midian. Her name was Zipporah. When Moses was eighty, God appeared to him in the burning bush, called and consecrated Moses to Himself, and launched his ministry. At long last, Miriam, Aaron, and Moses were reunited, when it pleased God, and to accomplish His purposes. But, as we shall see, Miriam's great love for Moses was eclipsed by her tremendous love for Israel. Commentators suggest she was quite a patriot. That's why she found Moses' marriage to the Ethiopian, a Cushite, so despicable. How dare Moses marry, again, and outside the family of faith! Her struggle with Moses was more than that! Miriam was bent on undermining the plans of God. She wanted Moses' job. Miriam wanted to lead Israel!

1. It appears Miriam was covetous. She wanted what God had not ordained for her. Patriotic pride had captivated her heart. Define covertous/covetousness.

2. Read Exodus 20:17. Record the last phrase of the verse below. Miriam was present at the giving of the Ten Commandments. Surely, she had seen the tablets up close.

3. God's word has given us scripture to safeguard us against intentional sin. Below is a list of seven biblical steps to avoid sin. Provide a scripture you think best represents each step listed.

    1. Pray: _____

    2. Use the Word of God: _____

    3. Recognize your weaknesses: _____

    4. Flee temptations: _____

    5. Be accountable to someone you can trust: _____

    6. Don't be discouraged: _____

    7. Confess, repent, and respond: _____

Anne Nicholson

Read Numbers 12:1-10 and answer the following questions.

4. "Then Miriam and Aaron spoke against Moses…" (Numbers 12:1). From the original language, this verse begins with the feminine singular form of the verb *wa tĕ dabber* implicating or identifying Miriam as the leader in this conspiracy. What does scripture teach us about submitting to the authorities which God has placed over our lives? Record a verse.

5. Aaron was the Priest of Israel, and he may have been a good spokesman for Moses, but he was a weak leader. He was easily swayed. He had already succumbed to the people's provocative erection and worship of the golden calf. Now, he will make another poor decision. In your opinion, when Miriam raised questions about Moses and started murmuring against him, what should Aaron have done and why? Record a verse to support your thoughts.

6. Read Numbers 12:2. Moses was called and anointed by God. However, Miriam's question implies God has spoken to them [Miriam and Aaron] in the same manner. What, if anything, does this verse reveal about Miriam's faith? What about her pride?

Miriam's faith:

Miriam's pride:

7. Moses was an extraordinarily humble man who had served the Lord well. Numbers 12:3. Commentators agree, this verse asserts there was nothing Moses had done to provoke an attack

by his siblings. The dissension which starts between them will quickly spread throughout the camp. What a painful situation for Moses. Who was really behind this attack? Have you been betrayed by members of your own family? If so, how did you respond?

8. In keeping with Moses's humble description of himself, he does not respond to their insurrection attempt. Instead, the Lord Himself handles the matter. Read Numbers 12:4-8. Record the highlights of Numbers 12:7-8 below.

v. 7

v. 8

9. Read Numbers 12:9-10. Complete the last phrase of verse 10 below.

"…suddenly Miriam *became* _____, as _____ *as* snow."

10. What does leper mean?

Meditation
Numbers 12:8 I speak with him face to face…

Miriam: Sister Of Moses

Day Five: How Did God's Love Redeem It All?

Memory Verse: Micah 6:4 For I brought you up from the land of Egypt, I redeemed you from the house of bondage; And I sent before you Moses, Aaron, and Miriam.

The unthinkable had happened. First, Miriam came against Moses and incited Aaron to join her folly. Next, God intervened on behalf of His anointed. We see in Numbers 12:5, the Lord came down…! What thrilling words! God was near to Moses! We are forewarned. God will deal with the enemy and his evil in whatever form it's embodied - even if it comes from members of our own family. Miriam is leprous! How startling is this? God will not allow us to push against His anointed - successfully or consistently, nor thwart His plans. The prophet Isaiah relied upon God and knew His power. The prophet inquired, "He who vindicates Me is near; Who will contend with Me?" (Isaiah 50:8).

1. Read Numbers 12:7. For Old Testament servants, there was only one acceptable response to God. That response? Faithful, steadfast obedience to the Word of God – period. Remember, biblical faith is confident obedience to God's Word despite the circumstances or consequences. This type of faith pleases God and is acceptable - always! As you review Numbers 12:7, what does this verse say about Moses but not about Miriam and Aaron? How do you think this statement from God made them feel? What information does it provide for you?

2. As stated above, biblical faith is confident obedience to God's word despite the circumstances or consequences. Does this describe your general submission to God's Word? If not, why?

Women of the Bible and God's Redeeming Love

3. What riveting question does the Lord ask in the last phrase of Numbers 12:8? Write the question.

4. Review Deuteronomy 34:10 in light of Numbers 12:8. Moses was not only called, chosen, and anointed by God for ministry - God was with Him. How exciting! Do you think this was news to Miriam and Aaron? Record the words of Deuteronomy 34:10 below.

5. Read Numbers 12:11-14. Who first cried out in Miriam's defense? Who first cried out to God?

6. Don't you know they were all stunned at Miriam's leprous state, including Miriam herself? This was an outright and immediate judgment of Miriam's opposition to Moses - God's anointed. What do you think about this? In your opinion, was her punishment just? Why or why not?

7. Turn to Leviticus 13:45 to discover how the leprous individual must identify himself or herself.

a. Record Leviticus 13:45.

b. After having such a prominent position among the leadership of Israel, this must have been terribly humiliating for poor Miriam! Have you ever experienced painful, embarrassing, or humiliating consequences following a poor decision? What did you learn through it?

8. Record Numbers 12:13 below. What does this tell you about Moses, the man?

9. Read Numbers 12:15-16. The entire camp of Israel came to a screeching halt while they waited on Miriam. What happened in Numbers 12:16?

10. Unconfessed, unrepentant sin causes spiritual leprosy which renders us ineffective to the purposes of God. A vast multitude waited seven days while their beloved Miriam was restored to health. Unfortunately, she was never fully restored. Her prophetic voice was silenced. Her gift of prophecy was finished. Our incredible worship leader who had once danced with rhythm and poetic passion was seated and still. How Miriam lived, the remainder of her days is not revealed in scripture. Nonetheless, she had learned a life-changing lesson. Why do you think Aaron, the Priest, was not stricken with leprosy as well?

Epologue: Miriam Died In The Wilderness.

Then the children of Israel, the whole congregation, came into the Wilderness of Zin in the first month, and the people stayed in Kadesh; and Miriam died there and was buried there. Numbers 20:1.

Tradition holds Miriam was mourned for thirty days by the Israelites. One commentator suggested her death was not from old age, or from complications of leprosy, but perhaps from a broken heart. Scripture is silent on the matter. The good news for us is like the other women in the Bible, Miriam was redeemed. God answered Moses' prayers! God spared her, redeemed her life, and restored her relationship with her brothers. Nevertheless, there were consequences. Wanting what God had not ordained for her, as well as her public rebellion and criticism against God's anointed proved to be humiliating and painful - spiritually and naturally. Ministry can get the best of us if it becomes our focus instead of Jesus. When this occurs, unless we're repentant and restored, we are no longer useful for God's purposes. When God's searchlight revealed Miriam's heart, she saw the reality of her sin. Thankfully, the revelation led Miriam to a broken heart of repentance. A contrite heart is pleasing to the Lord. The words of the psalmist David when confronted by Nathan: "The sacrifices of God are a broken spirit, A broken and a contrite heart—These, O God, You will not despise." (Psalm 51:17).

Forgiving Ourselves.

Although forgiven and restored, loved by God, by her brothers, and millions of Israelites, I suppose Miriam never forgave herself – that is, entirely. Sometimes, we can forgive others with ease, but ourselves, not so readily. Deep regret must have washed over her daily, as her prophetic voice was silenced. I speak from personal experience. Long years after my salvation regret overwhelmed me. I still struggled to forgive myself for harmful and hurtful mistakes, and at unexpected times - random times - regrets and sorrow would wash over me. Although I know, I am the Beloved's, and He is mine! I can genuinely relate to Miriam's heartache and deep regret. Perhaps you can too!

May her life serve as a reminder to us all. When we sin, it affects the lives of those around us. Most often, those whom we love best. And, if or when we covet what God has not given us, whatever it is, including ministry, it's a sin. God will forgive us, but painful consequences can last a lifetime.

The Old Generation.

Unrepentant jealousy, envy, covetousness, deceit, etc., can rob us of finishing strong. It was a somber ending for such an anointed life; as a result, all of Israel was deprived of her gifts. Ironically, none of the leadership entered the Promised Land. Neither Moses or Aaron (who died at the end of the 40th year) came into the land of Canaan. So, too, Miriam died in the 11th hour, just short of the promises of God. Tradition holds that her death served as a symbol the old generation could not enter in. Aaron's death is noted in Numbers 33:38-39. As for Moses, he struck the rock, misrepresenting God. To which God responded: Then the Lord spoke to Moses and Aaron, "Because you did not believe Me, to hallow Me in the eyes of the children of Israel, therefore you shall not bring this assembly into the land which I have given them." (Numbers 20:12).

Saving Faith.

Although they did not enter the physical promised land, I believe they had saving faith – all of them. Remember, Old Testament saints were saved because they *believed* in the promise of a coming redeemer. Most assuredly, these saints of old trusted God would redeem them, and all of those who called upon the name of the Lord. Romans 10:13. Few, if any, have seen and witnessed God's glory and marvelous works like they did. How could they not believe?

Thanks to God, we have His inspired Word. It not only helps us to know Him better, but it also strengthens us for the journey. According to the psalmist, it's a lamp unto our feet and a light unto our path. (Psalm 119:105.) It leads and guides us, encourages our faith, and is the most loving rebuke on earth – as needed. Remember, it is our source for life and godliness. So, keep your eyes on Jesus and spend time with Him - daily, and stay in His Word. For your hope is in Him! Moving forward, it is my prayer that the Spirit establish and confirm God's Word in your heart and bring it to fruitful performance in your life.

Meditation
Numbers 12:13 So Moses cried out to the Lord, saying, "Please heal her, O God, I pray!"

Notes - Miriam: Sister of Moses

Rahab

Rahab: A Woman On The Wall

Occasionally, God uses the most unlikely people to accomplish His work. We've all heard jaw-dropping tales of heroic rescues and unselfish acts of sacrifice or bravery which border on unbelievable. Sometimes the actions and accomplishments are too much for us to grasp or process. I believe it's true because we can't predict how we might respond under similar circumstances, and because we know, generally speaking, people are pretty ordinary. In fact, I heard of a pastor who once said, "God must love ordinary people a great deal because He sure made a lot of us." Look around you. We are ordinary people. Even though we are the pinnacle of God's creation, His masterpiece and image bearers, we are all ordinary sinners wholly incumbent upon God's grace for forgiveness and salvation. We need a Savior, every last one of us!

Our heroine of the week is Rahab, and she is no exception. This week's lesson will push against our sensibilities because God will partner with the most unlikely candidate. He will use an unlikely woman, her occupation, and defiled home to accomplish His divine purposes. In fact, He will redeem every aspect of her life. In all of scripture, this is perhaps the most remarkable tale of salvation, transformation, and redemption. Overall, it is a story of grace. It's a story of the power of God's grace revealed through the faith of an ordinary sinner.

The Truth Of The Gospel.

Rahab's story is God's loving and living testimony of the truth of the gospel. I have a personal affinity to this story because, quite frankly, her story is our story. Although I love all the women of the Bible, mention of her name always makes me smile. Indeed, hers is "a rag to riches story" - spiritually and naturally. Right before our eyes, God elevates Rahab to a position of honor and privilege as her defiled body is cleansed through and through. Only God can make the unclean clean, the untidy tidy, the unforgivable forgiven and the lost redeemed. That's His job, His focus, His work, His goal - the bottom line - it's His plan. Salvation and transformation. His Spirit is busy, even now, conforming us to the image of His son, Jesus. Because it was God's plan, Rahab holds the esteemed privilege of being the only other female listed alongside Sarah in the Hebrews record of those with noteworthy faith. But even more, from her very body, a kinsman redeemer will come. That's right! How great is our God?

If you have any history with the Lord, I'm sure by now you've figured out God is in the people business. He's into people! We are the benefactors of His grace through faith which saves us. Only humanity can make that claim. When He redeems us, He redeems the whole of our lives, not just the pretty pieces. Sometimes we don't see the results of His work instantly. Nonetheless, His Spirit is always working to accomplish His plan. He can't clean up the outside until He's dealt with the inside. Plainly stated, His life-changing spirit works in us before it works through us. A theologian of old once referred to this as the ministry of the interior.

When God's spirit manifested Himself in Rahab, she experienced an interior change – a heart change. Faith awakened, and she believed. The evidence of the effects of her conversion exposed her faith. If we merely attempt to change bad habits or a sinful lifestyle, it will never last. We can never affect an authentic or lasting change within ourselves.

On the other hand, when real faith - saving faith comes, it's always accompanied by God's power unto works. There is no other explanation for what occurred. It is the same with us. You might say, God has an inside connection with us all! Just in case you're wondering what's the igniting force behind all tales of heroics, sacrifice, and extreme bravery, it's God. That's right; it's always our merciful God and His amazing grace through faith which saves us, keeps us, and empowers us.

Living Under Condemnation.

Before we look closely at Rahab, let's get the backstory in place. Rahab was a condemned woman. Even though she was not aware of it, she was living under triple condemnation. First, she was condemned individually because of her sin and sinful lifestyle. In addition to her original or indwelling sin, she had adopted a lifestyle of sin and was benefiting from it financially. Since it takes two to tango, so to speak, her sin reached into the lives of others causing them to sin as well. Remember, we never sin in a vacuum. Every time she lay with someone she defiled her own body in addition to theirs. According to Paul, sexual sin is the only sin we commit which we commit against ourselves. Paul forewarned the church at Corinth: "Flee sexual immorality. Every sin that a man does is outside the body, but he who commits sexual immorality sins against his own body." (1 Corinthians 6:18).

Sexual sin is a hot topic, but it's not our purpose. Suffice it to say, God created sex and it was meant exclusively for a husband and his wife and no other. Any other sexual encounters are sexual sin. If that statement is offensive, remember only God's opinion matters. Mine and yours are irrelevant. God is serious about all sin, and sexual sin is no exception. In fact, many times I have seen the pain and destruction created through sexual promiscuity and adulterous relationships. It hurts, kills, separates, divides, and destroys - like all sin. When we operate outside the will of God in this fashion, we can rest assured it will come at a high price accompanied by painful consequences. For clarity, let's define sin. *Sin is any failure to conform to the moral law of God in act, attitude, or nature.*[9] There we have it. Sin would most assuredly include sexual sin and all sexual immorality. Jesus shocked the hearers when He spoke revolutionary words in the Sermon on the Mount concerning adultery, among other things. He called the unfaithful into account when He said, "But I say to you that whoever looks at a woman to lust for her has already committed adultery with her in his heart." (Matthew 5:28).

---

[9] Grudem, W. A. (2004). *Systematic theology: an introduction to biblical doctrine* (p. 490). Leicester, England; Grand Rapids, MI: Inter-Varsity Press; Zondervan Pub. House.

Secondly, her religious choices and idol worship were condemning. The entire region was overflowing with false gods, idols and idol worship. They celebrated and worshiped false gods like Baal, Dagan, and Ashteroth – gods of war and violence, or sex and fertility. In other words, violence, war, and sex were the order of the day; they were part of ordinary life. As hard as it might be for us to accept, they sometimes sacrificed their infants on the altars of fire to appease their awful gods. Although scripture strictly forbids infant sacrifice. Numerous Old Testament verses explicitly forbade the inhumane ritual. As an example, a harsh warning from God is found in Leviticus 20:2-5.

Lastly, she and all of the residents of Jericho lived under condemnation because they inhabited the land God had condemned through the covenant with Abraham in Genesis 15. We will examine these passages a bit later. For further study, you may wish to review Deuteronomy 18:9-14 which highlights God's message to Moses concerning the lands which the Israelites were instructed to conquer and possess. Here we discover the abominations before God that preceded their condemnation. Remember, God is merciful and patient. He has waited 470 years for the "days of the Amorites to be complete" as per His covenant words to Abraham from Genesis 15:13-21.

Sin and Condemnation.

Before we move forward, let's take a quick look at sin and condemnation. Rahab, her family, the residents of Jericho, and the inhabitants of the surrounding lands were living under condemnation, even though they were unaware of it. In fact, we're all living under condemnation, unless we belong to Jesus. How so? The Bible tells us we are conceived in sin and born in sin - our inheritance from Adam. That's why we need Jesus, to save us, for we could never save ourselves. To have right standing before a Holy God, we must believe in Jesus. Then, His righteousness becomes our righteousness - we are justified and declared not guilty of transgressing against God's law.

Unfamiliar with God's law? They are the Ten Commandments. The original commandments were written by the finger of God on tablets of stone, and given to Moses on Mt. Sinai. (Exodus 20.) They were delivered in love to set boundaries, define our relationship with God and others, and for our overall good and protection. They recorded God's holy standard to teach us right from wrong. However, over time, the Rabbis expanded the list of restrictions, further burdening God's people. The number ultimately climaxed at a staggering 613 laws. No one could keep them, not even Paul, the Pharisee of Pharisees. God knew we would fall short. According to Romans 3:23, we've all sinned and fall short of the glory of God. Because He loves us, and in His infinite wisdom and gracious mercy, God made a way. Jesus! He is the way, the truth, and the life. (John 14:6.) If Jesus is your Savior, you have nothing to fear. You're forgiven, and you're under no condemnation whatsoever – past, present, and future. Even the eternal consequences of your sin are settled. Because of Jesus, you have a new relationship with the law. You are governed by God's grace instead. What marvelous news! Thanks to God, there is no condemnation for believers. Paul assures the Romans and us, "There is therefore now no condemnation to those who are in Christ Jesus..." (Romans 8:1).

Who is Rahab?

In Joshua 2:1, we meet Rahab. A *harlot* who lodged in Jericho. The verse says: Now Joshua the son of Nun sent out two men from Acacia Grove to spy secretly, saying, "Go, view the land, especially Jericho." So they went, and came to the house of a harlot named Rahab, and lodged there.

From the verse, we can see Rahab was a working girl. Was she a harlot? That's what the Bible records. Although through the years many Bible teachers have tried to pretty her up by merely stating she was an innkeeper. It's true, "innkeeper" is one of the meanings of her name, but the New Testament writers of Matthew, James, and Hebrews confirm her harlotry. We'll be looking at these passages in our study guide. What you need to know is the original language makes it clear. Let's take a look. The Hebrew words for *a harlot* are ʾiššâ zōnâ. In the combined words, we have ʾiššâ meaning *female;* and zōnâ (from the primary root word *zanah*) which means *adulterous, prostitute, harlot, to commit fornication, commit adultery, be unfaithful.*

Now you can see why some have attempted to clean her up a bit. It was simply too much to accept a real-life harlot might be found in the bloodline of Jesus. But God thought otherwise. There are three other Gentiles in Jesus' genealogy as well and one Jewess, Mary - the virgin mother. God makes no mistakes. He allowed us to see, through Jesus' genealogy, Gentiles played a role in the birth of our Lord and Savior Jesus. How astounding!

In Matthew's record of Jesus' genealogy, we find five women. Matthew 1:1-16. Although it was uncommon to record women in genealogies during this period of history, God's inspired word has intentionally done so. Here we find one authentic harlot or prostitute – Rahab. Another who wasn't a harlot or prostitute, but disguised herself as one to lure her father-in-law into her bedchamber – Tamar; a widowed Moabitess – Ruth; and another who is not mentioned by name. She was the love of King David's life - his bathing beauty, Bathsheba. In the genealogical record, she is listed as "...her who had been the wife of Uriah." (Matthew 1:6). She was Uriah's wife, that is when King David took her for himself, impregnated her, and had her husband moved to the front line of battle where his death was imminent. It's plain to see, Rahab's not the only scandalous woman to make the divine list. Is she? The truth is Jesus had real people, real sinners in His bloodline. There is no other option. We are all sinners. Paul said, "for all have sinned and fall short of the glory of God." (Romans 3:23). We were all conceived in sin and born into sin - our inheritance from Adam. I've already said, we need a savior, every last one of us! We are justified when we believe. "So then faith comes by hearing, and hearing by the word of God." (Romans 10:17).

What else can we know about Rahab? She was not only living a sinful life but profiting from it as well. But, to the astonishment of onlookers, she was useful to God anyway. I find that hopeful. Are you wondering what made her valuable to the purposes of God? God did it! It was an infusion of His grace. How much grace? Enough! Enough to save her from herself, first, and then sufficient to ignite saving faith, change her destiny, give her a future and a hope, and enable her to accomplish His plan. That's thrilling! God always gives us exactly what is needed when it's needed. It would be enough grace by faith to save her family as well. When a way is made for her salvation, she will plead mercifully for her family's too. How interesting! On the surface, she appeared self-indulgent and self-obsessed, but here we see something entirely unexpected and remarkable. It's interesting to note, too, just before she becomes useful to the purposes of God, it appears she's not even aware she's the recipient of His saving grace, nor His electing love.

Commentators suggest she was profiting from her sinful lifestyle right up until that fateful day. The day she collided with a Holy God and His spies. Until God intervened, she was doing what she could, what she knew, and using her own body to survive. But like all heroic tales, everything changed in an instant. One might say Rahab's conversion tale is dramatic. Her new life was a drastic change from her old one – for sure. There's always a before and after story; Rahab is no exception. In an instant, her life and world transformed. This moment – her moment - has been coming since before the foundation of the world. She will respond accordingly. Without a moment's hesitation, she will spring into action and reveal her faith. Our unlikely heroine will risk life and liberty in response to God's call.

Take note, Rahab was resourceful and exercised initiative. She was bright, a quick thinker, and a problem solver of sorts, who possessed excellent instincts and discernment. She was very courageous, without apprehension, agenda, or false motives. Additionally, she was truthful to her pledge and followed through. Most importantly, she was open, willing and available to respond to God's call of electing love. Her heart was not hardened. God's spirit had sweetly wooed her. He does the choosing! He can and will save anyone of His choosing and propel him or her forward to accomplish His plan. He still saves to the uttermost and uses the unexpected. I like that! I told you she was an unlikely candidate. When it matters most, she will practice saving faith in the God of Abraham, Isaac, and Jacob. She will receive the spies "with peace" which takes faith to a heightened level. We read in Hebrews, "By faith the harlot Rahab did not perish with those who did not believe, when she had received the spies with peace." (Hebrews 11:31).

Astoundingly, Rahab had the peace, comfort, confidence, and surety of salvation. But it was more, she believed for her household as well. She believed all those inside would escape peril. The scarlet threads hung from her window would alert the assailants to the surety and protection of the blood of sacrifice. Just like in Egypt. The Israelites survived because the blood of the spotless lamb marked a cross on their doorposts. In Jericho, the scarlet threads in the window secured Rahab's safety, and her family's as well. Faith had come to the home of a harlot, and all her family survived. Isn't that our story? We believe, and in an instant, we have the surety of salvation. Our harlot, Rahab, will hide the spies and lie to save them without any regard for her safety. She will merely submit to God and look to Him for success - that's faith. With every fiber of her being, she will pledge allegiance to the one true and living God. Our unlikely heroine, Rahab, doesn't have faith and works, instead, faith that works. Astounding! Your study guide will help you navigate these exciting passages.

So, who was Rahab? A practicing harlot who was saved by God's amazing grace. She was God's faithful servant who became an ancestress of Jesus; the wife of Salmon, a real-life prince of Judah; the mother of Boaz; the mother-in-law of Ruth; a survivor of the battle of Jericho; and the first Canaanite convert commemorated in the Bible. It appears that our unlikely heroine was an exceptionally keen woman who was useful to the purposes of God!

A New Era Of Faithfulness.

When Moses died on the plains of Moab an era ended. At the appointed time, God installed and confirmed Joshua as the new commander of the Israelites. (Joshua 1:1-9.) Let's review the verse: "Have I not commanded you? Be strong and of good courage; do not be afraid, nor be dismayed, for the Lord your God is with you wherever you go." (Joshua 1:9). What a promise and what a call! Joshua was ready; he had passed the test of faithfulness. God had given him marching orders and blessings as well. Just so you know, as His child, you have the same blessing. Be strong and courageous; do not be afraid or dismayed, the Lord your God is with you, wherever you go! How could Joshua fail since God would go with him? Joshua was ready, at last! He was free to conquer the land of promise.

Notice although God's vision had not changed, a new spiritual leader would see it through. Let's remember, God's work never stops. He is always and forever advancing His kingdom work. I hope that gives you comfort. Until the end of time, our Lord's plan marches on through those He has called and chosen. It is Joshua's season. Is this perhaps your season as well? If so, you are ready. God equips us to accomplish His plans. He prepares us for the task at hand. Just like Joshua. He had learned well from one of the best. As you may recall from our study of Miriam, under the command of Moses, the family trio had led perhaps the most densely populated congregation in history. As his right-arm man, Joshua witnessed faithfulness, obedience, follow through, and blessings – for forty plus years. For the most part, Moses was an exceptional leader. But, it's a new day, and the spiritual baton has passed. At long last, it was Joshua's turn.

It's interesting to note, it was his turn, but it was not his first rodeo! It was not his first physical and spiritual challenge. Forty years earlier, Moses had commissioned twelve men and sent them to survey the land of Canaan. The spies were to observe what they saw and report back to Moses. As it would happen, ten men saw giants in the land, while Joshua and Caleb saw the opportunity for God's strength and glory to be revealed. Joshua and Caleb had spiritual eyes. Did you catch that? While ten men saw the giants or obstacles and impossibilities through natural eyes, Joshua and Caleb had a different vantage point. They had spiritual eyes. They saw the opportunity for God's grand reveal, by His grace and for His glory. They saw victory in advance. They had faith in God's ability to take the land. But, the other men lacked faith, and unbelief plagued them. As a result, a whole generation of Israelites perished in the desert. Joshua and Caleb were the only two who survived the captivity of Egypt and 40 years of wilderness wanderings to enter the promised land. Not in an attempt to oversimplify, but this is a classic example of God's faithfulness to the faithful. God blessed Caleb and Joshua! Their story unfolds in Numbers 13.

Why Jericho?

Geographically speaking, Jericho was between the Jordan River and the promised land. As you might have guessed, the Israelites would have to conquer the city of Jericho, and others, before they could possess the land God promised Abraham. Today, it is located in the region of the West Bank. The area is under Palestinian control, not the Israeli government. It is believed to be the oldest inhabited city in the world. I found it interesting to consider Rahab was living in the oldest occupied city in the world while performing the oldest profession in the world. Fascinating!

Conquering Jericho will be Joshua's first challenge as the nation's new leader. He was trapped between the Jordan River and the walls of Jericho. It was time to lead. Like his predecessor, Joshua called and anointed two spies to check out the land. Joshua 2:1. His desert training proved invaluable. He had seen Moses lead and guide God's people spiritually and naturally. Joshua's unshakeable faith in God will prevail. The time has come, and he is ready - for Joshua, there is no other option.

In the natural world, this was their conquest, but it was a spiritual battle as well. What we experience in the natural has a spiritual counterpart. All our battles, conflicts, and struggles are fought and won in our minds first, through our wills. Will we obediently trust God at His word? Will we believe God and obediently follow, trusting the consequences to Him? Remember biblical faith is confident obedience to God's word despite the circumstances or consequences. Joshua had that faith. Do you? It is yours for the asking!

A spiritual challenge loomed large before them. To move forward, naturally and spiritually, Joshua and company must defeat Jericho because it obstructed their path to the promised land. Even though the fortress walls stretched skyward, Joshua knew they were no match for God. This story is a fantastic example of fighting and winning battles spiritually. Joshua, too, proves to be an exceptional leader. It should come as no surprise. The name Joshua has the same meaning as Jesus, which is *Jehovah or Yahweh is salvation.* Indeed, salvation had come to Jericho.

Where Is Rahab In God's Redemption Story?

Rahab resides where God ordained - precisely. Her life, her profession, and her location were no surprise to God. By His divine providence, Rahab was living in Jericho and working as a harlot. God had not called her into this sinful lifestyle, but He is aware of everything about her and has allowed her to continue to fulfill His plan. At the appointed time, He will use it all to accomplish His purposes. Remember, what the enemy intends for evil, God can change for good. His work in the area of restoration is always exceptional!

Rahab lived in Jericho, a walled fortress city located east of the Jordan River on the plains of Moab. In its day, it was a vibrant place of commerce and culture. It was ideally situated on the main trade route which provided easy access to the walled city. Since the city overflowed with merchants peddling their wares, day in and day out, the spies assumed two more strangers would be quite ordinary. They believed it would be quite the norm for two strangers to arrive in town and seek lodging in the brothel. It's always about location, and Rabah's brothel proved to be a prime piece of real estate, indeed. It was much better than they thought. An exterior city wall supported the back of Rahab's brothel. It's location and business made her home the perfect spot to surveil the city. However, much to their surprise, their presence was detected. Even though they had planned carefully, they were not inconspicuous after all. Isn't it interesting, our best plans sometimes fail?

Subsequently, the King's alerted, "An enemy is among us." Imminent danger is the catalyst which ignites Rahab's newfound faith. Her quick actions prove beneficial. As God would desire, she quickly conceals the spies in the flax stalks drying on her roof. As if with blind eyes, the king's men fail to root them out, and God's men remain on the roof undetected. When it's safe, they escape the roof through a window in the exterior wall and head north a short distance. There, in the Judean hills, they remain three days as Rahab instructed. (Joshua 2:22.) As God ordained, the location of Rahab's house was perfect for a rapid escape when His spies fled the city.

What Did Rahab Get Right?

She believed in the God of Abraham, Isaac, and Jacob and followed through. Her word was true. She saved the spies. She protected them with her very life, even though, the King had sent men with a message to have her send them out. If discovered, it would have been her end. Her actions were treasonous, punishable by death. If her deceit became known, death would be her family's fate as well. When it mattered most, she was brave in the face of danger. She had courage. She let her heart and newly awakened spirit be her guide. Rahab was found faithful! In the process, she partnered with God. How thrilling! What does the end of Hebrews 11:31 confirm concerning her faith? Rahab "had received the spies with peace." What does that mean? We will be taking a closer look at this in our study guide.

Let's examine Rahab's honest and humble confession of faith:

Now before they lay down, she came up to them on the roof, and said to the men: "I know that the Lord has given you the land, that the terror of you has fallen on us, and that all the inhabitants of the land are fainthearted because of you. For we have heard how the Lord dried up the water of the Red Sea for you when you came out of Egypt, and what you did to the two kings of the Amorites who were on the other side of the Jordan, Sihon and Og, whom you utterly destroyed. And as soon as we heard these things, our hearts melted; neither did there remain any more courage in anyone because of you, for the Lord your God, He is God in heaven above and on earth beneath. (Joshua 2:8-11).

How astounding is her confession? We are all saved the same way: by the means of grace through faith. God's grace awakened her spirit, and in an instant, she believed. Just like the apostle Paul. When it pleased God to reveal Himself in her, Rahab had faith – authentic saving faith. As God enabled her to believe - it was accomplished. In the ninth verse Rahab says, "I know." In Hebrew, the word is *yada*, and the original meaning is *to understand, grasp or ascertain; especially to be familiar or acquainted with a person or thing.* In essence, her confession assured the spies, "I know this God - your God - I have faith, I believe in God." We shall see her bold confession was substantiated by faith that works. We will examine her entire confession in our study guide.

Genuine Faith.

Rahab, the prostitute, was saved and immediately sprang into action. Being moved by the Spirit, she hid the spies, made a noble confession of faith, and sent the townsmen away in the opposite direction. Although this was treason, she didn't care. Next, when it was safe, she let the spies down through a window of her house on the exterior city wall. Her actions would prove her faith was indeed genuine. Our unlikely heroine, Rahab, had authentic faith - an active and living faith. It would attest to her newfound spiritual awakening from God. How did it occur? Just like in us.

First, God's grace awakened her spiritually, and then He gave her faith to believe. Salvation from start to finish is a spiritual work from God. Our unlikely heroine, Rahab, is listed among the faithful in God's inspired list of Hebrews 11 for this very act. She believed with the heart, confessed with the mouth, and at the risk of significant peril, she acted on her verbal profession. In light of what she believed, she responded. Sadly, many of us talk the talk but don't walk the walk. But, not Rahab, she got it! Her life lined up with her lips! She confessed it and responded accordingly. How thrilling! May our daily responses to God be as genuine and faith-filled!

What Did Rahab Get Wrong?

When I wrote the introduction to this series, I mentioned some of the women in our study were decadent. That means they lived a lifestyle polite company would consider offensive. Some defining words for decadent are degenerate, corrupt, depraved, sinful, unprincipled, and immoral. In general, they are pleasure seekers and self-indulgent. It's difficult for us to imagine someone with the above-defined character traits, habits, or lifestyle was in the family tree of Jesus, isn't it? But as you know, it's true. That's amazing grace!

We've looked at Rahab, but as I said earlier, this lesson is really about God and His amazing grace. In fact, every time a sinner comes to faith, it's all about God and His grace. We are all on a collision course with God, and the lesson is also about the spies and their safety and the Israelites. It's about a pledge and promise and a scarlet thread, about men marching and marching, and trumpets and seven times and pervading silence against a backdrop of thundering footsteps and the dust rising in clouds from beneath their sandals. It's about their silent, unending prayers, and anticipation in their God who was able and sufficient. It's about the wandering eyes of those marching and their wonderment, amazement, and hope in God alone. It's really about victory and God's miracle work of salvation because ultimately, casting all else aside, it's God's work and His ultimate goal. That is why He sent us Jesus - to save the lost, to awaken our dead bodies and raise them to life, abundant life in Him, hope and faith in God and nothing else. It's always been in Christ alone.

This day in history was about God's work of grace through faith for Rahab. That's God's unmerited, unearned favor and plan to save her. That's right. In this lesson, we see the grace of God collide in the heart of a woman, who from all outward appearances, looked to be beyond God's reach. It should remind us no one is beyond the love and grace of God. Rahab, a new believer, was compelled into action by the grace of God, and for His glory. Within an instant, she proved useful unto the purposes of God. I love this story because God is in the business of redemption. He saves us. In some instances, He also rescues us from ourselves. That's Rahab's story, and it may be yours as well.

I feel for Rahab, but I'm uncertain about what prompted her decisions concerning her occupation of choice. Some have suggested she was the sole support of her entire family. Maybe or maybe not. Only God knows. As I was thinking about this lesson, it occurred to me that no young girl ever said, "When I grow up, I want to be a prostitute - I want to be used and defiled for sexual pleasure, yet never loved." I just bet that's nowhere on the list of dream jobs for anyone. But, for whatever reason, they do exist. Since the garden, women have allowed their pain and heartache to be masked in sexual desire and fulfillment, forfeiting the authentic for the counterfeit. Most certainly, they have believed the lie of the enemy. But, even this lie is not too difficult for God. He is, even still, rescuing, loving, and saving sinners to the uttermost!

How Did God's Love Redeem It All?

God loved Rahab, regardless. What she got wrong is probably very different from your sin or my sin. But guess what? Even though we categorize sin into major sin or minor sin, God doesn't. To Him, one sin is like another. All sin is sin and separates us from Him. Who cares if Rahab was not welcome in her neighbors' homes or at the Jericho corner market? God embraced her, the great I AM, the creator of heaven and earth. A man looks at the natural, but God looks at the heart. His electing love rested on Rahab. He chose her! He rescued her and welcomed her into the family of faith! But even more, God's love and grace placed Rahab in the family tree of Jesus. It's jaw-dropping and unthinkable. Those words cause me to giggle. Isn't that just like God to do the most unexpected thing? Our Rahab is in the royal genealogy of Jesus. In Matthew's inspired gospel, we find her name. Only God can take an ordinary prostitute and transform her into an extraordinary symbol of faith. If she would receive the privilege of motherhood in the line of Jesus, then surely nothing is impossible with God. Recalling the pivotal question of Genesis 18, "Is anything too hard for the Lord?" (Genesis 18:14). Most certainly not!! Anything in our lives that needs to be redeemed is redeemable by our Lord. He can do it, and He is willing. There is nothing too sinful for Him to handle. His blood has covered it all.

A Royal Bloodline.

Jesus' genealogy in Matthew's gospel lists Rahab as the wife of Salmon. Their loving union brought forth a son named Boaz. Boaz grew to become the kinsman redeemer who married Ruth, and their love and union produced a son named Obed. From Obed came Jesse, the father of David who was the favored King of Israel. From King David - through that line - Our Lord Jesus would come. Who was Salmon? He was a prince, an ancestor of the lineage of Judah. It appears when Rahab, the one-time heathen harlot married, she married into one of the honorable families of Israel. And, then because it was God's plan, Rahab became an ancestress of our Lord Jesus. Do you see God's amazing grace here?

A Happy Ending.

As Rahab's family assimilated into the family of Israelites, her blossoming faith flourished and matured. Over time, sanctification transformed Rahab into a model of faithfulness. Undoubtedly, Salmon's heartfelt gratitude for Rahab grew and bloomed into love. When grace expunged Rahab's former life of shame and desperation, prince Salmon made her his wife. One commentator suggested Salmon may have been one of the two spies. Only God knows for sure. It would make an excellent ending, but I couldn't find evidence to support the claim. Nonetheless, what a fantastic testimony to the purifying work of Christ. What He cleanses and purifies is as white as snow. Rahab's name became sanctified and dignified.

Speaking of Jesus' genealogy, except for Mary, the virgin mother, only those whom the scriptures would condemn made the inspired list. We looked at the list: Rahab, Tamar, Bathsheba, and Ruth. Why? So He who came on behalf of sinners, becoming sin - Himself, could destroy the sins of all. What love, what mercy, and what grace! That was the Trinitarian plan from before the foundation of the world. How thrilling! God loves us so! He came to sinners - He came to Rahab - He came to me, and if you're open and willing, Jesus will come to you!

No sinner is too sinful for Jesus. No sin is weightier than the blood He shed. Just before Jesus died, He said, "It is finished!" (John 19:30). When Jesus declared these words, He meant them! He has covered it all. He knows who are His and precisely what it will take for them to come to saving faith. And, so much more. He has known from the before the foundation of the world all those who would call upon the name of the Lord.

I find Rahab's life such an interesting dichotomy. Men had apparently been her weakness, her downfall, so to speak, all of her adult days. But the day God intervened, it was a different story. On that day, God's electing love would send two spies into her brothel, awaken her spiritually and provide salvation. Not just for Rahab but for her family, who would look to God and His scarlet thread for deliverance. From before the foundation of the world, this moment in time was coming. On this very day, God's love would embrace her, fill her heart, awaken her spirit, and within an instant, she believed. Her confession is passionate, and her actions back it up. Perhaps it's your day as well. Our Lord God is still saving to the uttermost!

That's the gospel, which means good news. Rahab's story of salvation is our story. God picked her up from the gutter, renewed her life, and gave her a future and a hope. He gave her Himself. That's the redeeming love our hearts can understand. We can know and trust: if He can and will do it for Rahab, He will do it for us.

Be blessed this week as you study Rahab: A Woman On The Wall.

Next week - Ruth: Blessed Submission.

Rahab's story unfolds in Joshua 2, Joshua 6:17-25; Matthew 1:5; Hebrews 11:31; and James 2:25

Rahab: A Woman On The Wall

Day One: Who Is Rahab?

Memory Verse: Hebrews 11:31 By faith the harlot Rahab did not perish with those who did not believe, when she had received the spies with peace.

God still chooses who He will partner with to advance His kingdom. In today's lesson, we will encounter the most unexpected ally imaginable. God typically works in ways that surprise us. We must never lose sight of the fact it's His work. To that end, He is raising up and taking down leaders to accomplish His plan, regardless of how things might appear to us. He is sovereignly bringing about His purposes. Remember our overarching verse for our study: "And we know that all things work together for good to those who love God, to those who are the called according to His purpose." (Romans 8:28).

1. Reading Joshua 2:1. How is Rahab identified? What does that mean?

2. The spies entered the brothel. In your opinion, what if anything made the house of a harlot a safe place to "go view the land," as Joshua commanded?

3. To the natural, there is a spiritual counterpart. From our text, in the natural, the spies entered the brothel, but in the spiritual, God was at work. He had big plans for Rahab. What was going on behind the scenes to change her life?

4. Read Joshua 2:1-5, paying special attention to Rahab words and actions of verses 4 and 5. Rahab lied! Now she's a harlot and a liar. Yet, God has chosen to partner with her anyway. Read Romans 3:23. In light of this verse, who would God use?

5. Jericho had many inhabitants, but we only know the name of one - Rahab. Write our memory verse below. Underline the first two words of the verse. Why are these words so significant? What will they mean for Rahab, and the Israelites?

6. What gave Rahab the courage to hide the spies and lie to the authorities?

7. Write the definition for faith from Hebrews 11:1.

8. From our memory verse, Hebrews 11:31, we discover Rahab made the big list. She is recorded forever as one of the two women in scripture of noteworthy faith. What made her faith so noteworthy?

9. How much faith is enough faith? Read Matthew 17:20. What does the verse tell us about the size of our faith?

10. The Bible tells us all things are possible with God.

    a. Record Luke 1:37 below.

b. Prayerfully recall God's faithfulness. In the space below, please share how God has been faithful to you in the most unexpected way?

Meditation
1 Corinthians 1:9 God is faithful, by whom you were called into the fellowship of His Son, Jesus Christ our Lord.

Rahab: A Woman On The Wall

Day Two: Where Is Rahab In God's Redemption Story?

Memory Verse: Hebrews 11:31 By faith the harlot Rahab did not perish with those who did not believe, when she had received the spies with peace.

When we encounter Rabah, she's a sinner in need of salvation. Unbeknownst to her, she's on a collision course with God. In all of Jericho, one person would come to faith – Rahab. Instantly, her fantastic faith would impact the lives of God's spies and her family. God had preordained to save Rahab and use her mightily, right there in Jericho. We might assume she was an unlikely candidate for God's electing love and partnership in His work, but she proved to be the very one! Salvation, from start to finish belongs to God. He alone makes the choice. In Jericho, God was not choosing based on who she was, instead who she would become once she believed.

1. Rahab was living in a condemned land. God had pronounced its sentence to Abraham in Genesis 15:16. Evil and perversion were rampant in the land. Everywhere its inhabitants were living according to their wicked pleasures and desires. What does Judges 21:25 confirm?

2. The evil extended to include Jericho. As a prostitute, Rahab was profiting from the depravity of the day. Read Romans 5:20. How do you reconcile her life with this verse?

3. Sexual sin is unique. Paul is clear about its consequences. "Flee sexual immorality. Every sin that a man does is outside the body, but he who commits sexual immorality sins against his

own body." (1 Corinthians 6:18). Do you think knowledge of this verse is a deterrent against sexual sin? Why or why not?

4. There are consequences to all sin, and sexual sin is no exception. Based on Paul's warning in 1 Corinthians 6:18, sexual sin, although forgivable, is unique in its nature. What is it? Record the verse below.

5. By divine grace and when it was pleasing to God, Rahab had a spiritual awakening. This awakening or revelation of God enabled her to see Him for who He is. Subsequently, when impending danger threatened God's servants, her newfound faith sprung into action. No one was probably more surprised than Rahab as she hid the spies and lied to the authorities without hesitation. Have you ever responded by faith to a difficult situation? All the while, having never predicted such a courageous response was within you? You are invited to share.

6. Rehab's faith was genuine! All believers are called to be a witness. Read Acts 1:8. Write the verse and underline the instructions to all believers.

7. Rahab lived inside the "impenetrable" walls of Jericho. Even though the walls were "supposedly impenetrable," she had heard about God's power. Read Romans 10:17. What does the verse tell us?

8. Rahab heard, and what she heard changed her life. Read Joshua 2:10-11. Record the highlights of each verse.

v. 10

v. 11

9. Rahab didn't let the newness of her faith prevent her from being useful unto the purposes of God. Once she sprang into action, there was a testimony in the land! How does this encourage your faith? Does it make you more inclined to look for unlikely opportunities to be His witness? If so, explain.

Meditation
Romans 10:17 Faith comes by hearing, and hearing by the word of God.

Rahab: A Woman On The Wall

Day Three: What Did Rahab Get Right?

Memory Verse: Hebrews 11:31 By faith the harlot Rahab did not perish with those who did not believe, when she had received the spies with peace.

Despite her colorful past and seductive sexual practices, Rahab became the recipient of God's divine grace. She experienced true peace which can only come from God. Paul explains what happened to Rahab. "Therefore having been justified by faith, we have peace with God through our Lord Jesus Christ,..." (Romans 5:1). Instantly, Rahab knew the settling peace of God. With newfound peace, she was strengthened and encouraged to jeopardize herself to save the spies of God.

1. Using a dictionary, define the word *peace*.

2. Rahab received the spies with peace. Even though her actions would be considered a treasonable offense, she exhibited *freedom from worry*. How do you explain this peace? For sharing, record your favorite verse that defines the believer's peace.

3. With a heart of peace, Rahab contended for the faith. Although she was a new believer, and the situation was potentially dangerous, she acted for the greater good to accomplish God's plan. Have you ever contended for the faith in circumstances which could have been costly to you personally?

Read Joshua 2:12-14. Answer the following questions:

4. What specific request does Rahab make in exchange for her kindness?

5. Review Joshua 2:13. Rahab requests six things. Record them below.

1.

2.

3.

4.

5.

6.

6. The spies responded in Joshua 2:14 giving Rahab the surety she had requested. Can you find the *"surety"* within the verse? Write the entire verse and underline the surety.

7. Then, what happened next? The word "then" in scripture is an indicator of a series of events which result in a climax. Tell what it was from Joshua 2:15.

8. Giving special notice to the number of days, what did Rahab instruct in Joshua 2:16?

9. Read and review Joshua 2:17-18. What additional condition must Rahab fulfill in order to be saved, she and her household? Be specific.

10. Give the highlights of Joshua 2:19-21.

v. 19

v. 20

v. 21

11. According to Rahab's instructions, the spies hid in the hills for three days. "The pursuers sought them all along the way, but did not find them." (Joshua 2:22). Then they returned to Joshua, son of Nun, to give their report. Unlike their predecessor spies of some forty years past (of which, Joshua was one), their favorable report was received. Record Joshua 2:24 below to discover the contents of the spies' favorable report.

Meditation
Joshua 2:9 "…and said to the men: I know that the Lord has given you the land, that the terror of you has fallen on us, and that all the inhabitants of the land are fainthearted because of you."

Rahab: A Woman On The Wall

Day Four: What Did Rahab Get Wrong?

Memory Verse: Hebrews 11:31 By faith the harlot Rahab did not perish with those who did not believe, when she had received the spies with peace.

What did Rahab get wrong? Lots of things, every day she sinned. We all do. Although her sin might be unique or different from yours or mine - to God, all sin is equal. The issue is not merely our sin but unrepentant sin. That's what condemns us, and eternally separates us from God. We still sin, as Paul said: "…for all have sinned and fall short of the glory of God…" (Romans 3:23). But, because we have believed in Jesus, His righteousness becomes ours. Although we are as guilty as guilty can be, we are declared NOT GUILTY! The blood of Jesus has covered all our sins, regardless of how big or how small. It will continue to redeem us until we stand in His presence. Rahab sinned – but, when she believed, faith washed her sins away. So, before you place a scarlet letter upon her forehead consider this. Though her sins are as scarlet, Christ's blood made Rahab white as snow.

Like us, Rahab got many things wrong. But God used every facet of her life – messes, shortcomings, poor choices, and a scandalous profession to shape her salvation story. He takes it all and makes it something useful unto His purposes. He exchanges ashes for beauty! Nothing is lost, and no two stories are alike. I'm confident my story is not like yours. Only God can take a broken life and make it something beautiful - something worth redeeming. Who knew Rahab's life of prostitution would be the gateway for her salvation - and her family's? Or ours? Only a merciful God. Just think, her life had been of little value before, but now it would become instrumental in the salvation of others – all others. Every time a sinner comes to faith, Rahab has played a part in it. How beautiful - even yours and mine.

Beautiful Salvation.

Salvation is a miracle. Every time someone comes to faith, God writes a beautiful salvation story. Each is a testimony of the faithfulness of God and His radical love for humanity. When God's gaze came to rest on Rahab, He saw the beauty of her life in partnership with Him. He didn't focus on her before; He saw her after! Thanks be to God. "Is anything too hard for the Lord?" (Genesis 18:14). Is any life too hard, too vile, or too far gone for God? Of course not. That's His job! He is in the business of taking the wrongs of our lives and making them into rights! What marvelous love – what amazing grace!

1. Salvation is from God. God's electing love came to rest upon Rahab in spite of her past performance, ungodly character, and lifestyle. Who we are when He chooses us is immaterial

to God. He has plans for our future. Read Jeremiah 29:11. Next, read Philippians 3:13. Record the verse which most speaks to your heart below. How do these words comfort you?

2. When the spies entered her brothel, Rahab had no idea what lie ahead. The miracle of God's salvation plan was about to unfold. Not just for Rahab, but for her family as well. Read Ephesians 1:4-5 and 1:11-12. What does Paul assure us from these passages?

v. 4

v. 5

v. 11

v. 12

3. What comfort. Review Ephesians 1:4. Write the verse. What do these words mean to you?

At the first opportunity, Rahab begged the spies to show kindness toward her family in exchange for the consideration she had demonstrated. Joshua 2:12. I find this exciting. New to the faith, yet, wanting the lives of others redeemed as well. Suddenly knowing whatever God had planned for the future was better than their present or their past. How encouraging, to plead for the salvation of your family. Have you done that? Pause for a moment and consider people who are not saved, particularly within your immediate family. Make a mental list or jot it down, and pray daily for their salvation. It never hurts to ask God to intervene by awakening them spiritually. Rahab did, and the results? They were all saved. Wouldn't it be wonderful to know God made you part of their salvation story? Jimmy and I were a part of my mother's salvation story. When she entered God's Kingdom in March of 2016, I smiled broadly behind quivering lips and salty tears. Knowing she's safe with Jesus still gives me great comfort.

As we move forward, take the time to intercede for the lost whom you hold dear. Do it daily. There is no time better spent than that upon our knees. That's where all ministry begins, and that's where our battles are fought and won. Prayers for the lost link us to God's work of salvation. When the opportunity arose, Rahab jumped at the chance to play a role in her family's salvation story. Maybe you could too. Pray about it. God will guide your prayers.

4. Not because of who we are, but despite that, God's electing love saves us. Remember, salvation from start to finish belongs to God. It has been His plan and work from before the foundation of the world. What comfort and peace! We owe everything to Jesus! Take a few minutes to thank Him. In the space below, write a prayer of praise and thanksgiving for your salvation and the salvation of those you hold dear. And, for those yet saved, thank Him anyway - in advance, trusting Him for their future salvation.

5. Rahab's influence within her family was considerably changed once God entered in. You might say her territory was suddenly expanded! She probably had very little, if any, influence over their lives up until this time. Now things were forever changed. As she bound the scarlet cord in the window, she assured the spies, "According to your words, so be it!" (Joshua 2:21). Rahab was confidently believing for her family! How did her family respond

to her instructions? They did not disappoint, but rather followed her instructions and did exactly as the spies commanded. The results? People were saved. Who? Let's review. Record Joshua 2:13 below.

6. Read Joshua 6:22. After the walls of Jericho crumbled the spies were given a new assignment. What was it?

7. Record Joshua 6:23 below.

8. Rahab's family followed her instructions, and they were saved. They believed Rahab and followed through – she was influential after all. If there was ever a time to listen to her instructions, this was undoubtedly it. What a testimony! Thinking biblically, what must they have seen in Rahab to prompt their compliance? Has God broadened your sphere of influence since your salvation?

The Take Away.

There's a critical take away from this lesson. You don't have to be a seasoned believer with seminary training or mission field experience to make an impact in the lives of others. You don't have to be a Sunday school teacher or an elder or deacon in the church either. You need not wait until you have all the answers because that day will never come. You have Christ in you, the hope of glory! What could be better ? He will supply all you need when He prompts you to share. You have a before and after story just like Rahab. Share your testimony. What is it? At its root, they're all the same. "I was like that, and now I'm like this." That's your before and after story. You may not have the nail-biting, cliff-hanging conversion like Rahab's just before the walls crumbled. Nonetheless, there is always a change because He changes our hearts first! The moment of salvation He invades us and fills us with His Spirit. He will never be taken from you. You didn't have to wait 90 days or audition for a position in God's kingdom. He found you and saved you! He filled you, then and there! Trust it and go with it! Yield to His Spirit.

One more thing. There is no such thing as "a little Jesus!" It's a myth. Similarly, you can't be a little pregnant either. You either are, or you aren't. You either have salvation, Him and His Holy Spirit or you don't. There are only two options. Not to oversimplify, but I used to be terribly selfish, unkind, and often thankless. But, that's all changed. I didn't do it, Christ's Spirit in me changed me. He did it! It's recognizable to me and others. About five years after my conversion, a family member said, "This must be God, no one could have made these lasting changes in you, but Him!" Others do take notice and, over time, our sphere of influence broadens, and our new life which is hidden with Christ in God reigns in us and shines through us – by this grace and for His glory and for the benefit of the Gospel. Rahab was recognizably changed – immediately. She trusted it, and she went with it. She didn't wait on all the conditions to be right or to have all the theology down. She must have simply said, "Look, you matter to me, I love you, I'm heaven-bound and I don't want to go without you! Don't delay. The end is near!" I would say the same for us. The end is near, don't delay. Don't wait to share! We are saved to be His witness from day one, and all the remaining days of our lives – wherever you are. Go and be a witness. Acts 1:8.

Our time is short! Don't leave things to chance. Only God knows who are His. Reach out in love and leave the results to Him. Better to err on the side of sharing with those already saved than not sharing with those who have never heard the gospel. Pray for the lost, particularly those you hold dear. Lastly, pray for boldness, discernment, and divine appointments. God will faithfully answer your prayers!

Meditation
Revelation 21:5 Then He who was sat on the throne said, "Behold, I make all things new."

Rahab: A Woman On The Wall

Day Five: How Did God's Love Redeem It All?

Memory Verse: Hebrews 11:31 By faith the harlot Rahab did not perish with those who did not believe, when she had received the spies with peace.

Today, we come to the dramatic conclusion of Rahab. She and her family will have an action-packed deliverance into the family of faith. They will find themselves standing in a fiery rubble as smoke and steam rise heavenward. Everyone in Jericho will come face to face with the judgment of God. The results? As promised, Jericho and her inhabitants will be utterly destroyed. That is, everyone but our unlikely heroine, Rahab, who *knew God and believed* – and the members of her immediate family.

Read Joshua 6:15-17 and answer the following questions:

1. What day was it? How many times did they march around the city?

2. In Joshua 6:17, the words *"doomed by the Lord to destruction"* means *damned, condemned, lost.* Jericho had been preserved by God for His divine purposes. The city was a tribute belonging to Him for the purpose of destruction. What does this tell you about the justice of God?

Women of the Bible and God's Redeeming Love

3. For six days, the Israelites had been marching around the city. What do you think the residents of Jericho thought about their battle plan? What was God teaching the Israelites?

4. Read Joshua 6:20. How did the Israelites shout?

5. Read the second phrase of Joshua 6:17 and Joshua 6:21. In your opinion, was God's plan accomplished?

6. Describe what happened in Joshua 6:22-23.

v. 22

v. 23

219

7. Complete Joshua 6:24-25. But they _____ the city and all that was in it with _____. Only the _____ and _____, and the vessels of _____ and iron, they put into the treasury of the house of the _____. And Joshua _____ Rahab the harlot, her _____ household, and _____ that she had. So she dwells in Israel to this day, because she hid the messengers whom Joshua sent to spy out Jericho.

8. Read Joshua 6:26-27. According to God's word, something can never be done. What is it? What was the penalty?

Rahab Finished Strong!

"Salmon begot Boaz by Rahab, Boaz begot Obed by Ruth, Obed begot Jesse, and Jesse begot David the king." (Matthew 1:5-6a).

The grace of God revealed! Rahab assumes her position in the royal genealogy of Jesus. Only God can change a life so radically. Her body once used for sexual indulgence and pleasure was cleansed and purified for a holy work in God's great redemption story. And, what a work it was! Ultimately, to bring forth a king. How amazingly wonderful is this? Indeed, God makes all things new.

Epilogue.

A broken girl from Jericho found herself in the mighty grip of God. He would not let her go. The results would be more than personal, they would be profound. They have impacted believers throughout Christendom into eternity. God transformed Rahab's soiled life into something priceless and beautiful, something that was useful, with kingdom purpose. He prevailed. God always wins! As a result, she has left her mark on humanity forever. From start to finish, salvation is God's work. It serves as a faithful testimony to all He can do when our lives are messy and broken, and we're living on the edge. That's where He found Rahab. Living on the fringe of town, walled in by shame and deception, trapped in a self-indulgent merry-go-round of sin. She was hopeless and helpless, "but God" sent two spies to her rescue. When the men of God entered the brothel, God's light invaded the darkness and hope came. It was her day, her moment in time - the day Rahab's broken, used up, lonely heart collided with the love of God. Mercifully, this day had been coming all the days of her life.

You know how I love a good ending! Rahab has one of the most beautiful finishes in scripture. Who was this Salmon that married Rahab? Salmon was a Prince of Judah. One commentator suggested he may have been one of the spies. Who knows? Only God can write a love story like that! But what a beautiful finish that would be. I wouldn't be at all surprised. "But God" changes everything. He found our lost Rahab and called her into a life of faith. Then, He partnered with her to save her family, married her off to a Prince of Judah, and placed her in the genealogy of Jesus. Wow - how astounding! Her story makes me smile in amazement every time I read it! Though her sins were scarlet, Jesus washed her white as snow!

Meditation
Romans 8:28 And we know that all things work together for good to those who love God, to those who are the called according to *His* purpose.

Notes - Rahab: A Woman On The Wall

Ruth

Ruth: Blessed Submission

Today, a family means different things to different people. Divorce and remarriage have enlarged the family circle. As a result, our culture consists of countless blended families. Once considered unthinkable, divorce and remarriage, is now quite the norm - even among believers. That means the traditional family structure has morphed into something more challenging and complex. Many families have expanded to include folks like half-siblings or stepbrothers and sisters or step-parents and grandparents, etc.

In the traditional sense, you become part of a family through birth, adoption, or marriage. The dictionary's first meaning for the family is just that. It defines family as a group of people related to one another by blood or marriage. This simple definition covers it all. It's interesting to note, however, neither marriage or birth can guarantee love within the family. Let me say that another way. Being part of a family does not guarantee loving relationships among its members. Be honest for a moment. Do you enjoy a warm, amicable fellowship with all your family members? If you do, you are blessed. Suffice it to say, that's unique.

Years of ministry and missionary service, foreign and domestic, have led me to conclude that enjoying and maintaining lasting, loving relationships within the family is one of our most significant challenges. In most families, an estrangement of some type exists. It seems most families have a black sheep or two, or possibly a member on the outside. That would be one that no one talks to, talks about, or hears from. It's like they dropped off the face of the earth or "were taken" like Enoch. I have encountered parents alienated from adult children and vice versa, as well as siblings estranged from siblings. Occasionally, it was strife between sisters and sisters-in-law or brothers and brothers-in-law. It occurred to me because we are all tainted by sin, and live in a sinful world, which is presently gripped by Satan, quite often we don't rub along well together. In some cases, decades passed without communication or reconciliation among the estranged parties. Tragically, in some cases, not even death's doorway reunited them. I would be remiss if I didn't confess, most of the anger-fueled rants I've encountered occurred between family members. That's right, full-blown, five-alarm, hair on fire tirades among and between blood relatives. I was once told, "It's easier for me to love and serve a drunk in the gutter, than members of my own family." Wow, what a mouthful!

There it is, I've exposed the elephant in the room. Loving relationships, even within the family, can be difficult and challenging, at best. Birth or marriage into a family does not guarantee love, regardless of what you might think. Albeit true, as believers we are called to love all others, it's not an easy task. After loving God with all our heart, soul, mind, and strength, we are commanded to love our neighbor as ourselves. Mark 12:30-31. Curious about our neighbor? Simply defined, *our neighbor* in this command is *everyone other than you*. Yes, it most definitely includes your family members. This is not a stretch at all. According to Bible dictionaries, brother and neighbor were synonymous and interchangeable within many Old Testament passages. Let's look at an example from Leviticus. "You shall not hate your brother in your heart. You shall surely rebuke your neighbor, and not bear sin because of him. You shall not take vengeance, nor bear any grudge against the children of your people, but you shall love your neighbor as yourself: I am the Lord." **(**Leviticus 19:17-18).

Similarly, James referred to this as *royal law*. The verse states: If you really fulfill the royal law according to the scripture, "You shall love your neighbor as yourself," you do well. (James 2:8). Please note the caveat at the beginning of this verse. The word *"if"* sets the tone for success. If you love your neighbor as yourself, you do well. According to James, this fulfills the royal law of scripture. I believe the problem is an improper understanding of this love. Let's make it a question. Do you understand loving your neighbor as yourself? Ponder that question. We'll look closer at this momentarily.

It's All In The Family.

If you're wondering what all this has to do with the story of Ruth, this is where it collides. The story of Ruth evolves through family relationships. Interestingly, our family relationships reveal or expose our relationship with God. At its core, I believe it's about love. We know, "God is love." (1 John 4:8; 16). As believers, knowing God's love, receiving God's love, and dispensing God's love becomes our challenge. Our unconfessed self-loathing and inferior self-worth, coupled with our unrealistic understanding of how God views us is at the root of this problem. Sometimes we feel unworthy of love on both the giving and receiving end. That's what makes the story of Ruth and Naomi quite amazing. Theirs is a story of faithful love, devotion, and commitment which displays God's promise, "I will never leave you or forsake you." The story of Ruth reveals the tender side of God. It's a real-life story of the gospel lived in real time through an unlikely duo, a mother, and her daughter-in-law. Most importantly, the story of Ruth paints a beautiful picture of our kinsman redeemer. Of course, that would be Jesus.

As I've already stated, family relationships are challenging, at best. But, of all the family relationships, none is perhaps as competitive and strife-filled as the mother and daughter-in-law relationship. Historically, it gets bad press. It has been the brunt of jokes and comedic, eye-brow raising storytelling since the beginning of time. We've all heard some pretty intense accounts of their struggles. Think about it a minute. Perhaps you, too, know of mothers and daughters-in-law who are bitter rivals, hardly speaking at all, much less uttering a polite or kind word about each other. Makes for tense times during holidays gatherings, doesn't it? I can't imagine the anguish of a son who loves his mother, the great love of his youth, against the backdrop of his wife and bride who now captures his whole heart, to whom he is charged to love and protect until death when they part. According to God, a son is called to leave his father and mother and cleave to his wife, as they become one flesh. Genesis 2:24.

Just The Three Of You.

In all good marriages, there is only room for three. That's right THREE. As we studied in Eve, when you enter into Christian marriage, you form a love triangle with God. It's the formula not only for an excellent beginning, but the key to matrimonial bliss throughout the ages. When God rules and reigns in both hearts, all the parents involved can be equally loved and respected. It's always best to obey God rather than man. When temptations come, stop and pray. Remember how God feels about you, and what He tells us about love. Next, choose love, joy, and obedience. Your obedience will foil the devil's plans. Remember, if you're a mother of a son, you are not his wife. You have done your part. A woman governed by God knows how and when to let go. At the appointed time, your son will answer for the state of his marriage before a holy God. Let go and allow your son to be the man God has called him to be. He doesn't need your help or unnecessary meddling. Instead, hands-off, let go, and let God be God! Then, trust in Him wholly. I can promise, God loves your son much more than you do. He knows what's best; He's got the plan.

On the flip side, if you're a wife, don't fear your mother-in-law. God never intended this be a competition - He's yours, you can relax. Instead, love her and set boundaries with confidence in her son's devoted love for you. Do so in love, with gentle kindness and great joy. Remember, she has played a significant role in raising the man of God that you now adore. Thank her because thanks are due. Let her know what a significant influence she has been and how grateful you are for her guidance. After all, her voice was the first voice of feminine candor, wisdom, and encouragement in his life. Then, leave it at that. Your gentle words spoken in tender sincerity will help her to let go, if need be, with grace and dignity! Lastly, don't forget to temper it all with prayer. Invite God to lead and guide your steps. If possible, pray together - all of you. When hearts are united in prayer, it's hard to be divided. Best of all, as God's love fills your collective hearts, a multitude of sins are covered!

There Are Exceptions.

Before we move forward, I'd like to go on record by stating there are exceptions to bitter rivalries. I'm a member of what I refer to as the sandwich generation. That means I am a mother-in-law who has a mother-in-law. On both counts, God has favored me greatly. I have a delightful daughter-in-law, and I pray for her daily! She is a real joy, and my son's whole countenance is elevated in her presence. She's an exceptional mother and the perfect wife for my son. God handpicked her. Enough said! I also have a marvelous mother-in-law. She has loved me like a daughter, and when my mother recently passed away, she tenderly said, "I know that I'm not your natural mother, and would never attempt to replace her, but as long as I live, know you have a mother who loves you." She is a solid believer, and I do not doubt she will be faithful to her pledge. I love her dearly and find great comfort in knowing she is there for me. God has blessed me indeed.

Anne Nicholson

An Unlikely Duo.

As we begin our journey in Ruth chapter 1, we find three grieving widows. One older, Naomi, and two much younger, her daughters-in-law, Ruth and Orpah. I can't even imagine the pain Naomi must have felt, still grieving the loss of her husband, and now, mourning for her sons as well. Grief to this extreme is unthinkable, yet, it is her portion. It is God's plan for her life this season. He will not leave her there, however. We will see as our story unfolds what great things God has in store for Naomi. What she deems as bleak at our story's onset will prove joyous in the end.

The incredible bond between Ruth and Naomi sets the bar high for all mother and daughter-in-law relationships. They share a genuine affection for one another. Early in our lesson, it will become evident the divine hand of God is charting their course. He is filling them up, and moving them about to accomplish purposes far beyond the benefits of their own lives. All believers are profoundly affected by their combined efforts. That's right, even us! Sometimes, we lose sight of God's work. He is weaving a beautiful tapestry of believers, worldwide since the beginning of time. We are not in this alone. The threads of our lives are intertwined and twisted together with multitudes of believers, from everywhere, to accomplish His divine goal. That would be His eternal plan to redeem and save humanity. We all have a role to play, and we shall see God enables Naomi and Ruth to execute theirs with precision and divine purpose.

Ruth's story melts into Naomi's. There will be times when it's hard to discern where Ruth's story ends, and Naomi's begins. As God would have it, neither of them had to face the pain and sorrow of widowhood alone. With God's hand to uphold them, Ruth clung to Naomi. She yielded wholly and loved unreservedly, eloquently restoring all that age and grief had stripped from Naomi. Ruth's inspiring devotion, love, and submission model Christ's relationship with His Heavenly Father who is our magnificent God.

Although the book of Ruth is the story of two women who truly loved one another, it is also the story of Naomi's kinsman redeemer and God's plan to save them. It's the story of their rise from abject poverty and widowhood to riches and eternal blessings. As you will see, from start to finish, *Ruth* which means, *friendship*, becomes our model for God-honoring submission and service within the family. She is not only the recipient of much love and grace but the purveyor of it as well.

Who Is Ruth?

Let's start by listing her character traits. Ruth was a faithful friend. She was a virtuous woman of noteworthy integrity. Whatever Ruth promised was as good as accomplished because she remained faithfully committed to her pledges. She possessed an excellent work ethic and gave attention to detail. Ruth followed instructions without complaining or deviating from the plan; was not only resourceful, but also remarkably selfless, appropriately submissive, and loved authentically, without guile. Generally speaking, she was a woman of impeccable character in every measure.

Although Ruth possessed many outstanding qualities, there were still challenges to be faced. Natural barriers like age, race, religion, and cultural differences could have easily divided them. "But God" had another plan for their lives. He planned to bless them individually and together. He intended to touch all believers, everywhere, throughout history, through their devoted lives of mutual love and commitment. They were strengthened by what could have divided them instead. You might say they had a "but God" moment which lasted a lifetime. Not familiar with a "but God" moment? It's a moment when God changes the course, the destiny, or the outcome of any given situation or circumstance. We were moving toward worldliness, but, and until, a faithful and loving God intervened. You see, Ruth and Naomi could have been enemies, bitter rivals, "but God" awakened Ruth spiritually and saved her. Now, they were on common ground and operated with a common goal. Among believers, that's always the common denominator. Remember, when Christ is ruling and reigning in hearts, all family relationships become a non-issue.

But God Saved Us.

Ruth's story is our story. We were going one way, our way, before salvation came. But God saved us; He awakened us spiritually. In so doing, He changed our destiny - our endgame, as well as our today game. Just like He did Ruth, and just like He did Naomi. They were wasting away in Moab, "but God" intervened. He gave Ruth a heart for Naomi, which birthed true love and devotion. Then God gave Naomi a heart for Bethlehem and moved her there. Because it was God's plan, Ruth followed.

Did you catch that? God changed Ruth's heart. He filled her with His presence, and in a moment's time, He gave her a new heart. A heart of flesh – one of love and devotion - a heart like His! That's where God's work begins in all of us, and that's how He exacts change in us. You might say, God gets right to the heart of all matters. To transform our minds, He goes through our hearts. That's why I call this a "but God" moment! In an instant, by the mercies of God, His grace saves us, and the journey begins. "But God" always changes everything, and it begins with a new heart.

Once God awakened her spiritually, although Ruth was a Moabite from Moab, she was Bethlehem bound! Our Ruth is a new creature, but who was she before? As you may recall, Moab was an enemy of Israel and occupied land situated just east of the Dead Sea. The people of the region were born of an incestuous sexual encounter between Lot, Abraham's nephew, and Lot's eldest daughter. We read in Genesis 19, "Thus both the daughters of Lot were with child by their father. The firstborn bore a son and called his name Moab; he is the father of the Moabites to this day." (Genesis 19:36-37).

Historically, the Moabites were a constant thorn in Israel's side. They pushed against the people of God from their inception. They were worshipers of the pagan god Chemosh, among others. Our story most probably occurred during the period of the judgeship of Jair. Most likely, their story happened around Judges chapter 10. The entire book of Ruth spans an eleven-year period. For ten of those years, their residence was Moab.

Yielded To God.

Ruth was a woman who had a choice, and she chose to follow God. She decided to do the next right thing. You will find this reoccurring theme throughout scripture. I have said before - it always comes down to choices. Each day, we make choices. Our decisions either align us with God or they are self-serving and frustrate the grace of God in us. Ruth will make a choice that is God's heart. I know this because it will stretch her and require submission and obedience. It will separate her permanently from her homeland and birth family. Like others in the Bible, she will abandon all she has ever known to go with Naomi and follow God. At this point, Naomi is Ruth's only connection to God.

God planned before He saved us to conform us to the image of Jesus. Although necessary, change can make us uncomfortable and take time. This growth does not happen apart from pain, loss, challenges, and difficulties. Unfortunately, this is when most of our spiritual growth occurs. Those who partner with God know this all too well. God is a jealous God and will tolerate nothing in our lives to eclipse our love for Him. Everything but God must ultimately be scraped away, sometimes little by little. It's often akin to prying a toy from a child's grip – one fanger at a time. You know what I'm saying. To follow God, we must be unencumbered by the world and its trappings. In order to "go with God," all of our idols, plans, and dreams have got to go! Only then, are we prepared to tackle the task at hand – the "good works" God predetermined before the world began. Paul assured the church at Ephesus God had plans to use them, saying: For we are His workmanship, created in Christ Jesus for good works, which God prepared beforehand that we should walk in them. (Ephesians 2:10). Ruth was about to collide with her destiny and "walk in those good works."

Confidently, Ruth will choose to move forward with Naomi as she affirmatively responds to the irresistible call of God. God will have His way. God does not change His mind; thwarting His plans are impossible. Noted theologian, pastor, and author, A. W. Tozer had this to say concerning the blessings of those used by God. "It is doubtful whether God can bless a man greatly until He has hurt him deeply." Both widows had experienced deep sorrow. They had endured pain and suffered a significant loss. Now unencumbered by the world and stripped of all its entanglements, including other relationships, Ruth (and Naomi) are at liberty to move forward with God.

Where Is Ruth In God's Redemption Story?

The book of Ruth develops the kinsman redeemer who is first introduced as follows: "If one of your brethren becomes poor, and has sold some of his possession, and if his redeeming relative comes to redeem it, then he may redeem what his brother sold." (Leviticus 25:25). In Hebrew, the word for redeemer is *goel* - meaning *kinsman or kinsman redeemer.* Simply defined, goel is the next of kin who can aptly redeem, avenge, ransom, revenge, receive, or buyback that which has been lost, stolen, etc.

In the Old Testament, Yahweh is the ultimate kinsman redeemer of His people. Not familiar with the term? Let's take a quick look. God made provision in the Law of Moses to provide for the impoverished person who was forced to sell part of his property or himself into slavery. According to Leviticus 25:47-48, God allowed the nearest of kin to step in and "buyback or redeem" what his relative was forced to sell. The kinsman redeemer was the closest relative who had the financial fortitude to cover the outstanding debt. By paying the ransom price, he erased the indebtedness which cleared the family name. How much would he pay; what was the cost? Whatever amount was needed to fully restore the poor or deceased's standing in the community. This buy-back not only redeemed the name but their land or old home place as well. Widows and their children could live and carry on as a result of the buy-back.

Further, if a family member died without an heir, (without a son), the kinsman gave his name by marrying the widow and rearing a son to pass down the family name. If or when death came at the hands of another, the redeemer would spring into action on behalf of the wronged family. Righting a wrong or avenging a disadvantage was always the kinsman's work. In other words, he's the good guy - their advocate - the one who had their backs. The Old Testament kinsman redeemer is a picture and type of Jesus who has avenged your life in every measure.

What Did Ruth Get Right?

Amazingly, Ruth chose God's path. Unlike Orpah who turned back, Ruth moved forward with God. She decided to love Naomi through the most challenging days of her life. Ruth chose to serve Naomi faithfully and with all her strength. Perhaps out of deep love and devotion for her deceased husband, Mahlon, she loved Naomi in his stead. Who knows for sure? Only God! But remember, widowhood was the worst fate imaginable for a woman in this time in history. Lest we forget, Naomi was elderly and unable to work to earn her support. Naomi is in dire straits, indeed! Astoundingly, Ruth chose to sojourn with the people of God, because she could not forsake Naomi. Deep within, she knew it was the better plan - God's plan. Our heroine, Ruth, chose joy, love, faithfulness, and obedience. You could sum it up with these words; Ruth decided to come into agreement with God.

Ruth, the former Moabite, joined the family of faith. She believed and submitted to the God of Abraham, Isaac, and Jacob. We shall examine her words of confession momentarily, but suffice it to say, Ruth believed wherever Naomi was going was far better than where Ruth had been. She had no doubt seen something quite beautiful in the lives of Elimelech and Naomi, and perhaps her husband as well. As a result, she longed for a place unknown to be with the people of faith. Ruth believed going with Naomi moved her closer to her God and was her heart's desire. When it's all said and done, Ruth will be tremendously blessed. How beautiful! Our study guide will examine these passages on day three.

What Did Ruth Get Wrong?

I can't find one thing in the Bible to suggest Ruth did anything wrong. She was a model of Christian character. She submitted in all the appropriate places and relationships in her life. She honored her deceased husband's memory well. She loved and provided dutifully for her mother-in-law and submitted to her authority and direction. She didn't ask why or insist on knowing the plan ahead of time. At every turn, she just did the next right thing. She walked by faith and not by sight. Ruth had authentic saving faith, an active and living faith! The book of Hebrews defines it. "Now faith is the substance of things hoped for, the evidence of things not seen." (Hebrews 11:1).

Ruth would not depart from Naomi. Remaining true to her name; she was a faithful friend and companion to an aged widow. Ruth's confession was not only eloquent and sincere, but it also exposed her heart of love. Her words have become familiar with each passing generation of the faithful. Wedding vows, lyrics of songs and poetry, etc., commemorate her words. Her conversion and confession occurred during a heart-wrenching scene. Tearfully, Orpah took her mother-in-law's advice, kissed her goodbye and departed for Moab. However, as God would have it, Ruth clung tearfully to Naomi and confessed her commitment in her famous pledge of faith. Out of the abundance of her heart, Ruth spoke these passionate words.

But Ruth said: "Entreat me not to leave you, Or to turn back from following after you; For wherever you go, I will go; And wherever you lodge, I will lodge; Your people shall be my people, And your God, my God." (Ruth 1:16).

Lastly, she was submissive to Boaz and open and available to the plans of God. That means she moved with God's grace instead of pushing against Him. Through actions which model Jesus, she placed the needs of all others before her own. What scripture reveals about her life provides a beautiful example of Christian character and humility. Our heroine, Ruth, was sacrificial in love, in service, and in submission.

Today's Choices Impact Our Tomorrows.

An indebted widow is tragic, even today. But, an indebted widow in Israel was the worst possible scenario. The death of spouses had left both women frail, weak, vulnerable, and destitute. Both were without a "covering." Let's look closer at this covering. God has given husbands headship authority in marriage. They cover us. The "covering" provides our protection spiritually, financially, and physically, according to God's plan. You may be the heart of the home, but God has given your husband authority as the head of the home. A woman without a covering is often prey to schemes, hardships, and deceits. Not because we aren't as smart as men, instead because the enemy knows our natural weaknesses and inclinations. Remember Eve? Satan tempted Eve, and she quickly fell when cunningly deceived. I don't care how smart or clever you think you are, alone, you are no match for the enemy. If you're married, go with the flow, submit to God's plan. Allow Him to use your husband to provide and protect, according to His plan. If you are unmarried, you are not alone. Christ is your covering. He is your spiritual head and His Word – the Bible, is your authority in all matters. Let Him lead and guide you. If your life is lined up with His Word, you are secure. You can trust Him with every area of your life. We may not know how things will work out, but we can know who is in charge. The mighty grip of God holds you! What comfort! You have "Christ in you, the hope of glory!" (Colossians 1:27).

If I asked you today, "Who's in charge of your life, how would you respond?" Think about it. Remember, Elimelech left Bethlehem and traveled to Moab of his own accord. Although he thought this was a good idea, it proved costly for his family. Because all choices have consequences, Naomi and Ruth were without hope, "but God" intervened.

Bethlehem Bound.

Word finally came, the famine was over. "Then she arose with her daughters-in-law that she might return from the country of Moab, for she had heard in the country of Moab that the Lord had visited His people by giving them bread." (Ruth 1:6).

Good news! The famine was over! Upon hearing the report, Naomi knew God was moving. Of course, she had seen His faithfulness before, but in Moab, His mighty work was only a faint memory. Then the word came, and she could recall His infinite goodness. God's Spirit was moving in and through Bethlehem, and there was life! Receiving the news caused Naomi to take stock of her life. Please note, God had not moved, Naomi had. Under Elimelech's direction, the whole family had moved, but now he was dead and gone and so were her sons. All three had perished and were buried on foreign soil. "But God" was living, and He was at work in Bethlehem! How thrilling it must have been to hear God was doing a new thing in the place she once called home. The moment of truth had come. This news would prompt a decision as God's truth always does. We either believe in God and submit, or we don't. These are our only two options. Similarly, as we yield to Him, behold all things in us become new.

Secrets Of The Heart.

Naomi searched her heart; she examined her life. What had happened? Where had she aligned her heart? In other words, where was her treasure? Take note, it's not uncommon for a crisis or family tragedy, like death or divorce, to prompt us to examine our lives. Through sorrow or a crisis, we often consider where we're going and where we've been. I believe all Christians should take a personal inventory from time to time, perhaps every day. It's a good thing to examine whether or not you agree with God. Are you living according to His word? That's agreement. People of faith obey God! In a moment of honest soul-searching, Naomi had an "ah ha" moment. It's a God thing. It's like a "but God" moment and we've all had them. It's the moment we come to terms with the condition of our hearts. In other words, Naomi came to her senses. Mercifully, God revealed the secrets of her heart.

The truth is until her heart was exposed, Naomi was a Jewess living in a foreign land, among unfamiliar people. "But God" instantly purposed her heart to long for home, her relatives, and her community of faith. That's when Naomi decided she can no longer travail in Moab. With good conscience, she could no longer align herself with the known enemies of God. Naomi came to an end, so to speak - her end. Isn't it fascinating to discover when we finally come to the end of ourselves that's where God begins? Poor Naomi, after ten years, she was empty and weary, "but God" had birthed hope in her heart. There was nothing left for her to do but humble herself and return to Bethlehem.

When we attempt to live in the world, so to speak, it beats us up. It always robs us of joy, and ultimately our witness. God is a jealous God. He has said, in essence, come out from among them and consecrate yourself - be separate - I have made you a peculiar people. But, when we live in the world, after its pattern and type, our vision becomes distorted. That's when we align ourselves with the enemy by compromising what God has said to seek our pleasures and pursuits. You may recall even Abraham, our father of the faith, was an unworthy witness when he lied to conceal Sarah's true identity. Although he was still God's man, with an irrevocable call, he proved ineffective in that time and place. Furthermore, God used a pagan king to reprimand him. How humiliating for Abraham and Sarah! Even Abraham had no testimony in the land of Egypt when his deceitful folly was exposed.

Weathered And Worn.

More than loved ones were stripped of Naomi while she languished in the world. When she returned to Bethlehem, she was weathered and worn – virtually unrecognizable. There it is! Did you see it? When the women of Bethlehem see her, they can't believe their eyes. Could this frazzled and worn out woman be Naomi? In astonishment, they inquire, "Is this Naomi?" (Ruth 1:19). Her bitter, brittle state was exposed. That is after she'd faced a personal famine of soul or crisis of faith. She had returned withered and worn, dry and parched. She was a living testimony of what happens when our spirits are left unnourished and unattended by God's Spirit.

Losing our way is easy. We must stay engaged with Jesus. Failure to rely on Him as our source of life and power depletes our strength and clouds our vision. Albeit true, Naomi had not left Bethlehem of her own accord, but with a husband who decided to move. Living in the "world" had its consequences. It caused her to move away. Away from God, His word, and the family of faith. If we move just one millimeter from His truth, it becomes distorted and is no longer true. We deceive ourselves if we walk away from God and attempt to finesse His Word to conform to our thoughts and ideas. That's when we make Him a God in our image, rather than bending our knee to Him - the Great I AM and lover of our souls.

On the contrary, if we remain focused, centered, and grounded in the things of God, we have strength and courage to live as He deems fit. Our ways become His ways. We think and move after a pattern of God. We think of Him and long for heaven. We have a kingdom vision. Then, we can agree with the writer of Hebrews, who in essence declared, "this is not our home, we're merely passing through!" Jesus must be the center of our lives and the reason for all that we say and do. We must not run from trouble like Elimelech when life's famines come. And, they will come! Death, heartache, disease, betrayal, poverty, etc., etc. Remember, whatever occurs, God has allowed into our lives. Instead, we must carry on faithfully looking unto Jesus, the author, and perfecter of our faith. Our kinsman will see us through!

God opened Naomi's eyes. With a humble heart, she was headed for heaven by way of Bethlehem. God can do great things when we humble ourselves. Christlike humility always changes our perspective. Once again, there was bread in Bethlehem. By the way, *Bethlehem* means, *house of bread*. Naomi knew it was time to go home. With deep longing, God had moved upon Naomi's heart to long for Bethlehem. Right before the harvest, the most joyous time of year, Naomi would reunite with the family of faith.

How Did God's Love Redeem It All?

Although Naomi and Ruth were perhaps the most impoverished women in Israel, God had a plan. And wonder of wonders, Naomi had a kinsman in Bethlehem. He had the financial prowess to secure their future. It just so happened, he was single and Ruth would catch his eye as she gleaned in his fields. Wouldn't you know our heroine, Ruth, would prove to be Naomi's best asset? Boaz would be taken with Ruth immediately. Her work ethic, kindness, and public devotion to her mother-in-law would win his heart. Boaz commemorates Ruth's devoted love for Naomi in Ruth 2:11-12.

God is bringing about a union with divine purpose. Ruth was never a liability to Naomi. Instead, she proved to be an asset, and the best hope Naomi had to secure their future. We will examine the thrilling conclusion in our study guide. You won't want to miss this! Ruth and Boaz will share a tender, romantic encounter on the threshing floor. Their romantic meeting is intriguing and unique because it could have easily backfired. In the moonlit night, Ruth will follow Naomi's detailed instructions. She will slip in quietly, where Boaz is sleeping, and gently uncover his feet. There, at his feet, she will lay cradled until he makes the next move.

What a touching scene. Her actions say in essence, "I am yours for the taking. I submit to you. I give my life to you, alone, if you will have me." A marriage proposal of sorts – but, in reverse.

Although Boaz was years older, and a wealthy Jew, he is overcome with the prospects of loving Ruth for a lifetime. Her impoverished state, widowhood, and foreign blood appear to be insignificant to Boaz. To some, this would be problematic, but Boaz sees something altogether different. He sees promise and potential; He detects life! When God is at work, there is always life, always promise, and always hope. On the threshing floor, Ruth unreservedly availed her heart to him, and he accepted. Boaz is thrilled. Before the break of day, Boaz assured Ruth's (and Naomi's) redemption. Boaz, the closest relative - a kinsman - has pledged to redeem it all. The enemy had plans for their death and destruction, "but God" had plans for their good.

Although this is a steamy scene with some sexual tension, nothing untoward or promiscuous has occurred. An honorable man like Boaz would protect Ruth's reputation at all costs. Ruth has irrefutably won his heart, and Boaz meant to have her as his bride. With his very life, he will protect and cover her until his dying day. Boaz will avenge Ruth and Naomi, regardless the price. No price was too steep to have her.

What a beautiful illustration of Christ's redemptive work on our behalf. He paid it all, giving His very life so He could ransom us. No price was too high, and no sin was so vile as to render His blood insufficient. Whatever the enemy planned for our death and destruction, Jesus has covered it all. What a Savior! What a friend we have in Jesus!

An Ending Twist.

To make the story a bit more interesting, just when we begin to think everything is worked out, another kinsman will come forward. Wouldn't you know he is a closer kinsman than Boaz? The man she has pledged herself to is not Ruth's redeemer, but he's won her heart, and this will prove problematic. Ultimately, the closer kinsman will determine he cannot fulfill the requirements and abdicate to Boaz. The couple will delight in his decision because they're a match made in heaven. In their hearts, they have already determined they have more than just a little chemistry between them. Boaz will ultimately pay the price. How much? All that it takes. He will redeem all that was lost and settle the score.

Our unlikely duo - Ruth and Naomi, had returned to Bethlehem bereaved and impoverished, "but God" said otherwise. Now, they will be full. *Naomi*, which means, *joy and my pleasant one*, will be joyful again. All her remaining days, she will rejoice in God, and have hope for tomorrow.

Our Redeemer And Boaz.

When Ruth marries Boaz, a little boy is born of their union. They named him Obed. How fitting. *Obed* means *worshipper or servant*, which reflects the character and nature of his mother, Ruth. According to God's plan, the line of the faithful continues. From Obed, Jesse will be born and from Jesse, the greatest king to reign in Israel, David - the former shepherd boy. You may recall, King David is identified in scripture as a man after God's own heart.

As we discovered last week in our study of Rahab, there are five women identified by Matthew's inspired record of Jesus' genealogy. See Matthew 1:1-16. It's interesting to note, all the women who made the inspired list have some sexual tension or scandal associated with their name: Ruth, Rahab, Tamar, Bathsheba, even Mary, the mother of Jesus. You may recall, while she was betrothed to Joseph, she found herself pregnant with Jesus. It could have been her end. "But God" said otherwise! We will be looking at her fabulous life in week ten of our study, so stay tuned. The redeeming love of our merciful God overrules all their humanity, their frailties, their mistakes and missteps, too. That's what makes each story so thrilling, and so utterly amazing.

I see glimpses of myself in all of their lives! How about you? Since God created Eve in the delightful garden, women are still women and always will be. God's blueprint for us, nor His plan has changed. Until the end of time, we will remain as the first one, loved and made in the image of God. Every one of the women in Jesus' lineage, even Mary, the virgin mother needed salvation. They needed a Savior, as do we! And, to every last one of us, He will be faithful. Jesus will see us through.

Our Redeemer Lives.

Our Lord Jesus lives and reigns. Before we turn to the study guide, let's take another quick look at our Redeemer. In the book of Job, Job was assured, no man came to redeem him! No human could do it. All of his comforters proved less than comforting. But, we see his faith reaches out and proclaims Yahweh will provide: "The things which are impossible with men are possible with God." (Luke 18:27). This passage reminds us salvation comes only from God. Job got it! Read his beautiful proclamation: "For I know that my redeemer [my kinsman or goel] lives and He shall stand at last on the earth." (Job 19:25). Job's hope looked to the coming Messiah. His words of hope affirmed his faith. How thrilling! Job knew His redeemer lived and He was coming! Are you aware of His coming? Look up! Your redemption draws near! Jesus is coming. Before His return, it's comforting to know He is redeeming us every day. Right this moment, Jesus is accomplishing His good, pleasing, and perfect will in your life. He is faithful and leaves nothing to chance.

Our Purposeful God.

It's no coincidence Boaz was related to Naomi and lived in Bethlehem. It was no accident Ruth found her way to his field when she needed work. Likewise, it was no mistake Boaz would be smitten with her. And, it's not surprising he had the financial prowess to pay the price. No, no, no! God was moving them about to accomplish His purposes - His plan. What was their part? Agreeing with God and His Word. Following Him and doing the next right thing. Trusting. Hoping in God, alone. Being faithfully obedient. Listening and yielding their hearts wholly to Him.

In closing, remember these two things. First, you can't give up things for God. "Behold, to obey is better than sacrifice..." (1 Samuel 15:22). There is nothing you can do to earn or win His favor. He couldn't love you any more than He already does and already has. What He truly desires is our obedience. According to Paul in Romans 12, that's our *reasonable service* in light of all that He has done on our behalf. So instead, love Him and obey Him. Jesus said, "If you love me, keep my commandments." (John 14:15). Essentially He means, "If you love me, you'll obey me!"

Next, remember Paul's words to the Romans. "The just shall live by faith." (Romans 1:17). As believers, we walk by faith and not by sight. That's the essence of what faith is. If we can see it, is it faith? Of course not! Faith is when we can't see where He's leading us or the outcome, nonetheless - we joyfully obey and follow - regardless. Now, that's faith.

Naomi didn't know how things would work out when she and Ruth returned to Bethlehem. How could she? Abraham didn't know where God was leading, but he followed. Countless others in scripture had saving faith, too. They simply obeyed God even though they couldn't see the benefit or the outcome. They were confidently obedient through unprecedented peril and some, upon threat of death. Remember, those of great faith obey God and trust the results to Him.

Is He calling you to get beyond your comfort zone? Maybe He's leading you to a foreign land or a soup kitchen or a homeless shelter. Could He be asking you to open your home to an orphan, a homeless veteran, or a foster child? Sometimes, God does that – the unexpected, and the most exciting thing conceivable. Why? Well, first to fulfill His kingdom plan. Next, to mold and shape us – to conform us to the image of His Son. He wants to make us more like Jesus. Mainly, He wants us to have faith in Him and not ourselves or others. He likes to grow and stretch our wings of faith. He is preparing us for heaven. Even when it's challenging or seems impossible, remember this. Abraham was called to follow a God no one knew. He merely heard God's irresistible call and obediently moved forward. He simply did it. Ruth did it. So did Naomi, Rebekah, Sarah, and so on. That's faith!

He's Got Your Back.

If you get a little off track, relax, He knows your heart. He's got your back. He can and will reroute you if need be! You have absolutely nothing to fear. You're secure in the grip of a mighty God who loves you, entirely, just as you are. Trust Him fully and yield to Him at every turn. He will lead and guide you. Practice His presence, lay at His feet like Ruth did Boaz and let Him still your anxious heart. You will find solace and peace in the Prince of Peace.

He is worthy! Thanks to God, we are at liberty to join the anthem of the saints of old, like Job who testify, "I know that my Redeemer lives and He is coming!" Like Job, we can say, "He is coming again! Of that, I am confident."

Be blessed this week as you study Ruth. Years ago, this was one of the first books I had the pleasure of teaching. Each time I read her thrilling story, I recall Jesus' work in my own life. Everything the enemy intended for evil, Jesus has turned for good. I mean everything! The enemy has not profited through my life and its many mistakes. Instead, the Lord Jesus, my kinsman, has redeemed it all. Yesterday, today, and forever - I know my Redeemer lives!

Be blessed this week as you study Ruth: Blessed Submission.

Next week - Esther: Destiny Fulfilled.

Ruth's story unfolds in the book of Ruth and Matthew 1:5

Ruth: Blessed Submission

Day One: Who Is Ruth?

Memory verse: Ruth 1:16 But Ruth said: "Entreat me not to leave you, Or to turn back from following after you; For wherever you go, I will go; And wherever you lodge, I will lodge; Your people shall be my people, And your God, my God."

Famine came to the land. Famine is a widespread scarcity of food brought on by many factors, including drought caused by lack of rain, crop failure, and population imbalance. Typically, malnutrition, starvation, and increased mortality accompany famine. Nearly every continent in the world has experienced a period of famine throughout history. Under the sovereign hand of God, some regions have experienced more famine than others. During Old Testament times, famines recurred under the watchful eye of God. Don't lose sight of the fact He allowed the famines to accomplish His work. Nothing happens apart from the watchful eye of God. His plans will succeed.

1. Famine had previously come to the land, and the fear associated with it shuffled folks around. Fear of starvation most probably caused Elimelech to uproot his family from Bethlehem, Judah and relocate them to Moab. We have seen this life-threatening phenomenon before. Which two patriarchs responded similarly to catastrophic conditions caused by famine? In other words, who else moved "out of fear" to avoid the consequences of famine? Please record a verse which identifies each patriarch and his response to famine.

2. Read Ruth 1:1-5. Summarize what occurred in each verse.

v. 1

v. 2

v. 3

v. 4

v. 5

3. Read Ruth 1:6. What does this phrase mean? "…the Lord has visited His people by giving them bread."

4. Read Ruth 1:7-9. What was Naomi's plan? What suggestion did she make to her daughters-in-law?

Read Ruth 1:8-10 and answer the questions:

5. It appears Naomi has offered wise counsel to Ruth and Orpah.

    a. What did Naomi suggest in Ruth 1:8?

Anne Nicholson

    b. What did she suggest in Ruth 1:9?

    c. After Naomi kissed them, what occurred in Ruth 1:9?

    d. They replied to Naomi in Ruth 1:10, "_____we will return with _____ to your people."

6. Read Ruth 1:11-13. In part, Ruth 1:13 says, "the hand of the Lord has gone out against me!" Who is speaking and what is she referring to?

7. What did Orpah do in Ruth 1:14? What did Ruth do? What do you think made the difference in their decisions? Who was ultimately in control?

Women of the Bible and God's Redeeming Love

8. Read Ruth 1:15-17. Ruth's confession bore the evidence of her conversion. She was willing to "go" with Naomi to parts unknown to follow Naomi's God. Which Old Testament saint(s) come to mind when you discover Ruth's heart to "go with God" to an unknown place?

9. Read Ruth 1:19-22. It is estimated the two women traveled 60 - 75 miles to reach Bethlehem. Their journey would have taken more than a week. What is the alarming question asked in Ruth 1:19? Record it below.

10. What was Naomi's response in Ruth 1:20? What did it mean?

Meditation
Ruth 1:22 Now they came to Bethlehem at the beginning of barley harvest.

Ruth: Blessed Submission

Day Two: Where Is Ruth In God's Redemption Story?

Memory verse: Ruth 1:16 But Ruth said: "Entreat me not to leave you, Or to turn back from following after you; For wherever you go, I will go; And wherever you lodge, I will lodge; Your people shall be my people, And your God, my God."

Old Testament saints lived and died in faith. In other words, they died looking forward to the promise of the one who was coming to redeem humanity. In Genesis 3:15, Adam and Eve received the first redemption promise. They were the first humans to hear God's remedy for the plight of man and their sinful condition. In the book of Ruth, Boaz reveals the Redeemer in greater detail. Here, we see Him with heightened clarity, purpose, and sufficiency. Remember, from start to finish the Bible provides a progressive revelation of Jesus! It's all about Him.

1. In Ruth 2:1 we meet Boaz, Naomi's kinsman. *Boaz* means *"in him is strength."* What does the verse say about him? What is significant about the meaning of his name?

2. Read Ruth 2:2-3. Answer the following questions:

    a. What did Ruth ask?

    b. How did Ruth come to glean in the field of Boaz?

    c. From whose family does Boaz come?

3. Timing is everything and Ruth and Naomi returned to Bethlehem at a significant time. They arrived at the onset of the barley harvest. Why do you think this would be significant?

4. Read Ruth 2:7 and Leviticus 19:9. Ruth asked to glean in the field. What does this mean? How is her work described?

5. Read Ruth 2:8-9. Briefly outline the first verbal exchange between Ruth and Boaz.

v. 8

v. 9

6. The word *favor, ḥēn* in Hebrew means *grace, compassion*. The word also has the essence of kindness, approval, goodwill, favoritism, partiality, and bias associated with it. Ruth has found favor with Boaz. Read Ruth 2:10, noticing Ruth's humility. Why is she amazed at this favor? What does she ask at the end of verse 10?

7. Who is a *foreigner*? In Hebrew, *gēr* – also translated stranger, alien, foreigner. Record Leviticus 19:34 below. What does this verse mean? Why is this significant?

8. Our witness is so important. Note the things Boaz has learned about Ruth and her character from observing her actions. Ruth 2:11-12. Be specific.

v. 11

v. 12

9. In Ruth 2:12, *refuge* means to *seek shelter, safety, security, asylum, or to flee for protection*. Biblically speaking, that's placing our trust wholly in God, rather than man or ourselves. For some of us, it's challenging, because we want to control our destiny. In our misguided thinking, we believe we do. Ruth thought otherwise. What is the significance of these words from Ruth 2:12? Record the verse below, underlining the last phrase.

10. Have you placed your hope and trust in the Lord? Is all your confidence resting upon Him? Record a brief testimony of the refuge you have found in Jesus.

Meditation
Psalm 91:2 I will say of the Lord, "He is my refuge and my fortress; My God, in Him I will trust trust."

Ruth: Blessed Submission

Day Three: What Did Ruth Get Right?

Memory verse: Ruth 1:16 But Ruth said: "Entreat me not to leave you, Or to turn back from following after you; For wherever you go, I will go; And wherever you lodge, I will lodge; Your people shall be my people, And your God, my God."

1. In chapter 2, we discover some aspects of Ruth's character. Three key verses begin with these words, "Please let me" or "Let me..." What does Ruth ask in v. 2, v. 7, and v. 13 which display her determination, dedication, and commitment? Each of these character traits is interchangeable between verses.

v. 2

v. 7

v. 13

2. Review Ruth 2:2; 2:7; and 2:13. Notice on the surface, Ruth's requests appear personal, but they are much more. Thinking biblically, what is the motivation of Ruth's heart?

Women of the Bible and God's Redeeming Love

3. Submission means to voluntarily place oneself under the authority of another. Do you see submission in Ruth's actions? Why or why not?

4. Ruth was not only submitted, but she was also a servant. Jesus was the servant of all. Read His words of Matthew 23:11-12. Record the verses. According to Jesus' definition, who will be exalted? Underline your answer.

5. Believers are to model the character of Christ. His nature or Christlikeness is formed in us as we yield to His spirit and conform to His Word. That's part of the sanctification process. As a result, we become recognizably, "servants of the Master." How would you describe a servant of the Master?

Anne Nicholson

6. Generally speaking, there are two types of folks — those who serve and those who desire to be served. We have an excellent example in Jesus, who came to serve. Read the words of Jesus in Matthew 20:26-28. In light of Jesus' description answer these questions: Are you a servant? Would others identify you as a servant?

7. Read and record Ruth 3:9. How does Ruth define herself? Underline her descriptive words.

8. Define *maidservant*.

Women of the Bible and God's Redeeming Love

9. Our actions speak volumes. In fact, they reveal more than words. There are times when words are unnecessary, and a tender touch or a warm smile says it all. Yesterday, we noted Ruth's humility in Ruth 2:10. Today, let's review the verse and examine her actions. What does Ruth do? In a one word response, describe what her actions conveyed to Boaz.

10. Read Ruth 2:22-23. Briefly note Naomi's request in verse 22 and Ruth's submissive response in verse 23. Do you recognize a pattern in Ruth's life? What is it?

v. 22

v. 23

11. Ruth will do it again. Read Ruth 3:5-6. Outline what happens.

v. 5

v. 6

251

12. Ruth had received wise counsel from Naomi. We are not on this journey alone. At times, God uses others to impact our lives. Has this happened in your life? You are invited to share.

Meditation
Psalm 37:23 The steps of a good man are ordered by the Lord, and He delights in his way.

Ruth: Blessed Submission

Day Four: What Did Ruth Get Wrong?

Memory verse: Ruth 1:16 But Ruth said: "Entreat me not to leave you, Or to turn back from following after you; For wherever you go, I will go; And wherever you lodge, I will lodge; Your people shall be my people, And your God, my God."

Scripture gives a glowing testimony concerning Ruth. There is no evidence her life was not above reproach. In fact, commentators agree she is a beautiful example of a life well lived to the glory of God. She was submitted to God's plan every step of the way. It appears, every time a decision was needed she purposed in her heart to honor God by doing the next right thing!

1. Read Ruth 3:1-4. Naomi has given Ruth specific instructions regarding Boaz. Record the words of verse 4 below.

2. Ruth is prepared to take a risk even though she is unsure of Boaz's response to her overtures and proposal of marriage. She is obediently walking by faith and not by sight. Significant risks require big faith! What was the source of Ruth's confidence? Record a verse which highlights blind faith.

3. Read Ruth 3:9. What do the words, *"take your maidservant under your wing,"* suggest? On the surface, this appears seductive, perhaps inappropriate behavior, but it is not. Read Leviticus 25:25. Based on this verse, what does Ruth hope to accomplish from her actions?

4. In all respects, Ruth personifies excellence as a submitted servant who is willing to go the distance. Similarly, Boaz is identified as a man of great wealth. *Great wealth* in Hebrew is *gibbôr ḥayil*. *Gibbôr* meaning *mighty man;* and *ḥayil* meaning *might, strength, power; able, valiant, virtuous, valor; army, host, forces; riches, substance, wealth.* What a glowing description of Boaz. It would appear from our discoveries Ruth and Boaz make a good match. In your opinion, what makes them well suited for one another? Who has made this match?

5. In Ruth 3:12, a dilemma develops. What does Boaz reveal to Ruth?

Women of the Bible and God's Redeeming Love

6. Ruth 3:13-14 highlight redemption. What does Boaz promise in Ruth 3:13? Thinking biblically, what is the meaning of these words, *"as the Lord lives!"*

7. Even though Boaz has instructed Ruth to lay at his feet until morning, no immorality has occurred from the original text. In this tender scene, what is demonstrated and revealed by the fact Boaz had an opportunity but insisted on the appearance of no evil? What was at stake?

8. Boaz cares deeply for Ruth; his intentions are pure. He plans to protect and provide for her, not to harm her in any way. Read Psalm 91:4. Record its promise below. How does this verse reflect the words and actions of Boaz in chapter 3?

Meditation
Psalm 46:1 God is our refuge and strength, A very present help in trouble.

Ruth: Blessed Submission

Day Five: How Did God's Love Redeem It All?

Memory verse: Ruth 1:16 But Ruth said: "Entreat me not to leave you, Or to turn back from following after you; For wherever you go, I will go; And wherever you lodge, I will lodge; Your people shall be my people, And your God, my God."

1. In order to serve as Naomi's kinsman redeemer, Boaz must present his case at the gate. Read Ruth 4:1-2. List the significant facts found in verses 1 and 2.

v. 1

v. 2

Verses 3 - 8 highlight the court proceedings at the gate. According to the times, this was as legal and binding as any court of law today. An irrevocable decision would seal their fate; the decision would be final. During the testimony of performance, Boaz speaks 93 words to establish his desire and ability to serve as the kinsman redeemer. His counterpart speaks a mere 19.

2. In Ruth 4:6, the closer relative disqualifies himself from performing the task of redeeming Naomi and Ruth. Why does he make this choice? What would this mean for Boaz?

3. What important information is revealed about Elimelech in relation to Boaz in Ruth 4:3?

4. The verses of Ruth 4:4-5 are crucial to the outcome of our case. Read Deuteronomy 25:5-6 to review the law concerning the performance required by the kinsman. What performance does Boaz request and require in Ruth 4:4? What further evidence does Boaz make public in verse 5?

v. 4

v. 5

5. What is the custom identified in Ruth 4:7?

6. What significant event occurs at the end of Ruth 4:8 to seal the deal?

Anne Nicholson

7. Read Ruth 4:10-11. Who are the witnesses?

8. Ephrathah (Ruth 4:11) is the ancient name for Bethlehem. See Gen. 35:19. Commentators agree, this public remembrance reaches back into the rich Israelite history some 900 years, to approximately 1915 B.C. This confirms the Jews' ability to preserve their rich heritage and traditions. That's significant because all of the witnesses are familiar with its reference. Read and review Ruth 4:11-12. From verse 11, "the witnesses" name two women in connection to Bethlehem. Who are they? Which was laid to rest near Bethlehem?

9. Read Ruth 4:13-22. God's work is amazing, redemption is accomplished! To sum it all up, Ruth and Boaz become the great grandparents of King David! Record Ruth 4:21 below.

Epilogue.

Since Solomon memorialized the Proverbs 31 woman in scripture, we've marveled at her. Generation after generation, for centuries, particularly women, have been captivated by his eloquent description of this lone female. But it's much more. We've been inspired and challenged by her excellence as well. She was amazing! Truth be told, if her virtuous nature is the overall standard for women, most of us would be found wanting.

From Solomon's description, I have a hard time picturing her chasing the dog or her kids down the street with curlers in her hair, sporting a worn out bathrobe and fuzzy slippers! I mean truly! It appears she had it all together. She found a sweet balance and reflected peace and poise, tempered with clever ingenuity and loving kindness. Even her kids couldn't say anything but good about her. In verse 28 of Proverbs 31, they called her, *"blessed,"* which means *to consider fortunate; call happy*. This happiness or blessedness is associated with wisdom influence. A review of the original text reveals the source of her happiness. This associated wisdom stems from one who conforms to God's established order, rather than pushing against it. She agreed with God! Her satisfaction, peace, and happiness are linked to faith or hope in God and His promises - regardless, not in her circumstances.

She lived beyond the moment, the minutia, and the here and now. You might say she walked above it all. It appears she had a kingdom vision. Even her husband had good things to say about her, "...he praises her." (Proverbs 31:28). He admires her and boasts about her. He sings a "joyous song" of praise concerning her. How awesome? He tells all the guys at the gate, "She's a real keeper - a joy, my joy, a true helper, indeed." Now, that's something to aspire to, isn't it? Have you ever wondered about her identify? Was she a real woman? Some have suggested she is merely a composite of the ideal woman. While others have indicated, no woman could ever embody all these good and honorable traits. However, I disagree. I believe like many others; the Proverbs 31 woman sounds an awful lot like Ruth. In fact, she may have been Ruth! Let's take a closer look.

Ruth is commemorated as a woman of *virtue* in Ruth 3:11. In Hebrew, this is the same word used to describe the *virtuous* wife of Proverbs 31:10. When used of women, *virtue* (and its forms) means *having a noble character*. It implies the *virtuous* one is: *always engaged in doing good*, as in, *"to be good to,"* or *"to benefit others."* Some Bible scholars believe Ruth is personified through the woman of virtue described in Proverbs 31:10.

In this context, it's interesting to note, the word, *ḥayil - (virtuous),* appears 245 times in scripture. When used to commemorate women, we find only three passages. Ruth 3:11 and two verses penned by King Solomon - Proverbs 12:4 and Proverbs 31:10. It's no coincidence our heroine, Ruth, was the great-great-grandmother of King Solomon. Both women share eight amazing parallels as revealed through the book of Ruth and Proverbs 31. The scriptural references are listed below:

Loyal and devoted – Ruth 1:15-18 and Proverbs 31:10-12

Motivated and driven - Ruth 2:2 and Proverbs 31:13

Detail and task-oriented - Ruth 2:7, 17, 23 and Proverbs 31:14-18, 19-21, 24, 27

Devout and reverent - Ruth 2:10, 13 and Proverbs 13:26

Wholly dependent on God - Ruth 2:12 and Proverbs 31:25b, 30

Demure and modest - Ruth 3:3 and Proverbs 31:22, 25a

Cautious and guarded - Ruth 3:6-13 and Proverbs 31:11, 12, 23

Generous and charitable – Ruth 4:14; 15 and Proverbs 31:20; 31

Was the Proverbs 31 women really Ruth? We won't know until the great reveal, but I'd like to think King Solomon was told of her and marveled at her noble character from his youth. How fitting! At the appointed time and upon inspiration of the Holy Spirit, he has commemorated her eloquently. What a picture of love and faithfulness.

In closing, may we prayerfully aspire to agree with God as Ruth did, and live a life noted as "happy and blessed."

Meditation
Ruth 3:11 And now, my daughter, do not fear. I will do for you all that
you request, for all the people of my town know that you are a virtuous woman.

Notes – Ruth: Blessed Submission

Esther

Esther: Destiny Fulfilled

When I was a young girl, I often dreamed of being a princess, tiara and all! But, if you could see me now, in my p.j.'s before daylight, drinking coffee, and surrounded by papers on my dining room table, you'd know it didn't happen. It was not in the cards for me. I've always had a vivid imagination, though, and as a child, I enjoyed playing dress-up. Sometimes, I'd coronate myself queen for the day. Everyone ignored me and my commands, however, because it was mere make-believe. I didn't care; I loved fantasy and pretending to be someone other than myself. (As I type those words, I know there's a deep story there, but this story is about Esther, so for now, we'll put that on a back burner.) Of course, I outgrew those childish dreams, for the most part. But, just between us, I loved the Walt Disney castle and when I thought about it, my friend, Cinderella lived there! It was her happy ending.

When I was a young mother, Prince Charles married Princess Diana. The event was widely televised, offering the world a front row seat to observe history in the making. I confess I watched every minute of it - every last detail. I marveled and oohed and awed at her magnificent dress, cathedral length veil, and beautiful horse-drawn carriage. It was like watching a fairytale in real time. I thought, how amazing is this? One day, they would be the King and Queen of England. (Since we don't have royal families in the U.S., this is as close as it gets.) But, as we all know, their story didn't entirely turn out as we imagined, or them, either, I'm sure. Their marriage proved to be an unhappy one, although I recall Diana confessing in a television interview how much she truly loved Prince Charles. I'm sure she did, at least in the beginning. Nevertheless, to be a "royal" brought honor and privilege, but it also carried with it duties and responsibilities. I'm sure their list of dos and don'ts is quite staggering. I dare say, it's why they are born into these positions, rather than applying for the job. I am certain, it requires something only God can do. I mean to put it in a heart, country comes before family, after God, and duty is always first - that's a high call and a tall order. Yes, most definitely, men and women must be born to serve God in this capacity. Most of us would be unable to do it. This call must come through our DNA.

Today, of course, we enjoy stories and pictures of Prince William and Princess Kate, the future King and Queen of England and their darling family. They are modern royals, to be sure. Like William's deceased mother, Princess Diana, the couple is genuinely loved and adored.

You know I love a story with a twist, and theirs definitely has one. As God ordained, scandal and public uprising over Prince Charles' conduct through the years, may compel the Queen to circumvent her eldest son altogether. If this occurs, the man who would be King, won't be after all. Instead, he'll have watched his lifelong dream, and vision slip right through his fingers. It happens that way, sometimes. The thing we want most remains just beyond our reach, and never comes to pass, it merely eludes us. The tragedy is, sometimes we author our misfortune, and our comeuppance is our just dessert. When it's all said and done, we find ourselves humiliated, and in utter despair, perhaps living with deep regret. It's sad when we are our own "undoing," but it happens. My sweet grandmother had a word for things like this. She would say, "It's like a dog who chases it's tail until he catches it, then bites it." Much to the dog's surprise, it's painful and humiliating! Nonetheless, when Queen Elizabeth II slips into eternity, the most desired post in the land might go to Prince William, Princess Diana's oldest son. After all, he was born for this, and I do not doubt he's the man for the job.

I have shared all this to set the tone for the story before us. It's about a King and his Queen. But, before we go there, I'd like to say one last thing about kings and their children. There is a King like no other king. He is the King of kings and Lord of lords. His name is Jesus. Through Him, you are a daughter of The Most High God - the Great I Am, the one true and living God. He is the creator of heaven and earth - and all its kings and queens. So, the reality is, I truly am a princess! In the eyes of Jesus, that is, and so are you. If you have called upon the name of Jesus for salvation, you are His princess and His most precious treasure. He adores you - everything about you - just the way you are. Sweet ladies, we are daughters of The Most High God and King of it all. We are His princesses!

Who Is Esther?

In Esther, we have another rags-to-riches story with a happy ending. You all know how much I love a story with a good finish! Esther's story is about the sovereignty of God and a beautiful orphan He used to prevent the inevitable annihilation of the chosen people of God. That would be the entire Jewish nation, those whom He affectionately called, "…My people, My heritage Israel…" (Joel 3:2).

Our story is about her destiny as she yielded her life to God and availed herself to His service. In so doing, she fulfilled our greatest commandment and the next one like it. Curious about these words of Jesus? You might review Mark 12:30-31. Simply said, Esther loved God with all her heart, soul, mind, and strength and her fellow Jews - that would be all of her neighbors as herself. She accomplished this by esteeming the needs of others more significant than her own and doing the next right thing. How did Esther come to this astounding conclusion? After fasting and prayer, and soliciting the collective prayers of all the Jews in the land, she determined to do the will of God. Esther agreed with God. Our heroine, Esther, was on board with God's perfect and pleasing will.

Although she was a queen, Esther was a servant. God's servant. She is a fantastic example of a woman who finds joy in serving God. But, it went much deeper. When she sought guidance from God, she could see the bigger picture. She knew and understood God's love reached far beyond herself. In other words, she concluded, "It's not all about me." We would all do well to remember God's love and work extends far beyond our comfy-cozy lives. He's always more concerned about our obedience than our comfort. Can you see it? Esther did. As she sought His guidance and direction, she aligned with Him. With vivid clarity, she could see the greater good and unselfishly moved toward it. Her partnership with God was life-changing and life-saving - literally. In the end, God wins as He always does. In the end, because of her faithfulness, she and her family were richly blessed. And lastly, the Jewish people were saved! Amazing things do happen when we are obedient to God. I've said it before, and I'll repeat it, "Behold, to obey is better than sacrifice..." (1Samuel 15:22).

Esther was a Jewess, the daughter of Abihail. Her family made their home in the Persian Royal City of Susa. Her parents died, leaving Esther orphaned at a young age. Scripture is silent on the cause or circumstances surrounding these events. We do know, however, when her parents died, she came under the guardianship of Mordecai, an official of the Persian palace. He was her older, unmarried, and childless cousin. Mordecai had a deep affection for little Esther and reared her as his daughter. In the security of his home, she was deeply loved and protected. Her doting cousin saw to her every need. No doubt, her education, and proper training prepared her for the tasks ahead. God never calls us to a work we are unsuited for or unprepared to accomplish. He plans that we succeed! He always equips those He calls. Esther was obedient to her cousin, and even when she became queen, she sought his practical and spiritual guidance. She trusted him immensely. She recognized his gentle sensibilities and remarkable wisdom. From her youth, Esther's discernment enabled her to distinguish between her enemies and her allies.

The Enemy.

Yes, Esther would have an adversary. A bitter enemy, just like all believers. His name is Satan, and he is waiting to devour us. (See 1 Peter 5:8.) He is not new, nor his tactics. Remember Eve? She had a tasty encounter with him in the midst of the garden. The enemy deceived her, and she enticed Adam to sin. Although God's plan for humanity was challenged, it was not circumvented. As always, consequences would follow disobedience. What was the sin? It was disobeying God, and the root issues are still the same. Not to oversimplify, but sin stems from pride. It's wanting to be God instead of obeying God. As a result, Adam and Eve were banished from the garden and could never return. From that day onward, God's people have strived with the enemy — even until now. But, as they departed God's presence, our merciful God moved on their behalf. Eve heard a promise of hope. She would have "seed" - offspring! Yes, children were in her future, even though she and Adam sinned. God's plan to use them and bless them had not changed. As always, God was faithful to His pledge, and the results endure to this day. From "her seed," God sent a savior. His name is Jesus!

A Humble Servant.

To Esther's credit, she trusted Mordecai, a gentle Jew like a father. Bible scholars have long attempted to highlight the nature of their relationship. Some have suggested Mordecai poured his life into Esther. It would appear after Israel and the God of Israel, Esther was the great love of his life. He could not have loved her more if she had been his natural daughter. His heart undoubtedly soared as he watched God elevate his sister's only child to the queen of the Persian Empire. So that you know, this was no small post. According to historians, at this time, the Persian Empire dominated most of the Middle East. It's king and queen ruled over a massive population. More than any other empire in history. Of the top five empires recorded, this was number one. It's estimated in 480 B.C. its population amassed 49.4 million people. Unfathomable! It's projected, in the day, the number represented 44% of the world's population.

There was absolutely nothing improper about Mordecai's relationship with Esther. Instead, God used this humble servant to raise and nurture his young ward to great heights of position which prove more than coincidental. Nothing merely happens in God's economy. Esther truly captivated Mordecai's heart. The outcome? Our study guide will uncover the wonders of Esther, a wise young woman who yielded wholly to the voice of God, as heard through His servant, Mordecai. For such a time as this, Esther accomplished the purposes of God because she regarded her own life as expendable for the benefit of others. Her hearts cry was merely this, "If I perish, I perish, whatever comes may be. It's my life for theirs!" Esther was all in with God.

What Of Her Character?

To sum it up, Esther was discerning and clever, but not sly. She was adaptable, and a quick study. She was intuitive concerning people and circumstances. Esther was easy-going, with a kind and gentle spirit. She was a real beauty inside and out but was not conceited. To the contrary, her noble character more than equaled her beauty - it surpassed it. She was faithfully committed without fear. Her hope was in God, alone. To that end, she was prayerful and purposeful. After fearlessly counting the cost, Queen Esther was willing to place her own life in peril for the benefit of others.

Esther knew who she was. She possessed a keen sense of her religious heritage, although she didn't speak openly about her Jewish birthright. As instructed by Mordecai, she concealed her identity rather than foil God's plan. But, when trouble came, Esther turned to God seeking guidance and direction. Instead of talking about her faith, she lived it. That coupled with love, devotion, and a sense of duty made her ideal for her call. Our heroine, Esther was notably selfless, even though her sudden rise to power and position could well have made her otherwise. It's no wonder her rare beauty captured the eye of King Ahasuerus, and ultimately, his heart as well.

Good Versus Evil.

Esther's story has everything. Mystery and intrigue, love and romance, rags and riches, a king and a queen, and an evil enemy in their midst. That's right, the king's court includes an adversary! Wouldn't you know, there's an enemy on the payroll? I don't want to spoil the story, but he has an evil wife as well. Although this enemy thinks he has the king's ear, like most wives, she has his ear instead. Her counsel, however, will prove to be not only unwise and misguided but unforgiving, and lacking redemption.

At her recommendation, an evil plot proves fatal because, of course, their schemes are no match for God. I love it, don't you? God always wins! Never lose sight of that. Regardless of how things might look, at the moment - God is in control. He is immanent which means He is in all things. He is always working to bring about His perfect and pleasing will. And, His plan will not fail, regardless. Relax and look to Jesus – trust Him and remember, an enemy or two along the way, even in your own life, will not trump God's plan. He will prevail! Whatever the evil enemy has planned, God can change for good.

A Happy Feast.

It's no wonder the Jews read the book of Esther each year during the feast of Purim. Never heard of Purim? God invoked this memorial celebration in Esther 9:20-22. In simple terms, it's a lesser Jewish festival and accompanying feast which takes place in the early spring each year. On the Jewish calendar, it's the 14th and 15th of Adar, on our calendar it falls between February and March. The festival is launched on Purim's Eve, as the Jews gather at their synagogues to read and celebrate this beloved treasury of scripture. Their primary focus is God's incredible deliverance, through Esther and Mordecai, which foiled Haman's evil plot to secure the Jews' annihilation.

When we lived in Jerusalem, the days which led up to Purim teemed with excitement. As commanded in the Torah, Jews, young and old alike dress in joyful costumes and gather in their synagogues to read the book of Esther and exchange gifts and money. They also mark this occasion through donations and charitable giving in remembrance of the poor who live among them. On this day, Jews everywhere have much to celebrate - God's redeeming love which saved them! Again! Every time the enemy's name, Haman, is read, the youngsters squeal and scream with delight. They know his end is coming. God will prevail! Although Purim is a lesser Jewish festival, for the young and young at heart, this is a favored holiday each year.

Where Is Esther In God's Redemption Story?

As our story begins, the year is 483 B.C., and Esther is an orphaned Jewess who has been raised by her older cousin Mordecai. For the background, her family of origin and their immediate ancestors had been led into captivity along with King Jeconiah about 103 years earlier. It occurred, as prophesied when Nebuchadnezzar fettered and shackled the Jews and carried them away to Babylon. (2 Kings 24 & 25.) There, they remained in captivity. Fifty-four years later, King Cyrus issued a decree allowing the Jew's return to their homeland. As a result, Zerubbabel successfully led the first flight of Jews back to Jerusalem.

It's interesting to note, however, Esther's family of origin chose not to return. They preferred to remain in the land of captivity rather than return to Jerusalem. Although captive, the Jews in Babylon experienced and celebrated great freedom in Persia. As a result, many flourished in Babylon. When the time came to choose to stay or go, they decided to enjoy the fruits of their labors, rather than uproot their families. For many, thoughts of the trip back to the land of their ancestors had too many unknowns. At any rate, they knew the trip would be long and treacherous. Additionally, her parents' generation were only acquainted with Jerusalem through the traditional stories and testimonies. They had no firsthand knowledge of Jerusalem, the City of Peace. Therefore, it's not curious when it was time to leave Persia, many felt no allegiance or longing in their hearts for Jerusalem. You can't miss what you don't know! Since Babylon had been the birthplace of many, it was home sweet home! The Jews of Persia had dug in deep. They were planted in Babylon and chose to bloom where they were! I found this interesting because they flourished not only on foreign soil but in the land of captivity.

So that you know, the second group of Jews would return. Ezra chapter 7 chronicles these events. A third return, known as Nehemiah's journey, would take place in 445 B.C. As you might have guessed, Nehemiah tells their story. The books of Ezra, Nehemiah, and Esther preserve the history of God's people during the Persian Empire, but only the book of Esther shares the story of God's people who chose to flourish in Babylon, under Persian rule, rather than return to Jerusalem.

What Did Esther Get Right?

From the biblical text, it's plain to see, Esther was an amazing young woman. Although we know no one is perfect, from the book which bears her name, it appears Esther did everything right. She was prayerful, reverent, obedient, submissive to God's plan, resourceful, gave attention to detail, was patient, and showed genuine care and concern for others. It's interesting to note, she was willing to do for her people what they could not do for themselves. Sound familiar? It should! Let's look at some parallels between Queen Esther and Jesus.

First, Queen Esther would save them, because they could not save themselves. She was willing to do so even at the cost of her very life. What a foreshadow and type of Jesus' sacrifice, love, and devotion. Her actions reflect Jesus, who lived His whole life to meet His destiny for the deliverance of all. Of course, this is something we could never do for ourselves. Scorning its shame, for the joy set before Him, He endured the cross. Similarly, with a love only God can give, Queen Esther esteemed all others greater than herself. In sacrificial obedience, she honored God and rose to meet her destiny with courage and grace. She was not an "it's all about me kind of gal." Not one bit; not even when she became Queen. She didn't run from her responsibilities, ignore the challenge, or attempt to talk herself out of this calling. She was willing to see God was on the move! She stood firm with God-honoring courage and met this opportunity head-on. She stared danger and death in the face while wholly trusting in God, her maker.

Let Us Pray.

You may recall in the Garden of Gethsemane, Jesus invited the disciples to pray with Him in His greatest hours of need. Likewise, Queen Esther, knowing the magnitude of her call, solicited the Jews of the land to join her in fasting and prayer. Did you catch that? Like a seasoned spiritual leader, she asked others to turn to God in fasting and prayer. She never pretended to have all the answers, but she knew God did! With sincere humility, she allowed others to see her need for direction from the true and living God. Could it be Esther was familiar with these beautiful words of the psalmist, David? "Hear me when I call, O God of my righteousness! You have relieved me in my distress; Have mercy on me, and hear my prayer." (Psalm 4:1).

In God-honoring humility, Esther displayed the essence of her faith when she entreated others to fast and pray. It's important to note she wasn't asking them to pray on her behalf - instead, along with her. That's huge! A spiritual leader always guides others to God's throne. She humbled herself before Mordecai and all the Jews in the empire, and essentially confessed, "My hope is in God. Fast and pray with me! I will trust in Him for deliverance, direction, and protection." Our study guide will navigate these fantastic passages on day three.

What Did Esther Get Wrong?

Scripture records no error or shortcomings concerning Esther. That does not mean, however, Esther was perfect. As we already know, regardless of how amazing we think we are, in reality, we're all sinners. Every last one of us is wholly incumbent upon God's amazing grace for salvation, including Esther.

What we see in our text is not Esther in and of herself, or in her strength. Instead, to fulfill her destiny, to accomplish God's plan, and "for such a time as this," we see a yielded life which was useful to God. She placed the needs of others before her own. Her focus was outward, not inward. Esther's heart of love overflowed into meaningful service. The takeaway? Esther was doing God's work, God's way! That's why her life looks perfect and so utterly amazing!

If you're feeling a bit discouraged because she appears perfect, don't be. Remember, we are perfect too; that is - in the righteousness of Christ. If God calls you to a task, He will establish you to accomplish His work - His way. By first preparing your heart.

What can we learn from Esther's submitted life? Quite a lot. This study concludes a bit different from all the others. It's not because Esther's life was more useful than others, it's because aspects of her journey provide unique teachable moments. Let's examine five life lessons which highlight Esther's strengths and accomplishments.

Anne Nicholson

Life Lessons From Esther.

1. Inside Out. Esther was more than just a beautiful woman. She had a wealth of inner beauty which radiated God's love and goodness. In other words, her outer beauty was a reflection of God's love and kindness inside. That's what people see – initially, that is. Christ's radiance in us, or the lack thereof.

My grandmother was an amazing woman. Generally speaking, you knew what she though on many matters, including beauty. She'd say things like, "Pretty is as pretty does," and "Take care that pretty doesn't turn pretty ugly!" Both statements suggest our outer beauty (mannerisms, words, actions, and deeds) expose the depth of our inner beauty. i.e., the condition of our hearts.

She was a woman of real substance, wisdom, and grace. She was an incredible believer and a faithful servant of servants. I never heard her complain or say anything mean-spirited or unkind about anyone. She never listened to gossip and would leave the room if my aunts and uncles got cranked up. She just refused to be a party to it. Taking her quiet leave, however, subtly spoke volumes. Through her departure, it's as if she said, "I don't approve of this, and I won't be party to it, and neither should you!" Sometimes, as she departed she'd shake her head and calmly remark, "Take care, your insides are showing!"

As a bright-eyed child of 8, I didn't grasp the magnitude of what she was saying. But, at the appointed time, salvation came, and I got it - and so much more. She was clever and had wisdom well beyond her formal education. She had a keen wit and was genuinely interested in others. She was extremely gentle and kind. She had incredible patience. She knew her way around the kitchen, and was the best southern cook ever! She could take an ordinary pot roast and make a dinner fit for a king. I can still see the "mile high meringue" on her banana pudding. Yum! But, beyond it all, she had integrity and wealth, but not from riches – spiritual wealth – which stemmed from a life-long love for Jesus. She was not merely a Sunday Christian, either. Although she had an active church life, she was a believer through and through - every day. As you might have guessed, she was a real beauty. Even in her waning years, she still had an award-winning smile and a vibrant twinkle in her jet black eyes. She never made a big production about her faith or why she believed. She simply got up each day and lived it. She ministered with her whole being, through love and service. She was never critical, and never stood on her soapbox. Instead, she had a subtle, easy-going, matter-of-fact way of calling others out, as need be, and she did so with charm and grace. It was a mother's way of rebuking her grown children. Much like you'd tell your daughter or friend, "you've got lipstick on your teeth, or toilet paper stuck to your shoe."

I'll never forget her. She had a gentle way of reminding others, our hearts are always exposed. A little makeup, alone, won't mask the truth. Nor will tossing an extra dollar in the offering plate each week! We can give and serve all we like, in the flesh, and our deeds may benefit someone, but giving and serving won't resolve our deep-rooted heart issues. What's inside our heart always shines through. If tenderness is there, tender words are spoken. If kindness is there, kind words are heard. Likewise, if jealousy or envy, anger or hatred, criticism or judgment dominates our hearts, we can't conceal it. We can smile and attempt to mask it and say things like, "I love you," or "I'm there for you," but our hearts can't support those weighty promises if God is not ruling and reigning within us.

You get the idea. Our sin will find us out! It will expose our hearts, and the truth will come out. That's why God is more concerned about the condition of our hearts, rather than our comfort. If you don't believe me, consider the words of Jesus. In essence, Jesus told the disciples – "what fills the heart, one speaks." His exact words: "For out of the abundance of the heart his mouth speaks." (Luke 6:45). How true! From Queen Esther's words, we can see she had a heart of love for others. When Esther said, "If I perish, I perish," her heart could support her pledge. Her heart overflowed with love for others, and her focus was saving others, not herself. Queen Esther had a pure heart which God could use.

Real Beauty.

Esther was a real beauty, but she was so much more. Something about her elegant purity and grace elevated her above all the others. Not only her words, but her overall character and gentle spirit captivated the heart of the most powerful man in the world. When he beheld Esther, every other candidate paled in comparison. As we shall see, he had his pick. In kingly fashion, he held an empire-wide audition to fill the post vacated by former Queen Vashti. How thrilling! Above all the women in the land, King Ahasuerus chose our Esther, an orphaned Jewess to become his bride.

Choosing Esther was God's plan. He picked her first - He chose her! Then He guided the entire selection process for His purposes. Nothing happens randomly. God is always in the mix. He is immanent. That means He not only created all things and exists in all things, but purposely holds all things together. Although Esther was the most beautiful woman in the land, it wasn't merely for beauty's sake. God would use her beauty - her entire package, to attract the King, and, ultimately, accomplish His plan. Yes, God was on the move, and He planned to move Esther into a position of power and influence to achieve His eternal purpose. Let's not lose sight of God's plan in Esther's incredible story. It is eternal and has never changed. It's the salvation of His people! In this case, the Jews! That was, after all, God's primary goal – saving us - from before the foundation of the world.

When Esther became Queen, all the accompanying benefits were secondary. We must remember, with position and power comes responsibility. So, too, with Esther. As God's sovereignty ordains, she will take her place as Queen, just in the nick of time. That is, in her people's time of greatest need. Our quintessential beauty, Esther, met her responsibility in a way which honored God.

Our Life Lesson: Want to be more beautiful? Fill up with Jesus, and you will be more attractive every day. Spending time with Jesus changes you from the inside out, beginning with your heart. Your walk and talk will change; your thoughts and actions will change. His Word transforms us as it renews our minds. (See Romans 12:2.) When we are filled with His spirit and guided by God, others will say, "I see Jesus in you!" Isn't that our goal, to be conformed to His image? It's God's plan for us - all of us. That the Redeemed of God "be conformed" to the image of His Son, Jesus. (Romans 8:29.) When He is ruling and reigning in our hearts, we become more beautiful because His love, mercy, and goodness always shine through!

2. Lean On God. Esther undergirded her courage with prayer. It's not coincidental the more she prayed, the more strength she possessed. Great courage and strength come from faith in God. Always has and will. Daniel prayed, Paul prayed, and our Lord Jesus prayed! The disciples never asked to learn how to feed the multitudes, heal the sick, or raise the dead, but they did say, "Lord, teach us to pray." The scripture from Luke's gospel: Now it came to pass, as He was praying in a certain place, when He ceased, that one of His disciples said to Him, "Lord, teach us to pray, as John also taught his disciples." (Luke 11:1).

It's not curious this was their urgent request. The disciples had seen, first-hand, the incredible power of prayer. They were witness to Jesus' unfailing confidence in prayer, as well as His devotion to prayer. They knew it was the source of His undeniable strength, wisdom, and power. They had been with Jesus and watched him retreat to places of solitude to pray. He never forsook time with His Heavenly Father. No one could have been busier than Jesus, yet, He took the time to pray! He needed fellowship with God and guidance from God. The disciples had heard Him declare, "For I have come down from heaven, not to do My own will, but the will of Him who sent Me." (John 6:38).

If Jesus needed prayer, how much more should we? Our faith is encouraged, guided and empowered through prayer. Through prayer, we are not only commissioned, but we also talk with a friend closer than a brother with whom we can commiserate or celebrate. Whatever the occasion, in joy or crisis, take the time for committed prayer. He's an every day God! You can't surprise Him. You might just as well tell Him all things because He already knows it anyway! Unburden your heart; lighten your load. Remember, confession unburdens the soul and helps us move forward.

On the contrary, unconfessed sin binds us, keeps us down, and prevents us from moving forward, spiritually, as well as naturally. Additionally, and most tragic of all, unconfessed sin breaks our fellowship with God. Confess it all, tell Him everything. There's nothing you can't confess to Him, or He can't handle. Remember, He is always at work. He's a big God! He loves you passionately and unreservedly, without end. How much? He loved you enough to die for you! His plans will succeed! Paul reminds us, "And we know that all things work together for good to those who love God, to those who are the called according to His purpose." (Romans 8:28).

Our Life Lesson: We cannot know the will of God or accomplish it apart from praying God's word and waiting on Him for direction. Esther sought God's counsel, and He guided her success! Why? Prayer changes everything. It invites God into every situation or circumstance. It aligns us with God, and if necessary, it changes our hearts. Esther believed in the power of prayer. So much so, in her hour of greatest need, she turned to God. We see her heart for God and their intimate relationship exposed through her instructive words to Mordecai, "Go, gather all the Jews who are present in Shushan, and fast for me; neither eat nor drink for three days, night or day. My maids and I will fast likewise. And so I will go to the king, which is against the law; and if I perish, I perish!" (Esther 4:16).

How powerfully exciting! Esther knew and understood the power of collective prayers and fasting. When she invited others to partner with her in prayer, I dare say, this was not an inaugural prayer to an unknown God. Esther enjoyed a relationship with God. She knew Him, and He knew her. Take the time to pray. Get into the habit of seeking Him daily. Then, like Esther, when life's troubles come, and they inevitably will, prayer will be familiar and comfortable for you. It should be like speaking confidentially to your spouse or closest friend. He is faithful.

I talk more to Jesus than anyone else! He is my closest friend and greatest love. Early in our marriage, when I confessed it to my husband, he smiled tenderly and replied, "That's why you're the one for me, I wouldn't have it any other way." If prayer is new to you, put Him to the test. Over time, you will see His faithfulness again and again. Then, like Esther, you will be equipped, encouraged, and empowered to be His witness - no matter what.

3. Making Plans. Following three days of faithful prayer and fasting, Esther was ready. Her Gethsemane moment revealed her faith. Gethsemane moments are all the same. They occur in our lives when whatever we're facing is so weighty we can't see straight. Generally, they occur in or around a crisis of faith or despair and heartache. They come when lives are at stake or when we face peril, or as some tragedy unfolds, or immense fear grips our fragile human hearts. They happen when we don't know how to stand and don't know which way to go. Every believer will come to this place sometime on his or her journey, maybe more than once.

The commonality? A Gethsemane moment always calls for a decision. Jesus agonized in the garden of Gethsemane the night of His arrest. The battle between flesh and spirit is real. All spiritual matters were settled as our Lord lay prostrate before His Heavenly Father. While unburdening His heart, He came into agreement with God. In other words, Jesus suffered the cross before He ever went there. When Jesus said, "...yet not my will, but yours be done" - it was finished; complete; accomplished! When He rose to His feet to meet His destiny, the victory was His. He never looked back. Neither did Esther. We are sufficiently supplied for the task before us when we seek God's counsel. When we rise from our knees, we have the victory, the answer, the power, the provision, the healing, etc., which only comes through prayer.

Prayer accomplishes everything spiritual, and then it transcends to the natural. In these moments of humility and surrender: 1) God always attends us; 2) we find the courage and strength to do the will of God, and 3) we are prepared to face whatever God's providence has planned.

Esther's Gethsemane moment had come full circle. Her fervent prays availed much! They were fruitful and beneficial! But, how did she respond?

Our Life Lesson:

We can follow Esther's model for God-honoring service.

- She devised a plan - Esther 4:16
- She committed her plan to prayer and fasting
- She invited others to partner with her
- She waited for God's timing prayerfully and patiently, with confidence, poise, and grace
- She moved forward at the appointed time; without delay or changing her mind

The sum of it all? Queen Esther did God's work, God's way!

4. **Godly Wisdom And Counsel.** Don't despise Godly counsel. Esther received advice from Mordecai when it came. Although Esther was discerning in her own right, she was open to the Godly counsel of others - namely Mordecai. That's wise. But, let's temper it with a word of caution. Take care who is advising you. Are "your advisors or comforters" endeavoring each day to look more like Jesus? Do they have your best interest at heart? In other words, look for counsel from those demonstrating the hallmark traits of Christian faithfulness. You know who they are. Those whose lives look like Jesus! It's that simple. When I want counsel, I obtain it from those whom I know are friends of God.

Our Life Lesson: We are not on this journey alone. God can and will use other believers to help mold and shape our lives. The best example of this comes through marriage. As we gently rub through life together, we smooth out our mate's rough edges, and vice versa. I can't always see my error, but my husband has absolutely no difficulty detecting it. No doubt, he's not silent on the matter, either. Thankfully, he's direct and scriptural without being unkind or abrasive. Godly counsel not only looks like Jesus, but it also sounds like Jesus too! In other words, it's full of love and goodness. It has your best interest at heart. It is never critical, harsh or hurtful. When God uses him in this fashion, I am open and prayerful concerning his words of wisdom. If God is in it, you will not only hear Him speak, but your spirit will testify to it as truth, and confirm it as well.

You may recall, God used Paul to rebuke Peter when needed - once in the City of Antioch. For the sake of time, we're not going to delve into the story. That's another lesson for another time. If you're curious about what happened, you can read this account in Galatians 2:11-21.

When someone offers me advice, even my husband, I generally respond by saying only, "Thank you." Then, at the first opportunity, I pray through their words and ask God to reveal His heart on the matter. If need be, I turn to God's Word for further confirmation and correction. God's Word never fails. It is without a doubt, the most beautiful and truthful rebuke on earth. It's amazing how tenderly His word brings us back into harmony. What's that? That would be His perfect and pleasing will. Once the matter is settled in my heart, and sin confessed as need be, I let it go and merely trust God. He is faithful. Once that's done, it's finished. I trust God's Spirit to bring His Word to performance in my life. That's part of the Spirit's job. He is faithful. It's my daily prayer, by His grace, "I mature into the woman He desires as He brings His Word to performance in my life." I'm confident He will see me through.

5. Seeking The Greater Good. Esther was willing to risk her own life for the lives of others. As God's servant, she esteemed the needs of other Jews higher than her own. They would not know of their near annihilation until the crisis was averted. When it was over, grand celebration accompanied by much pomp and circumstance occurred. Your study guide will take an in-depth look at these verses on day five.

When Esther rose to meet her destiny, it was not out of selfish motivation, but the total lack thereof. She had nothing to gain. Esther didn't do it for fame or fortune. She already had those - she was Queen, for heaven's sake! When word came from Mordecai, perhaps this was her destiny, something spiritual occurred in Esther. In a spiritual awakening of sorts, Esther had a "but God" moment. Haman planned to kill the Jews, "but God" planned to use her to save them. It was not the word God would use someone else, if she was unwilling, which gripped her heart and aligned her with God. Instead, Esther didn't want to miss one thing God had planned and prepared for her. She was ready to get outside herself, get beyond her comfort zone, so to speak, to see God's plan accomplished.

Nothing is more thrilling or satisfying than partnering with God to do His work. I can confess without hesitation, this is true! Let's review Mordecai's warning from Esther 4.

And Mordecai told them to answer Esther: "Do not think in your heart that you will escape in the king's palace any more than all the other Jews. For if you remain completely silent at this time, relief and deliverance will arise for the Jews from another place, but you and your father's house will perish. Yet who knows whether you have come to the kingdom for such a time as this?" (Esther 4:13-14).

Our Life Lesson: Close your eyes and say these words, "For such a time as this… for such a time as this." Have you ever pondered those words? Have you ever thought about where you are, right now, this very moment? Have you considered your married or single status in light of God's divine purpose? Or, your state of motherhood or lack thereof? Each journey is unique. We are individuals, fearfully and wonderfully made, all with purpose and intent. Your existence is God's intentional work. You were born in this time and place in history because it was part of God's overall sovereign plan. Look around you. Your physical address, your location, and your present circumstances are all part of His sovereign plan. You are where you are, doing what you are doing because God ordained it. We learned in our story of Eve, from before the foundation of the world, God conceived you in His mind, called you into existence, and then, at the appointed time, molded you with His loving hands before placing you in the womb He chose to use to bring your forth. Did you pick your parents? Of course not. Did you have any impact on your birth? Of course not, but God did! God guided it all. You didn't have anything to do with your spiritual birth, called being "born of the Spirit," (God's Spirit) - either. That's a spiritual work from start to finish. It was all God, every bit of it was His plan.

God fills the book of Esther, although His name is not there. In every verse, in every chapter, He's there. In His sovereignty, He is accomplishing His eternal plan. God is redeeming His Jews, the remnant which remained in Susa. His love is not defined or limited by location. He didn't forget them because they chose not to return to Jerusalem. He didn't punish them for staying in Persia and enjoying life where they were planted. They were still His people - God's chosen. God never lost sight of them, and He never let go.

It's the same with us. God will never let you go. You are gripped by a mighty God who loves you, unconditionally. He has a plan for your life! You are His treasure. Jesus died to have you. His plan will succeed! And, in the process, you will triumph! A faithful God will see you through.

Perfect Love.

God loves you completely just like you are. I know it's hard for some of us to grasp because in this world love is flawed. Sometimes human love proves not very loving and in the end, hurtful and unfaithful. But, God's love is so "other than" human love, which is flawed and tainted by sin. God's love is complete, holy and pure. It's not performance-based. You can't earn it or buy it. God's love is not for sale. It is given freely because that's who He is. "God is love." (1 John 4:8; 4:16). He is the embodiment of all that is love. He created it, and He gives it. Truthfully, you couldn't do one thing, better or different, to cause Him to love you more than He already does and already has. His love for you is undeniably complete and eternal. Rejoice, you are secure in God's love - it will endure forever! Jesus will never leave you or forsake you! Deuteronomy 31:6 and Hebrews 13:5.

It All Comes Down To Choices.

I've said it before, and I'll repeat it. It always comes down to choices, and Esther had two. She could either risk her life to save the Jews or face certain annihilation with them. She trusted God and made the better choice. That's the divine providence of God at work.

What an exciting week we have ahead. Esther's love for God climaxed in faithful obedience to the benefit of not only herself but others. She was all in with God. The results were amazing. They had a positive impact on her life, the king's life, and let's not forget Mordecai, as well as every Jew in the Persian Empire. Don't you find that exciting? I sure do. When her moment in time came, she was ready. She stepped into her destiny, wanting all that God had planned for her, and nothing less. As she prayed and counted the cost, she was empowered to rise above the obstacles and fear. Esther cast personal concerns aside, desiring instead to walk through the door God opened. Esther chose to "move forward with God," and to live beyond all she had hoped or imagined…. even for a Queen.

A Journey With God.

No one who partners with God can know the outcome with certainty. All you can know is, He alone is God. He is right and just, He has a plan, He's always moving, and He loves you! That's part of the thrill and the beauty of His work. Through the years, every time I thought I had Him figured out, He did the most unexpected thing. Sometimes, the outcome was far above anything I thought possible. But, guess what? It was always perfect. Our Lord God still does the perfect thing!

What's in your future? What's your destiny? It is my prayer that you will hear God speak through this study of Esther. Have you said yes to God? It's never too late to respond to your Gethsemane moment, which always calls believers to a place of decision. I hope that you will respond, like Esther, by essentially saying, "I'm moving forward with you God, and if it kills my hopes, and dreams to accomplish yours, for the greater good, so be it! Not my will, but thy will be done. I'm all in!"

How Did God's Love Redeem It All?

Day five of our study will guide you through the conclusion of Esther's thrilling journey. In short, God wins, again! He reversed the evil curse of Haman and executed His perfect and holy judgment. That reminds me of words from the psalmist: "The heathens are sunk down in the pit that they made: in the net which they hid is their own foot taken." (Psalm 9:15). God can handle all evil planned and plotted against His people. He will fight for us and avenge all wrongs against us. He is our protector. His eye is on us. As a believer, nothing can touch your life that has not first run through the loving hands of God. We must remember, He is a God of love and He is in control at all times and in all places. What a comfort! God loves you and is, even now, working all things together for good because you love Him and are called according to His purpose.

As you study this week, consider the following questions. Who is guiding your life? Are you walking in your strength, or are you wholly yielded to God? Esther was walking by faith and not by sight! But, until tested, she didn't know the measure of her faith. Neither will we! Moving forward, I pray when we're tested and our destiny calls we will be empowered to do His will, like Queen Esther, by His grace, and for His glory.

Be blessed this week as you study Esther: Destiny Fulfilled.

Next week - Gomer: Perpetual Prostitute.

Esther's story unfolds in the book of Esther.

Esther: Destiny Fulfilled

Day One: Who Is Esther?

Memory Verse: Esther 4:16 "Go, gather all the Jews who are present in Shushan, and fast for me; neither eat nor drink for three days, night or day. My maids and I will fast likewise. And so I will go to the king, which is against the law; and if I perish, I perish!"

Vashti is no longer the reigning queen as we open the book of Esther. For clarity, read Esther 1:1-20. What a dilemma! There is no sitting Queen for King Ahasuerus. Her public refusal to come before him at the royal banquet has caused quite a stir, including much consultation among the wise men who "understood the times." Fear has gripped their hearts because all women might come to despise their husbands when news of Vashti's unsubmissive behavior becomes known. The wise men concluded, as Vashti's behavior becomes public knowledge, "there will be excessive contempt and wrath," among the wives of the kingdom. Here we begin.

1. What do the wise men suggest from Esther 1:19-20?

v. 19

v. 20

2. King Ahasuerus liked their idea. How did he respond?

3. The decree was irrevocable. Read Daniel 6:8; 12; and 15, in light of Esther 8:8. Do you think the decree was important to the health and well-being of the Kingdom? Explain.

4. Using a dictionary, define *irrevocable*. Do you think their actions were excessive?

5. To grasp the full impact of the edict, write Esther 1:22 below. Underline the words that are most significant, in your opinion.

6. Read Esther 2:1. Note these words, "After these things… he remembered Vashti…" The King missed his Queen. A man without a woman is never complete, not even a king. Commentators agree, most likely this occurred during the latter portion of the King's disastrous war with Greece, between 481 and 479 B.C. Because we know the King's edict or proclamation was irrevocable, there could be no reconciliation between the two. In light of that reality, the wise men offer a remedy to the King. What do they suggest from Esther 2:2-4?

v. 2

Women of the Bible and God's Redeeming Love

v. 3

v. 4

7. Read Esther 2:5-7. Who was Mordecai? How did he end up with Esther (Hadassah) as his ward?

8. From Esther 2:7, what two words describe our orphan, Esther?

9. Read Esther 2:8-10. Esther's custody is transferred to Hegai. What does the first phrase of Esther 2:9 suggest to you? Why do you think this would be important?

Anne Nicholson

10. Review Esther 2:8-10, and answer the following questions.

    a. How many choice servants were given to Esther?

    b. Why were extra beauty treatments given to Esther?

    c. Do you think this points to God's providential control? Why or why not?

    d. Record a verse to share highlighting God's sovereignty.

Meditation
Esther 2:7 …The young woman was lovely and beautiful…

Esther: Destiny Fulfilled

Day Two: Where Is Esther In God's Redemption Story?

Memory Verse: Esther 4:16 "Go, gather all the Jews who are present in Shushan, and fast for me; neither eat nor drink for three days, night or day. My maids and I will fast likewise. And so I will go to the king, which is against the law; and if I perish, I perish!"

Esther and her family were Jews in captivity. As our story begins, the year is 483 B.C., and Esther is an orphaned Jewess who has been raised by her older cousin, Mordecai. For the background, her family of origin and their immediate ancestors had been led into captivity along with King Jeconiah about 103 years earlier. It occurred, as prophesied when Nebuchadnezzar fettered and shackled the Jews and carried them away to Babylon. (See 2 Kings 24 & 25.) Fifty-four years later, King Cyrus issued a decree allowing the Jews' return to their homeland. As a result, Zerubbabel successfully led the first flight of Jews back to Jerusalem. However, Esther's birth family did not make the trip. They preferred to remain in the land of captivity rather than return to Jerusalem. As a result, Esther and her family were Jews living in a self-imposed exile!

1. The Jews in Babylon were enjoying life. List several reasons you think Esther's family chose to remain in exile rather than return to Jerusalem. Can you relate to their decision? Why or why not?

2. Even though they chose to remain in exile, God was still with them. What does this say to you about the sovereignty of God?

3. The Persian King receives more than 175 references in 167 verses contained in the book of Esther. However, there is no mention of God - not one! There is also no mention of God in the inspired text of the Song of Solomon. What do you think God is attempting to reveal through this inspired omission of His Name? What, if anything, does it speak to you personally?

4. The enemy has long been working to eliminate the Jewish nation. In the book of Esther, all of God's unconditional covenant promises to Abraham and David were jeopardized. However, God in His sovereignty preserved His people down through the ages. He will do it again. From the scriptures listed below, briefly indicate what occurred to threaten God's covenant promises.

Matthew 2:16 -

Matthew 4:8-9 -

Matthew 16:21-23 -

Luke 22:3-6 -

5. Throughout history, God's keeping hand of providence has held us. He moved beautifully throughout the book of Esther on behalf of His beloved Israel. He accomplished this by raising an orphaned Jewess to a position of power and influence to circumvent the elimination of her people. This dramatic rescue serves as a reminder that He is working in the unseen to redeem and preserve all those who would "call upon the name of the Lord." Read Psalm 121:4. Record the verse below. What does this speak to you personally?

6. God will stop at nothing to save His people, even those who are living in a self-imposed exile. Choosing the world is not an option for believers. James said if you are a friend of the world you are an enemy of God. Record James 4:4 below. Have you ever chosen the enticing world?

Meditation
1 Thessalonians 5:24 He who calls you is faithful, who also will do it.

Esther: Destiny Fulfilled

Day Three: What Did Esther Get Right And Wrong?

Memory Verse: Esther 4:16 "Go, gather all the Jews who are present in Shushan, and fast for me; neither eat nor drink for three days, night or day. My maids and I will fast likewise. And so I will go to the king, which is against the law; and if I perish, I perish!"

From the biblical text, Esther was an amazing young woman. It appears she did everything right. She was obedient, prayerful, patient, reverent, resourceful, detail-oriented, and wholly submitted to God's plan. But, something more significant was going on inside Queen Esther's heart and mind. Her focus was others; she was utterly selfless. For a Queen, a woman of wealth, power, and influence, this was rare indeed. Even though she was queen of the most extensive empire in history, she esteemed others higher than herself. She expressed genuine care and concern for the well-being of others. In sacrificial obedience, she honored God and rose to meet her destiny with grace and elegance.

1. Read Esther 2:10. What significant information had Esther concealed about herself at Mordecai's request? Why do you think this was significant?

2. From Esther 2:12-14, what must be completed prior to "one night with the King?" Be specific.

v. 12

v. 13

v. 14

3. What significant phrase is found at the end of Esther 2:15? Record it below. Can you recall a male patriarch who received similar recognition in scripture?

4. After the initial visit with the King, no one returned without His express invitation. Review Esther 2:14. Read Esther 2:17. What did the King think about Esther? Why is this significant? Who is at work behind the scenes?

5. Read Esther 2:18. Esther became a bride. What five things does the King do in celebration?

1.

2.

3.

4.

5.

6. Mordecai was sitting at the gate which reveals his position of prominence within the kingdom. Apparently, he has already found favor in the eyes of the king.

   a. What is revealed to Mordecai in Esther 2:21?

   b. What did Mordecai do with this information according to Esther 2:22?

   c. What was the outcome from Esther 2:23?

7. The above scene alerts us to the political climate of Persia. Now comes Haman, an arch rival of Mordecai. The 1,000-year feud between the Jews and the Amalekites was a thriving reality since the Jews' exodus from Egypt. (See Exodus 17:8-16.) The feud's bitterness appears repeatedly throughout scripture. There was no hope of reconciliation between Haman, an Amalekite, and Mordecai, the Jew. Mordecai's public refusal to bow down to Haman has heightened Haman's hatred. So, he devises a plan. Read Esther 3:8-15. To understand the full measure of Haman's evil plan, record Esther 3:13 below. What does the first phrase of Esther 3:14 tell you about the decree?

v. 13 -

v. 14 -

The whole empire will receive the published decree. Undoubtedly, disbelief, chaos, and anger were the order of the day. *Perplexed – m^{e}bûwkâh, meb-oo-kaw'* - from the root word – *bûk* is the last inspired word in Esther, chapter 3. In its Niphal voice or stem, the word appears only three times in the Old Testament. It conveys reflexive action, where the subject of the verb both carries out and receives the action of the verb.[10] In Hebrew, its meaning is *bewilderment, confusion, uncertainty*. The verb has been translated as follows in the three passages: *bewildered* in Exodus 14:3; *are restless* in Joel 1:18; and *was perplexed* in Esther 3:15.

---

[10] Heiser, M. S., & Setterholm, V. M. (2013; 2013). *Glossary of Morpho-Syntactic Database Terminology*. Lexham Press.

8. Review Esther 3:15. Can you imagine the anguish of the Jews? They were stunned! "But God" will have the last word. He takes the things which perplex us and changes them into something He can use. Something which will ultimately glorify His name. In the end, everything points to Him! Has God comforted you in a perplexing situation? Has He brought clarity when you were bewildered? You are invited to share.

9. As we open Esther 4, Mordecai learns all that's happened. He responded through what actions from Esther 4:2-3? Thinking biblically, what is the spiritual meaning behind his behavior?

10. Hathach, the king's eunuch, facilitated conversations between Mordecai and Queen Esther. Ultimately, he provided her with a copy of the decree. Mordecai's decision to expose Haman's evil plot sets the tone for the rest of our story. Read Esther 4:8. What does Mordecai instruct Hathach to do? What does he hope to accomplish?

Meditation
Daniel 9:3 Then I set my face toward the Lord God to make
request by prayer and supplications, with fasting, sackcloth, and ashes.

Esther: Destiny Fulfilled

Day Four: Esther's Heroism

Memory Verse: Esther 4:16 "Go, gather all the Jews who are present in Shushan, and fast for me; neither eat nor drink for three days, night or day. My maids and I will fast likewise. And so I will go to the king, which is against the law; and if I perish, I perish!"

We find two significant themes in the book of Esther: God's sovereignty and God's deliverance. Esther provides a timeless record of His divine providence which is two-fold. First, it speaks of holding all of creation together as He intended, and second, it involves the eschaton or unfolding of final events. That would be the last things to take place according to God's divine plan. Although God's name is missing from Esther's 167 verses, (NKJV) the text displays God's providential care like no other book in the Bible. Every verse bears witness to God's presence, power, and control. To that end, He is the star of this nail-biting drama. Esther's story is the perfect setting to reveal the sovereignty and deliverance of God, as He works from the unseen. All the while, working all things together for good to accomplish His plan.

As we draw Esther's story to a close, days four and five will focus on Esther's heroic partnership with God and His divine deliverance of the Jews.

1. Read Esther 4:10-17. Record Esther 4:14 below to discover Mordecai's life-changing messsage.

Esther 4:14 —

2. Review Esther 4:15-17. What was Esther's sacrificial response? Record the verse. Note: With these powerful words, Esther comes into agreement with God, and steps into her destiny.

3. Esther 4:15-17 reveal Esther's Gethsemane moment. Every believer will come to this point sometime on his or her journey. A Gethsemane moment always calls for a decision. Jesus agonized in the garden the night of His arrest. The battle between flesh and spirit is real. Although Jesus was entirely God, He was also fully man. In the dark of the garden, He

Women of the Bible and God's Redeeming Love

sought His Father in prayer. With great humility, Jesus lay prostrate before God's throne and unburdened His soul. There, He accomplished all things spiritual. He came into agreement with God and rose to meet His destiny. That moment, it was achieved - it was finished! Jesus suffered the cross before He ever went there, and He never looked back. Neither did Esther. When a matter is settled in our hearts and confirmed in our spirits, we are ready to face whatever God's providence has planned. Have you ever had a Gethsemane moment? You are invited to share.

4. After three days of united fasting and prayer, Esther is ready. She dresses in her royal attire and prepares to face the king. Read Esther 5:1-4. Notice in Esther 5:2 "she found favor in his sight."

Thinking spiritually, what do these words mean? Who is behind it all?

5. What does the King offer in Esther 5:2? Do you think his offer is sincere? Why or why not?

6. At long last, Mordecai is honored in Esther 6:1-14. Five years after Mordecai foiled a plot to assassinate King Ahasuerus, his discernment, and unwavering faithfulness is rewarded. Unbeknownst to Haman, his plans for great fanfare and celebration were to bless his arch nemesis, Mordecai, rather than himself. With care and attention to detail, he prepared an event to remember. It would be, indeed! What a difference a day makes. One day Haman is riding high, having received an invitation from Esther to dine with the King, and the next, he endures horrible humiliation. Mordecai will mount the King's steed and wear the royal crown and robe. Poor Haman, he is ordered to parade Mordecai through the town square and herald him saying, "Thus shall it be done to the man whom the king delights to honor!" (Esther 6:11).

Afterward, in great humiliation, Haman shares details of the day's events with his wife and friends. She has an interesting response. Record his wife's prophetic words of Esther 6:13 below? Why are these words significant? Who is in control?

7. Esther responds by inviting the King and Haman to a banquet. In reality, there will be two banquets (Esther 5 & 7), but it appears things are moving along just as Esther has envisioned. Ultimately, she will defer her real request until chapter 7. Read Esther 7:2-4. Note in Esther 7:4, she repeats the exact language of Haman's decree from Esther 3:13. Esther is so very clever! In the space below, highlight the details of Esther's petition. Who is calling the shots? Esther or God?

v. 2

v. 3

v. 4

8. Haman erects gallows, upon which to hang Mordecai. However, God wins again! He intervenes, and Haman will hang there, instead of Mordecai. Read Esther 7:1-10. In light of grace and forgiveness, was God's justice served? Why or why not?

9. For further thought, in light of Esther 7:8-9, do you think the King's anger was escalated by Haman's inappropriate behavior? Why or why not? Describe his inappropriate behavior below.

Meditation
Esther 7:10 So they hanged Haman on the gallows that he had prepared for Mordecai.
Then the king's wrath subsided.

Esther: Destiny Fulfilled

Day Five: How Did God's Love Redeem It All?

Memory Verse: Esther 4:16 "Go, gather all the Jews who are present in Shushan, and fast for me; neither eat nor drink for three days, night or day. My maids and I will fast likewise. And so I will go to the king, which is against the law; and if I perish, I perish!"

Talk about victory! In keeping with Persian law, all property of traitors became part of the royal treasury - regardless. Ultimately, this would be good news for Mordecai. The King gave Haman's estate to Esther, and she passed it on to Mordecai. The results? Mordecai reigned over the house of Haman! And last, but not least, the King's signet ring was removed from Haman's hand and placed directly upon Mordecai's. Not only was Haman's evil plot reversed, but the one he sought to destroy came into possession of all that he had possessed. Makes me smile to think about it. You know I love a story with a good twist, and what a twisty-turn we have in the book of Esther. God wins again! His justice prevailed. As always, it's perfect.

1. Read Esther 8:1-4. Esther made a plea before the King. What humble posture does she assume and how does the King graciously respond?

2. What does Queen Esther request in Esther 8:5-6?

v. 5

v. 6

Women of the Bible and God's Redeeming Love

3. Read Esther 8:7-8. Verse 8 authorizes something pretty amazing. What does this verse provide? Does it overrule the King's previous edict of Haman or is it a counter-decree?

4. A decree was issued from India to Ethiopia, all 127 provinces. List the noteworthy points of Esther 8:12-14.

v. 12

v. 13

v. 14

5. Fill in the blanks from Esther 8:15-17.

v. 15 So_____went out from the presence of the king in royal apparel of _____ and white, with a great _____ of _____and a garment of _____ and purple; and the city of Shushan _____ and was glad.

v. 16 The Jews had light and gladness, joy and _____.

v. 17 And in every province and city, wherever the king's command and decree came, the Jews had _____ and _____, a _____ and a _____. Then many of the people of the land became _____, because _____ _____ _____ _____ fell upon them.

Prayerfully review the above passages. Consider how satisfying this must have been to all the Jews of Persia. Do you see God's mercy in these verses? Esther's parents and many others had decided not to return to Jerusalem and, instead, remained in exile. But God lavished His love and blessings upon them anyway. How amazing! Even in their self-imposed exile, God poured out His love, His favor, and His blessings. The story concludes with the Jews revenge over their oppressors.

6. Read Esther 9. Record the amazing highlights of Esther 9:4-5 below.

v. 4

v. 5

Read the remainder of Esther 9 to discover the further revenge Queen Esther requests. Commentators suggest God used this pagan King to eliminate the Amalekites as He had required in Exodus 17. God can and will use anyone available to accomplish His plan. Remember, Esther is a book of God's divine providence. Finally, a thousand years later the feud was ended. God's people remained in Sushan and experienced great peace and joy.

Let's review Queen Esther's instructions: "…according to the written instructions and according to the prescribed time, that these days should be remembered and kept throughout every generation, every family, every province, and every city, that these days of Purim should not fail to be observed among the Jews, and that the memory of them should not perish among their descendants." (Esther 9:27-28).

Epilogue.

To this very day, Purim continues. Jews worldwide read the book of Esther, annually, and practice its prescribed standards. Purim, a day of feasting and gladness, was instituted as follows. "… as the days on which the Jews had rest from their enemies, as the month which was turned from sorrow to joy for them, and from mourning to a holiday; that they should make them days of feasting and joy, of sending presents to one another and gifts to the poor." (Esther 9:22).

What about Esther?

Queen Esther finished well because her heart was devoted to God, and we have no reason to assume otherwise. Esther delighted to see the advancement of her beloved Mordecai. At long last, she revealed her identity. The King became aware of her Jewish heritage and loved her all the more. He showed his express love and devotion by elevating Mordecai and launching a worldwide celebration, Purim, in her honor. It appears that all's well that ends well. With no secrets hidden, her heart was pure before God and her husband. Together, they were free to love each other well and finish strong, ruling side by side in Persia.

What About Mordeai?

What about Mordecai? This passages below sum it up succinctly. God prevailed; good triumphed over evil - again! Not only was Esther blessed, and all the Jews of the kingdom, but Mordecai as well. God raises up and takes down leaders. (Daniel 2:21.) Good things inevitably come to those who wait upon the Lord and obey Him. According to God's word, Mordecai was blessed:

"And King Ahasuerus imposed tribute on the land and on the islands of the sea. Now all the acts of his power and his might, and the account of the greatness of Mordecai, to which the king advanced him, are they not written in the book of the chronicles of the kings of Media and Persia? For Mordecai, the Jew was second to King Ahasuerus, and was great among the Jews and well received by the multitude of his brethren, seeking the good of his people and speaking peace to all his countrymen." (Esther 10:1-3).

Meditation
Esther 10:3 For Mordecai the Jew was second to King Ahasuerus, and was great among the Jews and well received by the multitude of his brethren, seeking the good of his people and speaking peace to all his countrymen.

Notes: Esther - Destiny Fulfilled

Gomer

Gomer: Perpetual Prostitute

If you're married, chances are, it was not an arranged marriage. More than likely, you met in the traditional sense through an encounter, friends, or a blind date. Perhaps you first noticed one another in the course of everyday life - at church, the gym, or at work. There is no formula for finding the "one" God has for you. Typically, He brings your mate into your life at the most unexpected time, when you're not looking for a mate, or when you're too busy even to notice – that is, initially.

It's been interesting to discover God's unlimited resourcefulness to unite couples. Remember, He's always at work and uses everything to accomplish His purposes. Things like placing two people in the right place at the right time, (even though one of them made a wrong turn, or so they thought), or closing one door and opening another. He can change our location by changing our circumstances. A corporate downsize can look tragic, but it might position you not only for the job of your dreams but the man of your dreams as well. The bottom line is God moves us, spiritually and naturally. Things like a career change, a relocation, even something as simple as a trip to the grocery store or a new church can place you precisely in the right spot to encounter the love that's waiting for you. Sometimes our destiny is right around the corner. Anyway, you get what I'm saying. Over the years, it's been fascinating to discover the ways and circumstances by which God brings us together.

Here are a few examples. I once knew twins who married each other's twin. Their meeting was assured. I know of a girl who met her future husband on an airplane – in the next seat. One transatlantic flight was enough to connect their hearts. I knew a sweet girl who married the boy next door - literally. Their parents had been lifelong friends who watched their future son and daughter-in-law grow up right under their noses. I found that interesting. God strategically placed them next door to one another where their acquaintance was unavoidable. I once knew a nurse who married her patient's son. His tender concern and care for his mother undoubtedly got her attention. It ultimately won her heart. I knew a professor who married his teaching assistant – not immediately, but that's how they met. I heard of a barista who had a client drive ten miles out of the way – every day – merely to buy her coffee. Ultimately, a dialogue began – I assume over coffee beans, and the rest is history. The funny thing is, he never liked coffee. But, he became a faithful consumer to be in her presence. I've known lawyers who married former clients, and doctors – likewise with former patients or their nurses.

More than once, I've known in-laws who married the surviving spouse of the other in law. It just happened to one of my dearest friends who'd been widowed and believed she'd never love like that again, or marry. "But God," said otherwise. They are blissfully happy! Their story is beautiful and genuinely romantic. Who would have thought so? They're both in their late 60's! And just once, I met a widow who married the best friend of her eldest son. Now that's unique, probably the most distinctive of all. Although many years separated them, age was a non-issue. They were both missionaries called to prayer ministry in Jerusalem. When I met them, they had been married twenty years! Her hair was a creamy snow white, and she looked like an angel. Everyone loved her, and their love and devotion were unmistakable. They adored one another; it was apparent. Together, their work and Godly influence touched and changed lives! They were quite a unique team, indeed.

Regardless of the circumstances, when God brought couples together, they had chemistry! As a result, they were drawn to one another and looked for opportunities to be together. Over time, love bloomed, and ultimately, they were married. That's the way it goes for the majority of us. God simply does it!

Called To Love.

However, that's not the case with Gomer and her husband, Hosea. They are an unlikely couple and the focus of this week's study. We will watch their story unfold as Hosea answers God's outrageous call to marry a prostitute, and they begin their life together. Although their story ends beautifully, it gets off to a shaky, shameful, and sinful beginning. It was a rough go for quite some years, but God is faithful. That won't surprise you, if you know, personally, of His faithfulness. The entire story unfolds under a canopy of God's love and amazing grace.

When I read the Book of Hosea to write this lesson, I was stunned – again. I'm always stunned when I study about Hosea and Gomer! Not by the outrageous behavior of Gomer, or because God asked Hosea to marry a prostitute. Instead, I'm overwhelmed by the abundance of Hosea's unrequited love and grace-filled forgiveness. It seems his well of goodness knows no end. Sound familiar? It reminds me of the unfailing love and grace we have in Jesus. That's right, even when our behavior is outrageous and we have run after other loves and other lovers - as we all have - He is faithful, still. He is always waiting with open arms to receive us and forgive us. Regardless of the sin.

A Picture Of Christ.

In Hosea, we find a picture and type or a foreshadow of Jesus. The parallels are remarkable. In mercy which mirrors Jesus, Hosea forgave his bride, again and again. No matter what she did, or how she sinned, Hosea's love was deeper still. With passionate love and determination, he kept pursuing her, and kept after her, through all her follies and adulterous missteps, until at last, he had her. That's worth repeating. He never stopped pursuing his bride. That is, until, he exclusively won her heart. She was the prize; she was the goal. She was the conquest; she was his mission. She was the joy set before him. Sound familiar? You're that same joy. Did you know that? Even if no one has ever told you, you are Jesus' joy. You were the joy set before Him when He endured the cross. The last moments before He slipped into eternity; you were in His heart and on His mind. We'll visit that momentarily.

The Love Of God.

The Book of Hosea is a picture of God's amazing love for Israel, an adulterous, idolatrous, unthankful, complaining, and stiff-necked people - the lot them, with a few exceptions scattered throughout history. Two immediately come to mind. First, Enoch, who "walked with God and was taken," and Esther, whom we studied last week. There were others, too. And, of course, our Lord Jesus! He walked among men, yet, He was perfect. Lest we forget, He was the incarnate God made flesh, born for the deliverance of all humanity. What we have pictured before us, is a real-life story of Israel's (and our) unfaithfulness against the backdrop of God's faithfulness. Gomer's story illustrates God's unfailing, grace, mercy, and forgiveness. All of which is rooted in love. That's who God is - LOVE.

We've talked about the love of God in every lesson. You can't study the Bible, even the Old Testament, without discovering His love - it's everywhere. It's His story, and He wrote it, so naturally, His love is exposed. From the first word to the very last, the Bible is a heightened revelation of Jesus, who loved us enough to die for us. As Paul explained in Romans, "But God demonstrates His love toward us, in that while we were still sinners, Christ died for us." (Romans 5:8). How astounding is that? When we were God-haters running after everything imaginable in the world, and away from God, Jesus died for us! In your place, literally. We can see it clearly in scripture. God loved us and died for us. "For God so loved the world that He gave His only begotten Son, that whoever believes in Him should not perish but have everlasting life." (John 3:16). I've told you already; God is love. (1John 4:8 and 4:16).

Author and Holocaust survivor, Corrie Ten Boom, knew God's love firsthand. It kept her through hell on earth at Ravensbrück concentration camp. She had much to say about God's love, here's one example. "There is no pit so deep, that God's love is not deeper still." Look at that again. Now, prayerfully consider the following. Are you running from God? Are you sinning, knowingly, and hiding from God? Are you in a bottomless pit? If so, God's love is deeper and more profound - even still! And thankfully, He will pursue you until He has you. No matter what it takes - no matter how we've sinned, no matter where we've wandered, and no matter how much we've cheated - He aims to save! Thankfully, none of us are beyond His love, His reach, and His amazing grace. That's right - He adores us, fig leaves and all!

They Counted The Cost.

Surely the triune Godhead counted the cost within the Trinity. As I meditated and prayed about Gomer and Hosea, I considered the enormous cost God and Jesus suffered to ransom us, yet they were willing. Even then, they had foreknowledge of our adulterous behavior, stubborn mindsets, prideful attitudes, and wicked - evil hearts. And, sometimes the most unthinkable - the outright rejection of God!

As we move through our lesson, you will see Gomer's repeated outright rejection of Hosea. It's no wonder, with each episode of rejection and rebellion I saw God's love and grace clearly, against the backdrop of God's law. Paul defined it like this. "Moreover the law entered that the offense might abound. But where sin abounded, grace abounded much more, so that as sin reigned in death, even so grace might reign through righteousness to eternal life through Jesus Christ our Lord." (Romans 5:20-21).

I hope you can see God's unfathomable love in those verses. If not, look again. Just in case you don't get the real meaning of the passage, outlined simply, it's this. The Law was given as a schoolmaster to show us our sin. The law showed us the truth, that is, God's holy standard. And, that my friend, is the only standard which matters. Not my opinion on right and wrong or what's politically correct or what isn't. No, not at all. Only what God has said truly matters. His Word will remain and endure long after the mountains melt like wax. I'll repeat it, only God's opinion counts. In the end, you won't be judged by what your neighbor thought about you, or what your spouse or your kids thought - either, for that matter. Only what God has said will ultimately matter.

In that sense, The Ten Commandments were given to make us aware of right and wrong. It's like God drew a line in the sand and defined both sides. There were no gray areas either; right was right, and wrong was emphatically wrong. The Law showed us our trespasses by clearly identifying and unmasking our sin as well as our inherent sinful nature. Mercifully, where sin increased, God's remarkable gift of grace, which is His unmerited, undeserved favor surpassed it and increased all the more. That's amazing grace!

A Holy God knew we could never keep the law; only Jesus lived a sinless life. There was not one blemish on Him, although He was fully man when He lived among us. For the remission or forgiveness of sins, God has always demanded a suitable blood sacrifice. Our Lord Jesus was the perfect sacrifice. Moreover, He was willing and able! Only His blood was worthy to satisfy the wrath of God. To that end, Jesus died in our place. He hung on that tree for all humanity because it was God's plan.

Incidentally, the idea was born out of love in the Trinity, long before the world began. That's long before the first sin was ever committed. Why? God knew we'd never be able to save ourselves, but He was prepared to do it. Once the Law was given sin was identified, and our inability was exposed! Our need for a Savior revealed. That's why God sent His Son into the world because He loved us and desired to save us. Rejoice, your sin debt is paid. Jesus' righteousness is our righteousness to eternal life because we have believed in Him. That's our ticket to forgiveness, to freedom from guilt, to an outpouring of love that's unfathomable and inexhaustible, to unbroken reconciliation and fellowship with God — now and throughout eternity. Thanks to God, we are justified - declared not guilty, because we believe.

As we move forward in our study, keep God's love in mind. There is nothing you could have done to cause Jesus to love you more than He does, already has, and always will. His love is willing, able, and prepared, to forgive you and see you through! To put it in real time, let's look at a beautiful example of sin and disease in this fallen world, against the backdrop of God's grace and mercy, called love, that's deeper still.

Vulgar grace.

Simply defined, grace is the unmerited, undeserved favor of God. His grace is all over the Bible, in every chapter. You might say grace has captivated our hearts in that by grace through faith God saved us. (Ephesians 2:8). God's grace is not only amazing, its radical, and it perplexes us. Through the ages, volumes, and volumes have been written about saving grace. It has been preached about, prayed about and sung about since the Old Testament writings. You may recall, it was the topic of Miriam's Song of celebration and praise when the Israelites crossed the Red Sea. (See Exodus 15:21.)

Years ago, I came across the words of a repentant Catholic priest who died on April 12, 2013. His name was Brennan Manning. He is one of our favorite writers of all times, particularly my husband's. Although Father Brennan was a broken and sick man, He was God's man. He was loved by God, thoroughly, and he knew it. That's right; God loved him to perfection, warts and all. He exposed his heart of love and wonder of God through his many books. I believe, without a doubt, Father Brennan loved God as much as he possibly could. He understood God's grace - He got it. How so? He received it and graciously accepted it. He lived it through sickness and, ultimately, unto death. He loved God desperately, but he couldn't save himself. He knew God's Word, inside and out, he preached it for decades and wrote volumes and volumes about it. Nonetheless, he was still sick. Even in his illness, God used him powerfully.

His ministry of grace, worldwide, is remembered. He has touched the lives of many who serve as Christian leaders of this generation. Father Brennan knew he was forgiven much! Wholly and entirely – eternally! Do you? God's grace and forgiveness humbled him repeatedly. He wanted others to grasp the depth of God's amazing grace, that persevering grace, which held him through his sickness and sin. You might say, Father Brennan, loved much, too. So much so that he was willing to share his testimony of highs and lows - of pain, of shame, and sorrow everywhere he could. Not to expressly expose himself or his sin, instead, to magnify God's love and perfect grace. Father Brennan was a brittle alcoholic, and ultimately, he lost his earthly battle. But, in an instant, he was embraced and welcomed into heaven by the one who died for him – our Savior Jesus. Thinking on Father Brennan in light of God's incredible forgiveness and love brings the words of Jesus to mind. "Therefore I say to you, her sins, which are many, are forgiven, for she loved much. But to whom little is forgiven, the same loves little." (Luke 7:47).

Father Brennan understood the love and mercy called forgiveness. To that end, He spent his life sharing the love of God and God's profound mercy and grace wherever He sent him. He got it! He embraced God's grace! So does Hosea, and so will Gomer. Before we move forward, let me share his game-changing revelation about the love of God and His incredible grace. The following statement is just too perfect to neglect.

"My message, unchanged for more than fifty years, is this: God loves you unconditionally, as you are and not as you should be because nobody is as they should be."

He indeed got it, he understood and fully embraced God's grace. Those words come from the last book Father Brennan wrote before He entered God's presence. You won't be surprised to learn it's titled - *All Is Grace: A Ragamuffin Memoir.* If you're up for it, it's a marvelous read!

God's grace is not cheap grace either; it's marvelous grace - amazing grace! Father Brennan called it vulgar grace. It's the same grace which chooses to save the drunk in the gutter, and then lifts him up and makes him whole and complete. It's akin to the grace Jesus showered upon the Gerasene demoniac in Mark 5:1-20. When there was no hope and no help, he cried out loudly, in chains, day and night…then, grace came. He was delivered and became a marvelous witness, testifying throughout the region of Decapolis. Incidentally, this converted demoniac, formerly called Legion, was the first missionary Jesus ever sent out. As a result, many in the region were saved and healed.

That's grace. It's the same grace which saved you and me. It's the same grace which saved Paul. It's the same grace which saved all the disciples, and Billy Graham, and Mother Teresa, as well as presidents, kings, and queens. The same grace saves all those who live in captivity to sin, wherever they are. Mercifully, God's grace is no respecter of people. It's the same grace that will save our children, spouses, and unsaved family. In fact, it's the same grace that's been saving since the beginning of time. It's always been what it is today. Grace has never changed and never will. What it does change, however, is you. How marvelous, God's grace changes us!

From eternity past, God's electing love planned who would be His. He has been faithful to His plan. It has not changed, nor will it. He has known before the foundation of this world who would call upon the name of Jesus for salvation. His Spirit woos us, awakens us, and as God would have it, at the appointed time, guess what? We come to faith. Instantly, we are born of God's Spirit and our destiny changes. As I said before, we were headed one way, "but God" changed our destiny. He saved us! His grace through faith wiped away our sins because we believed. Now, we are heaven bound by way of this world which we are merely passing through.

Hosea Knew Grace.

I have said all this to set up this week's study. You will soon discover, our study of Gomer is the message of grace. It's always been the message of grace, mercy, and forgiveness. This grace is the life-shattering gift my heart received on a gurney in a hospital in August of 2002. I was a broken, rundown, scared, hopeless and helpless piece of humanity. I was a mess! I had been unloved and unlovable, shuffled about and discarded, I was all but forgotten, "but God" said otherwise. It was God's good pleasure and perfect and pleasing plan to pour His love and grace out on me. I didn't need a sermon or an altar call, and I didn't have a pastor ushering me to a prayer room. What I had was an authentic, life-changing, life-altering, staggering outpouring of grace and the revelation of Jesus Christ as Lord. I collided with God! He saved me - right then and there.

In the depths of despair and hopelessness, I'd taken an overdose because I wanted to die, "but God" had another plan. There it is! Did you see it? I had my "but God" moment! It changed my life. He spoke to my cold dead heart so distinctly. I felt His presence and immense unending love and forgiveness. It's as if He said, "I'm not finished with you yet! Don't give up on me; I've never given up on you! I will never leave you or forsake you!" That was it. I just knew that I knew that I knew. I had Christ in me, the hope of glory! From that moment forward, my life has been His. Like Esther, Sarah, Abraham, and all others of the faith, I received God's call, rose to meet my destiny, and I've never looked back. I must confess. I have no regrets whatsoever. God's grace by faith which saves us is the greatest gift of my life.

Who Is Gomer?

She was a living, breathing prophetic example of the spiritual condition of Israel - God's chosen people. You may recall God's thrilling showdown between Moses and Pharaoh which culminated in ten plagues, a Passover dinner, and a mass exodus from Egypt. We examined this story in our study of Miriam. God parted the Red Sea and millions of Israelites, and those who gleaned near walked through on dry land. Once their safety was secure, God released the waters, and it swallowed the enemy up. With exacting power and precision, The Red Sea claimed Pharaoh and all his horses, chariots, and soldiers as its own. These idolatrous, stiff-necked people I'm referencing in this lesson are these Israelites' descendants.

In real time, Gomer was the unfaithful wife of a man who loved her unconditionally. She is all of us, in some measure. Gomer was flat out, wide open running after the world and other lovers, with abandon. She was doing an excellent job of it, too! We all do, sometimes. Worldly pleasures will catch our roving eyes and cause us to fall. A favorite gospel song from 1997 reminds us, "we are prone to wander." God used Hosea's unconditional love and Gomer's pleasure-seeking, adulterous pursuits to mirror Israel's unholy pursuits and shameful idolatry, despite God's repeated profession of His unending love, protection, and provision. Similarly, I quite imagine as a loving husband, Hosea had done the same.

A Picture Of Faithfulness.

In our story, Hosea is a picture or symbol of God's love for Israel, and ultimately, us as well. The Israelites had seen God's deliverance and provision. Many had experienced it personally. However, they continued in willful defiance. I find it interesting, they were willing to take whatever grace God might offer when they called upon Him in crisis, and once delivered they returned to cultivating their interests and neglected God. He will deal with them through a harsh reprimand and temporary separation in Hosea chapter 2. You could say Israel's focus was the deliverance and not the deliverer! Sound familiar? But God always responded to them. That's mercy and grace! He continually came to their aid. With the crisis averted, they'd quickly return to unholy pursuits and shameful idolatry. Pretty thankless, isn't it? Nonetheless, unlike us, God is faithful. Paul reminds us, "If we are faithless, He remains faithful; He cannot deny Himself." (2 Timothy 2:13).

We're human. In our frail humanity, we are inclined to be selfish and self-seeking. We feed our flesh with what the eye sees. That's everything the world has to offer. The enemy is working overtime in these last days to set a delectable smorgasbord of sin before us – every day. It appears nothing, absolutely nothing, is off limits. But God does come to our aid when we call. Once delivered or rescued, we too, quickly forget God's marvelous deliverance.

You will recall the Israelites honeymooned with God only three short days after crossing The Red Sea. Then the bellyaching, murmuring, and complaining began. They longed for the world - in Egypt. Can you believe? They preferred to bake bricks without straw under the hot Egyptian sun, rather than follow God. They chose slavery under Pharaoh to a desert journey with Yahweh - the true and living God as their guide. How tragic. They missed their old life in the world, and all its tasty offerings. They wanted to be god, rather than submit to God. When their "Gethsemane moment" came and begged for a decision, as it always does, the lot of them opted out. They chose the world, and in the process, they shook their fists at Moses, the anointed man of God.

If left unchecked, our pleasures and pursuits will dominate us. Anything we long for more than God can quickly become an idol or idol worship if we're not careful. That's sin. The Lord Jesus knows this, but His grace and mercy are always right, always perfect, and still timely. Thank goodness, He sees our hearts! He knows, too, whose are His. To those, His keeping grace will endure until the end. He is patient with us, just like Hosea with Gomer. He is long-suffering, and His plans will succeed. Every last one of us will finish strong! He will see us through, and on that, you can rely.

An Unlikely Couple.

Let's examine God's command to Hosea.

When the Lord began to speak by Hosea, the Lord said to Hosea:

"Go, take yourself a wife of harlotry
And children of harlotry,
For the land has committed great harlotry
By departing from the Lord." (Hosea 1:2).

In this verse, the verbs, *"go take"* are a command. It appears God required Hosea to marry a prostitute. In Hosea 3:1, God repeats the directive, the words *"go again, love"* are imperative verbs as well. They, too, are commands or orders from God. God didn't say, "Hosea, if you don't mind, could you, or would you be willing to marry Gomer? Could you pray about it and get back to me?" That was not the case. These verses will require our attention. Our study guide will examine God's unexpected request concerning Hosea's future, and the challenges associated with His request.

When God commanded Hosea to marry a harlot, don't you know he was stunned? If his mother was still living, don't you know she was even more stunned? I'll just bet the news was met with a heated debate, flanked by discouragement and much argument. But, with biblical faith, he did it anyway. Lest I remind you, biblical faith is confident obedience to God's Word despite the circumstances or consequences. That's faith. At the moment, Hosea couldn't see the benefit, I'm sure. How could he?

Nonetheless, he was obedient to God's command. As I studied about Gomer, I was overwhelmed by Hosea's tender, unrequited love, and forgiveness. God gave Hosea the love he needed to succeed in his mission. He opened Hosea's heart and said, "Love her as I do," and Hosea did it. He truly loved Gomer, just as God loves us. And, Hosea forgave her just like God forgives us. Completely, over and over - again and again! Now, that's amazing grace.

Where Is Gomer In God's Redemption Story?

The Book of Hosea was primarily written to show God's love for His sinful people. Lest I remind you, that's all of us. It included the inhabitants of the northern kingdom of Israel and was written to them, and to God's people everywhere. It's a timeless story for humanity. Hosea wrote it, and the events recorded spanned 38 years and occurred between 753 and 715 B.C. Some have suggested Hosea was not a true story. I beg to differ. I have said before - I'm a literalist when it comes to scripture, and I believe with all my heart Hosea, and Gomer were real people, just like you and me. They were doing life in the northern kingdom until Hosea had a "but God" moment.

On what appeared to be an ordinary day, God spoke to Hosea and instructed him to marry a harlot. Here's where their journey began. For Hosea, it started when he said "yes" to God. For Gomer, it was quite a different story. Her "yes" appears to come from a divided heart.

Nonetheless, God handpicked her from the gutter, so to speak. In the end, it will prove to be the best blessing of her life, but it won't look like it in the beginning. She will push against God's grace which comes through her loving husband. She will accept his love and affection, and then reject it and run - repeatedly. From our text, it appears Hosea has done everything God has asked. He has showered her with love and affection, mercy and forgiveness. His love has endured, and Hosea remains faithful and steadfast, even though Gomer has not. After a fashion of Christ, He has loved her well, just like the Lord Jesus loves us. But, she ran to the world and took other lovers. Shameful – but, so have we.

A Prophet Of Love.

Who was this man who loved a harlot? Hosea was a prophet in ministry, serving, teaching and living in the northern kingdom known as Israel. I'm convinced Hosea did an exceptional job of loving Gomer because he has been characterized as a prophet of love. Nonetheless, Gomer will continue in a pattern of unfaithfulness. So, what's up with that? Our study guide will help us analyze their relationship in light of God's instructions to Hosea along with Israel's unfaithfulness.

Although this is Gomer's story, we cannot know it apart from Hosea's. Once united in marriage, the two became one flesh. As you already know, this is the closest relationship humans share this side of heaven. Like all husbands, Hosea will stand accountable for the state of their marriage. God chose Gomer to be Hosea's glory. In essence, Paul identified wives as their husband's glory. 1 Corinthians 11:7. In other words, we reflect their good standing, favorable reputation, and renown. Generally speaking, we agree with them and convey their opinion. At times, however, we don't fit the bill, do we? I know I fall far short myself. Eventually, Gomer would be it. But as our story opens, she needs to be made whole – she needs rescuing. From herself, first, and then from a terrible trap of sin swaddled in pain, self-loathing, and unworthiness.

Who was this man God called to love a harlot? Who was the man capable of such unfailing love? He is our model of Jesus. His name, *Hosea*, means *salvation*; the same thing as Jesus. A literal translation, *"Jehovah is salvation."* Pretty amazing, isn't it? What a beautiful picture of God's perfect and unfailing love for us.

A Broken Girl.

Gomer was a broken girl who felt unworthy of the love of a good man. How so? Only God knows. But for whatever reason, Gomer was unable, perhaps unwilling to receive the love of a good man. We know from scripture, Hosea was an honorable man. What could be better than marrying the prophet of love? Perhaps Gomer's unwillingness stemmed from a shameful past or fear of rejection or her inability to trust. How could she know and receive the love of a good man if she'd never known it? When we know the truth, the lie is exposed. Until then, we are unable to see clearly. Knowing and believing God's truth always sheds light on the lies of the enemy. God's Word is our first line of defense against the enemy. Remember, Jesus battled Satan in the wilderness armed only with God's Word. It was more than enough! (See Matthew 4:1-11; Mark 1:12-13; and Luke 4:1-4).

I believe with all my heart, Gomer's feelings of unworthiness and shame disqualified her from receiving true love or extending it in return. She was incapable. We can't give what we don't have. You can't draw water from a dry well. My grandmother used to say, "You can't get blood out of a turnip!" Where no potential exists, none is realized. Gomer was empty - void, except for pain, unworthiness, and self-loathing. Something deep within her was broken and empty. She was void of hope and possessed an insatiable desire for comfort and peace. She longed for it; she craved it. She searched for it, literally running after it. She needed love but didn't recognize it when she had it. Only God could heal her deep wounds. Only His love could enable her to know, give, and receive authentic love.

We live in a world gripped by the enemy and every evil thing imaginable. It's not heaven yet! People, although sometimes well-meaning, hurt us and leave us bruised and scarred. They will use us up, take what they want, and then discard us tattered and worn. How do I know? It's my story - perhaps it's yours as well. "But God" can heal the hurts and fill the void of emptiness and despair. Within every heart, there is a God-sized, God-shaped hole waiting and longing for God. Whether you know it or not, nothing else will satisfy. Could you possibly be waiting for Him to fill yours?

What Did Gomer Get Right?

Gomer's name is not mentioned again after Hosea chapter 3. She was full and satisfied. The full-time mother of three and the wife of a prophet. Gomer, no doubt, had her hands full. Commentators speculate Hosea does not mention Gomer, again, as an example of what God would do to the northern kingdom if they continued in rebellion. He would put them away in isolation.

What Did Gomer Get Wrong?

We've already stated the obvious. Gomer did a lot things wrong. She was unfaithful to her husband and played the harlot. Truthfully, Gomer was a harlot when he found her. She was what God ordered. She never pretended to be something she wasn't. She dared to be herself. I found that tidbit refreshing. She never hid who she was. Gomer was real. She wasn't wearing fig leaves! Gomer was in touch with who she was, and lived it out, unlike the Pharisees. In essence, she said, "I am not faithful" ...and, then she followed through.

And, so did Hosea. He received God's command and followed through, executing his call to perfection. How amazing! I find it thrilling, Hosea truly loved her. That was the bonus. He loved her as Christ has loved us, with an everlasting love. Paul issued husbands a biblical command in Ephesians 5: "Husbands, love your wives, just as Christ loved the church and gave himself for her..." (Ephesians 5:25). I don't honestly believe Gomer could have done anything wicked enough for him to forsake her - truly, I don't. Hosea would love her, wholly and exclusively, until he drew his last breath. It was what God had asked of him, and the prophet of love would be found faithful. We must remember, God will never ask something of us which we are unprepared to accomplish. He will equip you for the call – every task, large or small. God plans for our success! Hosea would effectively model Jesus to his unfaithful wife, up close and personal, every day. He would love her until He had her. He would display and dispense God's unfailing love, despite her behavior. That was Hosea's call.

Hosea 2 mirrors God's relationship with his unfaithful wife, Israel. Gomer's unfaithfulness is exposed right along with Israel's adulterous behavior. Through these passages, God openly addresses their sin. He tells it like it is, and uses Gomer's sinful lifestyle as a living example. What a visual! We must remember, forgiveness, restoration, and salvation is always God's focus.

This story may feel very familiar to some of you, I found it so. In fact, I got a lot of things wrong in my life. I came to faith later than some, but at God's appointed time. So naturally, I had years to run after pleasures and pursuits and encountered heartaches and disappointments on both the giving and receiving end.

When my husband vowed to love me like Christ loved His church, I'll confess, I was uncertain. Not because I didn't think he meant it, but because I had known unfaithful love on both sides. I feared being hurt or hurting him. But, I'll have to admit, to the best of his ability he has done an exceptional job. I was so stunned by his proposal, that initially, I declined. I felt unworthy of the love he confessed. I was fearful and doubtful that anyone could truly love me, "but God," said otherwise. I have known firsthand, the love of a good man - God's man, who was called to love a harlot!

Lost And Found.

Gomer was broken and lost, until Hosea came for her. It is clear, they were no longer together, but scholars disagree on whether or not he divorced her. I believe Hosea had put her away, just like God had temporarily done Israel in Hosea 2:2-13. However, God will display His grace and mercy in Hosea 2:14-23. His last reassuring words of affection to Israel from v. 23:

> "...And I will have mercy on her who had not obtained mercy;
> Then I will say to those who were not My people,
> 'You are My people!' And they shall say, 'You are my God!' " (Hosea 2:23).

Helpless, hopeless, and lost was Gomer. "But God" spoke words of mercy, restoration, and salvation in Hosea 3:1, instructing Hosea, *"Go again, and love"* ...*Gomer*. So, she was indeed lost and hopeless until the day she had a "but God" encounter with her husband. Once again, she would be the recipient of God's amazing grace! Hosea had come to the slave market hoping to find her. Her identity had been exposed, and Hosea was alerted to her whereabouts. How so? The details are not disclosed in scripture.

Nonetheless, can you imagine how Hosea felt when he found his bride in the slave market? Gomer had hit bottom. She was in a low place, spiritually and naturally. Perhaps weary from running, and out of desperation, she sold herself into slavery. "But God" had other plans for her. Just like He did for you and me. And, wonder of wonders, Hosea came and purchased her, redeemed her just as God commanded. Without shame and apology, he stepped right up and said in essence, "I'll take the little filly right there - Yes, the cutie with the brown eyes and worn and weathered look! I'm into frail and helpless. Yes, sir! She's the one for me!"

I picture him riding up on a white horse in heroic, John Wayne-ish type fashion. Genuinely gallant and incredibly romantic! (I told you I'm a hopeless romantic.) But, who doesn't need a little romance along the way? We are like Gomer in some measure. We're all in need of rescuring and redeeming, and Hosea did it. He ransomed his bride - he paid the price. Our worn-out Gomer was the love of his life! It's interesting to note Hosea could see what the world had missed. They saw her sin and screw-ups, "but God" enabled Hosea to see far beyond her mistakes and shame. God empowered Hosea to love an ungodly woman in a Godly fashion, wholly and entirely. How amazing! That's a love which gives and gives, asking nothing in return. After a pattern and type of Christ's sacrificial, unfailing love, Hosea's love was not performance-based either. Gomer didn't need to earn Hosea's love; she already had it - exclusively.

Dying For love.

When Hosea purchased Gomer, it confirmed he truly loved her – regardless. He didn't care about her yesterdays or her failures. He loved her, with abandon, and in an instant, her heart knew it. Hosea's actions said, "Gomer, I love you, regardless – you'll always be the one for me! I am hopelessly and helplessly head over heels in love with you!" Her heart heard, "I see you, I know you, and I love you – totally and forever, not as you should be, but just as you are!" It was real, it was passionate, it was purposeful, and it was tender. But above all, it was God's plan.

Hosea didn't care what anyone else said or thought about it, and at long last she got it. How great was his love? He was dying to have her, to rescue her, to pay the penalty to free her. Now, holding her in his arms, he was complete – his heart was whole and satisfied. No price would have been too much to redeem her, but the price Hosea paid was really quite small. It was the cost of an ordinary slave: fifteen shekels of silver and one and one-half homers of barley.

That's approximately 6 ounces of silver and 9 bushels of barley. Numbers 5:15 sheds some light on the emancipation price. The sum was the amount due for one accused of adultery. Interestingly, some commentators believe Gomer was enslaved for her illicit sexual activity, while others think she sold herself into slavery when she hit rock bottom. Either way, Hosea paid a pitifully small amount to redeem his bride. How much? The total price was about 30 shekels of silver.

If the price rings a bell or sounds familiar, it's because Judas received the same measly amount in exchange for Jesus. For the price of an ordinary slave, our Lord Jesus was sold and betrayed by Judas, the son of perdition. How much would our emancipation from slavery ultimately cost Jesus? It would require everything Jesus could give! Down to His last drop of royal blood. Giving His very life, Jesus paid it all.

If you're feeling unlovable or worthless, take heart. You are worth everything to Jesus. When Hosea paid the slave price, Gomer was no longer worth much to anyone except him. But, to him she was everything! She was the prize and the joy set before Him. He loved her just as God loved Israel - just as Jesus has loved you and me. Hosea's love was real, it was radical, and it was lasting. His love said, "I love you, you're worth everything to me."

How Did God's Love Redeem It All?

He sent the perfect mate to redeem a willful, adulterous wife who was looking for love in all the wrong places. God sent Hosea to save her because she couldn't save herself, and He aims to save. That's His plan from before the foundation of the world. He will not stop short of having those who are His. How fitting, how perfect, how amazing? What grace! This Old Testament book paints the most beautiful picture of God's love that never dies and pursues us until He has us.

When I was on that gurney in the hospital, I wasn't worth much to anyone either - no one was there for me. "But God" sent the most unlikely person just in the nick of time. He knew what I needed to come to faith. He sent a friend of the family, and she was there, but not one of those whom I had served to the best of my ability. Instead, so I could see the full measure of His love and grace, He sent someone I had treated unkindly, at times. Someone I had taken advantage of, at times. Someone whose feelings I had ignored, at times. "But God" used her most profoundly. She loved me in spite of me. She sang over me and prayed over me - she loved me into the Kingdom. I owe her a great deal. She is part of my salvation story! We are friends, true friends, today, even still. When there was no one left to love me, Jesus sent someone who knew my pride, my selfishness, my conceit, my sin - she knew it all, and she loved me still. The best words my ears ever heard were this. "Hang on, Jesus loves you. Your children need you; God's not finished with you yet."

In The Arms Of A Savior.

Can you get a visual of Hosea surrounded by slaves, holding Gomer in his arms, and saying, "Hang on, I'm not letting you go… ever! I have paid the price, and I love you with an everlasting love. Your children need you. God's not finished with you yet!"

I can; I've been right there. Hosea - which means, *Jehovah is salvation,* has come. Ladies, it's an individual thing, and I believe salvation came to Gomer on that very day, at that very moment. Do others agree? Some do. But I know Jesus is in the business to save the broken, the beat up, the used up, the forgotten and the neglected. He loves the marginalized! She was all of the above, and He aims to save! Sometimes we need rescuing from ourselves – first. I did, so have others, and I believe Gomer did too. Thank goodness, He is the God of Everyman – regardless. Whenever, wherever, Jesus loves the sinner, no matter how dirty, how sinful or how small. He is the God of all. What a savior!

God Of All.

Remember, Jesus could have had a royal birth, but He was born to poor Jews instead. We'll be looking at their fantastic story next week, but suffice it to say, Jesus' parents were two nobodies from nowhere. Jesus was born a poor carpenter's son. How poor? Very! Their temple offering at His dedication was one reserved for the poor. (See Leviticus 12:8). Next week's lesson will unpack the details.

Nonetheless, when Mary was advanced in her pregnancy, she and Joseph traveled to Bethlehem to participate in the first census, as ordered by Ceasar Augustus. Along the way, her labors began. They couldn't beg a room in the inn when her pains heightened, and His birth was imminent. Instead, a dirty stable welcomed them. After His birth, our little Lord Jesus was placed in a bed of straw called a manger. You can't get more common or ordinary than that. That was our Lord's humble beginning. And, when He paid our sin debt, He did so between two common thieves on a cross.

Our King Jesus came and went the same way. No fanfare - not flanked by nobility or pomp and circumstance. In fact, before His end finally came, even His disciples had fled. Alone and nailed to a cross, our Lord Jesus died. He did so for every man - for all of humanity - because God so love the world and that was the plan from eternity past. Our Lord Jesus has paid it all. When Jesus said, "It is finished!" He meant it. These powerful words were rooted in love, just like Hosea's. Gomer's heroic rescue and passionate acquisition is a picture and type of Jesus securing His bride, the Church. Rejoice, like Gomer. We are free from sin and bondage. Free from all shame and regret. It's all gone, settled, wiped away and forgotten, as far as the east is from the west. That's the good news, that's the gospel. Jesus loved us and died to save us. We are totally, and utterly LOVED and FORGIVEN. His blood has ransomed us. We are the Beloved's, and the Beloved is ours!

Just As You Are.

I believe when Hosea held Gomer in the slave market that day, it was truly settled and finished. The fight was over, and the battle won the moment her heart believed. That would be the moment her heart was convinced what his eyes said were true. Damp with tears, and twinkling with delight and the joy of victory and accomplishment, his eyes said "Now that I've found you, I'm never letting you go. You're mine, and I love you, not as you should be, but just as you are!" Rejoice, we are loved the same by our merciful God!

Hosea is one of my favorite Old Testament books. That's because it's all about God's grace. The Book of Hosea is God's way of letting us know His forgiveness knows no boundaries; it is unlimited just like His love. If you are struggling or running and hiding, it is my prayer God rescue you and reclaim you as His own. He is willing and able to pay the price. He would say to you today, "I love you with an everlasting love! Your yesterdays don't matter to me. I have found you, and I'm never letting you go!"

I am so thankful that the hounds of heaven chased me until God caught me! Of all the blessings in my life, knowing Jesus - being His - is the best blessing. If you've fallen into the trap of this world, call upon Jesus. He will faithfully come! Ladies, look up, your redemption draws near!

Be blessed this week as you study Gomer: Perpetual Prostitute

Next week - Mary: The Virgin Mother

Gomer's story is found in Hosea 1:1-3:5

Gomer: Perpetual Prostitute

Day One: Who Is Gomer?

Memory Verse: Hosea 1:2 When the Lord began to speak by Hosea, the Lord said to Hosea: "Go, take yourself a wife of harlotry And children of harlotry, For the land has committed great harlotry By departing from the Lord."

As we begin our study of Gomer, we come to a dark period in the history of God's people. Our study will examine those living in the northern kingdom of Israel during the latter days of King Jeroboam II. Hosea received his call to ministry near the end of a prosperous, but morally declining time in Israel's history. Although the upper classes seemed to be experiencing prosperity, they were oppressing the poor and running after false gods. The book of Hosea highlights the parallels between his relationship with Gomer, his bride, and God's relationship with the nation of Israel. Covenantal promises bind both; however, both brides are unfaithful. Nonetheless, God and Hosea will demonstrate constant and persistent unfailing love.

1. Throughout scripture God has made some unusual requests of His prophets. What curious command does God make in Hosea 1:2? How does Hosea respond?

2. Using a dictionary, define *harlot*. In your opinion, is this a suitable match for a prophet?

3. Read Hosea 1:2 again. Everything God does has purpose. Thinking biblically, what was the purpose of this request? Do you see the answer within the verse? Write the verse, underline the answer.

4. From the original language, the word *"Go"* was a common verb in the imperative mood or tense; it was a command. Understanding the meaning of the word, do you believe Hosea could refuse? Why or why not?

"Go...take." The two verbs together form a command which requires a response – Hosea's. It's interesting to see the command, *go*, followed by the command, *take*, within this verse. The word *take* in Hebrew is *qah*. In our text, they form the compound word *laqah* which means, *take (get, fetch), lay hold of (seize), receive, acquire (buy), bring, marry (take a wife), snatch (take away).*[11] Note the words, *"take a wife,"* within the definition.

5. Hosea got the message; God was speaking clearly. Although God's request appears unthinkable, Hosea obeyed. He chose God's way. Have you made a difficult decision to obey God even though it appeared strange to others? You are invited to share.

---

[11] Kaiser, W. C. (1999). 1124 חקל. R. L. Harris, G. L. Archer Jr., & B. K. Waltke (Eds.), *Theological Wordbook of the Old Testament* (electronic ed., p. 481). Chicago: Moody Press.

Women of the Bible and God's Redeeming Love

Commentators have long debated the reality of Hosea's relationship to Gomer. Is this a real story and if so, how could God require a man in ministry to marry an immoral woman? Here are some things to consider. First, Leviticus 21:14 prohibits the marriage of a priest and a prostitute. Note: Hosea was a prophet, not a priest. Nowhere in scripture does it suggest he was serving in the temple or synagogue. There is a distinct difference between prophet and priest. A prophet was an individual called and anointed by God who received and delivered God's inspired message. Next, some Bible scholars suggest Gomer may not have been immoral before their marriage. They assert Hosea 2:1 merely alerted Hosea to what was coming in the future. I believe Hosea married a prostitute. Either way, Hosea was obedient and married Gomer. God chose to use Hosea and his adulterous marriage to speak a powerful warning to Israel concerning its spiritual adultery. Remember, God will use extreme measures to restore us spiritually!

6. Read Hosea 2:1. The couple will be blessed with children. How are they described?

7. Gomer is the daughter of Diblaim. As with other Hebrew names, the definition reflects the character of the person. The meaning of *Diblaim* is *double layers of grape cake or two raisin cakes; double embrace.* On the surface, that doesn't tell us much, but more in-depth research does. The name depicts someone given over to sexual desires or the need or urges for the gratification of the senses sexually. Gomer would prove to be her father's daughter. The apple didn't fall far from the tree. Read Proverbs 22:6. What does this verse tell us about our God-given responsibility to our children?

Meditation
Proverbs 22:6 Train up a child in the way he should go, And when he is old he will not depart from it.

Gomer: Perpetual Prostitute

Day Two: Where Is Gomer In God's Redemption Story?

Memory Verse: Hosea 1:2 When the Lord began to speak by Hosea, the Lord said to Hosea: "Go, take yourself a wife of harlotry And children of harlotry, For the land has committed great harlotry By departing from the Lord."

Hosea's role was to show the northern kingdom's unfaithfulness to God. Instead of remaining faithful to their husband and provider, they had married themselves to Baal and other gods of Canaan. Hosea's message warned unless they repented of their sin and turned back to God, their destruction was imminent. The northern kingdom was plagued by religious apostasy, political intrigue, and foreign alliances. All of which were displeasing to God.

1. Hosea knew Gomer would be unfaithful. But, he obeyed God's command and married her anyway. Her immoral behavior was not only hurtful and humiliating, but it soon became public knowledge. God's prophet repeatedly dealt tenderly with his wife despite her sin and its painful consequences. Under Mosaic law, divorcing Gomer was an option, but in Christ-like fashion, Hosea dispensed mercy instead. It's a beautiful picture which demonstrates the Lord's tender dealings with us. Can you recall a time when you expected harsh consequences and received God's abundant grace instead?

2. Between 753 and 715 B.C. Israel was ruled by six kings who were particularly wicked. They promoted heavy taxes, oppression of the poor, idol worship, and total disregard for God. When leadership has no regard for God, the people suffer. It is no wonder the people, including Gomer, despaired and adopted lifestyles which dishonored God. Read Judges 21:25. Record the verse below.

Judges 21:25 _____

_____

3. In Hosea 1:3-4, a son is born. What do they name him and what does it mean?

4. Gomer conceived and birthed a daughter in Hosea 1:6. What name was she given and what does it mean?

5. Read Hosea 1:8-9. Gomer conceived again. After weaning her daughter, she bore a son. What name was he given and what does it mean?

6. God is writing a fascinating message to Israel through the names of Hosea's children. With the birth of Lo-ammi, God administers the final blow. *Lo-ammi* means *not My people*. In essence, God says, "I am not your God." A literal translation is "I am no longer 'I am' to you." These words symbolize God's rejection of Israel. The Israelites had known the I AM of God since Exodus 3. How do you think they felt when they heard these painful words? How might you feel?

7. God will restore. He is merciful in all His ways. Read Romans 9:26. Write the verse and underline the promise, as quoted by the apostle Paul in his letter to the Romans.

8. Read Hosea 1:10-11. In verse 10, God reaffirms the Abrahamic Covenant. Why is this significant to us? Does this give you comfort and hope? Why or why not?

9. Read and review Hosea 1:10-2:2. We see in these verses the grace and mercy of God. In spite of Israel's unfaithfulness and willful pride, He is faithful. God would save a remnant for Himself from Israel and Judah. Throughout history, God has preserved a remnant. He does so because it was His promise and He is a covenant-keeping God. Record your favorite verse to share about the faithfulness of God.

10. Abraham received the original promise. What was it? Read and record Genesis 22:17 below. We are forgetful, but God is not. Moreover, He will keep His covenant promises because God cannot lie; nor does He change His mind. He is faithful and true to His Word.

Review Hosea 1:10. For reinforcement and encouragement, underline the reoccurring words or phrases from Genesis 22:17 repeated in Hosea 1:10.

11. If you don't have a long history with the Lord, you may be uncertain of God's truthfulness. For reassurance, complete the old and new testament passages below.

Numbers 23:19 God is not a _____, that He should _____,

Nor a son of man, that He should _____. Has He said, and

will He not _____? Or has He spoken, and _____

_____ _____ make it good?

Remember, unlike people, God is faithful. Even when we are faithless, God is true to Himself.

2 Timothy 2:13 If we are _____, He remains

_____; He _____

_____ Himself.

Titus 1:2 in hope of eternal life which God, who _____

_____, promised before time began,…

Who was this God who commanded Hosea to marry a prostitute? Let's take a closer look at God's nature and character. When Moses cried out to God, he said: "Please, show me Your glory." (Exodus 33:18). God responded:

Then He said, "I will make all My goodness pass before you, and I will proclaim the name of the Lord before you. I will be gracious to whom I will be gracious, and I will have compassion on whom I will have compassion." (Exodus 33:19).

For fuller understanding, let's define Godly compassion: *rāḥam* means *love deeply; have mercy, be compassionate.* This root refers to deep love (usually of a "superior" for an "inferior") rooted in some "natural" bond. In the Piel [verb stem] it is used for the deep inward feeling we know variously as compassion, pity, mercy[12]

Let's look at the language and apply the definiton of compassion. In Exodus 33:19, as the created, we have a natural bond with God - our Creator. He (the superior) extends compassion on "whom (He) will" (the inferior) humanity - the created. That's us. We receive and enjoy the results and benefits of God's *compassionate* action. From the original language, the object (us, the created) of the Piel verb's action "suffers or enjoys the effect" of the action. We are changed, affected, or put into a state of being by this very action. *Notice, we have done nothing but receive.* Here we see the beauty of God's work revealed within the structure of the original Hebrew language. Amazing!

Next, God placed Moses in the cleft of the rock and passed by proclaiming the name of the Lord. The following morning, Moses met with God again. "Now the LORD descended in the cloud and stood with him there, and proclaimed the name of the LORD." (Exodus 34:5).

Below we find God's description of Himself. To this, and all of His Word, He is faithfully devoted – forever and ever - down to the last detail or jot and tittle. God cannot lie!

12. Complete God's description of Himself below:

Exodus 34:6-7 And the Lord passed before him and proclaimed, "The Lord, the Lord God,

_____ and _____,

_____, and abounding in _____

and _____,⁷ keeping _____ for

thousands, _____ _____ and

_____ and _____, by

no means clearing the guilty, visiting the _____ of the fathers upon the

children and the children's children to the _____ and the

_____ generation."

---

[12] Coppes, L. J. (1999). 2146 רחם. R. L. Harris, G. L. Archer Jr., & B. K. Waltke (Eds.), *Theological Wordbook of the Old Testament* (electronic ed., p. 841). Chicago: Moody Press.

Moses, God's man, the spiritual leader, and intercessor of Israel desired to know God better. To efficiently mediate and minister between God and His people, in Moses' mind this was essential. In essence, Moses said, "To represent you, effectively, I must see you and know more about you. I must know You will be with me." Moses had a tall task before him, and he knew full well without God's presence, they would never make it. Without the certainty God would "go before them," Moses wasn't going! God had *compassion* toward Moses and provided a beautiful picture of His essence, character, and nature. Thankfully, His living Word has preserved it permanently. As you conclude today's lesson, prayerfully review Exodus 34:6-7. In light of these words, settle the matter once and for all – Moses did. Upon hearing these words, Moses worshiped:

So Moses made haste and bowed his head toward the earth, and worshiped. Then he said, "If now I have found grace in Your sight, O Lord, let my Lord, I pray, go among us, even though we *are* a stiff-necked people; and pardon our iniquity and our sin, and take us as Your inheritance." (Exodus 34:8-9).

You are invited to prayerfully ask and answer the most significant question of this entire study:

Who is God and what's that to me?

Meditation
Hosea, 1:10 ...And it shall come to pass in the place where it was said to them,
'You are not My people,' there it shall be said to them, 'You are sons of the living God.'

Gomer: Perpetual Prostitute

Day Three: What Did Gomer Get Wrong?

Memory Verse: Hosea 1:2 When the Lord began to speak by Hosea, the Lord said to Hosea: "Go, take yourself a wife of harlotry And children of harlotry, For the land has committed great harlotry By departing from the Lord."

Today, we will study what Gomer did wrong. We will conclude our week of study on days four and five as we combine God's redemption with Gomer's repentance. What a fitting end to such a fantastic story. I heard it said many years ago, "Sinners make the best saints." How true!

1. Some Bible scholars suggest Hosea was not the biological father of Gomer's children. These words of Hosea 1:2, "children of harlotry," possibly support their claim. Regardless of her children's paternity, God used them as a visible expression of His utter displeasure with Israel. What does God's word teach us about adultery? Record a verse to share.

2. Read Hosea 2:2-13. God brings His charges against the spiritual adultery of Israel. Notice the detail with which God calls them out. He has left no stone unturned. He has specifically mentioned the overall unfaithfulness of the bride, and her relentless desire to pursue other lovers. As a final statement, God addresses Israel's biggest woe, "But Me she forgot." Israel abandoned God. Have you ever turned your back on God? You are invited to share.

3. Our God is a God of restoration and reconciliation. Always this is His aim. From the question above, if you abandoned God, how were you restored? Record a verse which highlights the beauty of God's restoration in your life.

4. Read Jeremiah 31:31-34. God revealed a new covenant through His faithful servant. These verses describe a new covenant with a spiritual and divine component. All those who knew God and called upon His name would participate in His blessing of salvation! In the space below, outline God's new covenant promises from each verse.

v. 31

v. 32

v. 33

v. 34

5. Read Hosea 2:18-20. God will do it. In these verses God gives the "I will…" pledge multiple times. Please list the promise from each verse below.

v. 18

Anne Nicholson

v. 19

v. 20

6. The grace of God is astounding. Even though Israel perpetually practiced spiritual adultery, God would restore them. What is more gracious than this? Read Genesis 12:1-9 to recall the promises of God to Abraham. Who was to bring the covenant to performance, God or Abraham? What does this mean to you?

7. We can all be thankful, God is a covenant-keeping God. Write a brief prayer of thanksgiving below. Praise Him now! You are invited to share your prayerful testimony which glorifies Him!

8. Although we are not given the details in scripture, Gomer was either forced into a life of servitude or voluntarily sold herself into slavery. Whichever the case may be, God will not leave her where she is. It is the same with us. He is the remedy, and He will come for those who are His. He had a plan for Gomer. He planned for her reconciliation to Hosea. His plan is beautiful. God used Hosea to pursue, save, and restore his bride. Is that not a picture of God's work on behalf of the redeemed, His bride – the Church? Read and record Ephesians 5:25 below to discover the depth of Christ's love for His Church.

9. Hosea came for Gomer. In Godly fashion, he pursued her until he found her! Repeatedly, Hosea revealed the depth of his unconditional love. Similarly, God wants to demonstrate His faithful, unconditional love for us. Especially when we feel unloved and unlovable. Are you familiar with God's steadfast, unconditional love? If so, you are invited to share.

10. To conclude today's study, read the parable of the lost sheep in Luke 15:1-7. Note the man's joy in finding his lost sheep. Can you imagine how much more Hosea's heart rejoiced when he discovered his lost bride? Feel the joy! Record Luke 15:6 below.

Meditation
Proverbs 18:22 He who finds a wife finds a good thing. And obtains favor from the Lord.

Gomer: Perpetual Prostitute

Day Four: What Did Gomer Get Right?

Memory Verse: Hosea 1:2 When the Lord began to speak by Hosea, the Lord said to Hosea: "Go, take yourself a wife of harlotry And children of harlotry, For the land has committed great harlotry By departing from the Lord."

There is nothing more beautiful than a sinner saved by grace, not because he or she is so beautiful, but because the grace of God is revealed! Today's study will look at the love of a man for an unworthy woman, behaviorally speaking. The truth of the matter is, Hosea would be faithful to the end. God had given him an assignment and planned for him to succeed. The results are amazing. Gomer would finally be made whole, her emptiness would be satisfied, and her unworthiness abolished. God was about to make all things new! What a marvelous God we serve.

1. Yesterday's lesson ended on a low note. Hosea's bride had hit rock bottom. To be restored, many of us must find rock bottom. At the end of us, God begins. Thanks be to God! What do you think occurred in Gomer to lead her to the sinful life she is living? Who was ultimately in control?

2. Have you or a family member ever experienced a "rock bottom" low? If so, what was the purpose and what was the outcome? Looking back, can you see the divine hand of God at work? For sharing, please record a verse which describes the sovereignty of God.

3. God would restore Israel. He is faithful even when we are faithless. Read and record the promise of 2 Timothy 2:13 below.

4. In one day's time, Israel will prostitute herself no more. God pledges marriage and provides the dowry. Watch closely. We, like Israel, bring nothing to the table. Our faithful God does it all. With increasing intensity, God declares His restoring love in Hosea 2:18-20. As the redeemed, we are the recipients of God's unlimited mercy and Godly compassion. That means we don't get what we truly deserve, neither did Gomer. On the contrary, we are the recipients of His unfailing love and abundant mercy and grace every moment of every day, just like Gomer. Although God asks nothing of us in return, Paul says that we have a reasonable service. Read Romans 12:1 to discover the desired reasonable service. Record Romans 12:1 below.

5. In Hosea 2:19 God lists four nouns to define how He intends to betroth us to Himself forever. List the nouns below and provide a definition for each in your own words.

1.

2.

3.

Anne Nicholson

4.

Recalling the promises of God not only keeps our focus on Him, but it also encourages our faith. Additionally, praying or claiming God's promises increases our knowledge of Him and keeps us adequately aligned with Him. It's interesting, as commanded by scripture (Deuteronomy 11:18) every orthodox Jew recites the following verses each time he places the phylacteries on his hands and forehead:

"Hear, O Israel: The Lord our God, the Lord is one! You shall love the Lord your God with all your heart, with all your soul, and with all your strength. And these words which I command you today shall be in your heart. You shall teach them diligently to your children, and shall talk of them when you sit in your house, when you walk by the way, when you lie down, and when you rise up. You shall bind them as a sign on your hand, and they shall be as frontlets between your eyes. You shall write them on the doorposts of your house and on your gates. (Deuteronomy 6:4-9).

The beautiful results? The love and mercy of God is always before them!

As New Covenant believers, God's law is written on our hearts. Our response? Obedience based on the foundation of love and relationship with Jesus. Remember, Jesus said, "If you love Me, keep My commandments." (John 14:15). We are obedient as an act of love, not for approval or in a legalistic fashion, rather with hearts of love and gratitude. Hearts that are wholly devoted to Him.

6. God planned to bless their obedience. Blessings always follow obedience. Read Deuteronomy 7:12-16 and record the highlights of God's beautiful promises in response to their obedience.

v. 12

v. 13

v. 14

v. 15

v. 16

7. Review God's pledge of Hosea 2:18-23. God is making a new covenant with Israel. It was more than a mere contract or treaty. The new covenant was made in love and relationship will be its center. Israel who had *"forgotten God"* [Hosea 2:3] would *"know"* Him like never before. Record Hosea 2:20 below.

8. In Hosea 2:20, the word *know - yā·ḏă‘* means more than to be aware of someone through observation. It speaks of relationship, intimacy, and familiarity. God's desire from the beginning. Review Hosea 2:8. It appears Israel did not know God was their benefactor, do you? Record a passage below which speaks of God's perfect provision - spiritually, naturally or both.

9. Moving forward, God planned to make it His business to ensure they *"knew"* Him. He plans that for us as well. Review Hoses 2:20. Matthew Henry's Commentary on verse 20 confirms God's remedy. "…therefore, to prevent the like, (apostasy) they shall all be taught of God to know him." God planned His Spirit would woo us, draw us, and keep our souls hungry for Him by giving us a good understanding and right knowledge of Him. To know Him is to love Him. Record the comforting pledge of Hebrews 8:11 below. Underline the last phrase of the passage.

10. Hosea's love for his wayward wife was not extinguished by her perverse behavior even though her betrayal was bitter and public. Has not Israel's, as well as our betrayal been bitter and public at times? Nonetheless, Hosea loved her! What a beautiful picture of Christ's love for us. Read Jeremiah 31:3. Record the verse. *Notice there are no qualifiers in this verse.* To all who will receive, God's love is free and available. What does this confirm in your heart about Him?

11. Thinking scripturally, does Jeremiah 31:3 remind you of another promise in scripture? If so, please record the verse below.

Meditation
Jeremiah 31:3 The Lord has appeared of old to me, saying: "Yes, I have loved you with an everlasting love; Therefore with lovingkindness I have drawn you."

Gomer: Perpetual Prostitute

Day Five: How Did God's Love Redeem It All?

Memory Verse: Hosea 1:2 When the Lord began to speak by Hosea, the Lord said to Hosea: "Go, take yourself a wife of harlotry And children of harlotry, For the land has committed great harlotry By departing from the Lord."

Hosea will stop at nothing to redeem his bride. What a beautiful picture of God's faithfulness in our lives. He will stop at nothing to redeem us. There is no sinner too vile and no shame too great - Calvary covers it all! The blood of Jesus has sufficiently paid the price! Whatever your past, He remembers it no more. He has cast it as far as the east is from the west. Consider this. If your sin was like fish in a lake, the Lord Jesus has posted a sign on the bank which forever reads, "Absolutely No Fishing Allowed!" Believer, you are free from your past. Jesus has paid your sin debt in full!

1. Read Hosea 3:1. *"Go again..."* was the command. Again, Hosea had heard the voice of the Lord. Pause for a moment and prayerfully consider Hosea's faithfulness in light of Gomer's unfaithfulness. What a contrast. God has asked the faithful one, yet again, to pursue, recover, and redeem his estranged wife! What does this command reveal and demonstrate to us about God?

2. Review Hosea 3:1. "Go again, love a woman who is loved by a lover and is committing adultery…" Hosea found hope embedded in the language of the command. From the original language, this was a command with a predicted or anticipated outcome. It meant the "latter would improve the former." In other words, as Hosea responded to God's command, he could anticipate the results of his next movement (his obedient going) to improve the former (her adulterous behavior). How thrilling! Hosea looked to God, expecting a good outcome through his obedience. What was he anticipating? Divine restoration and healing. Based on Hosea 1 & 2, do you think his confidence had a foundation? If so, what was it?

3. Continuing with Hosea 3:1, "…just like the love of the Lord for the children of Israel, who look to other gods and *[love the raisin cakes of the pagans]*." (Emphasis mine.) The Israelites preferred the pleasures and pursuits of the world to the things of God. How shameful, God's beloved Israel had taken other lovers, just like Gomer. Their pursuit of pleasure was likened to an aphrodisiac, sensual raisin cakes! The more they consumed, the more they wanted. It was euphoric. They were overcome with self! Have you desired worldly pursuits and pleasures more than God? Read this warning from James 4:4. Record the verse below.

4. Read Hosea 3:2-3. The matter is settled. Please outline what occurred in the verses.

v. 2

v. 3

Hosea purchased his wife for the price of a slave. "Fifteen shekels of silver and one and one-half homers of barley" – the equivalent of thirty pieces of silver. (See Hosea 3:2). For the same amount, Hosea would redeem his bride from bondage, and Judas would betray and sell Jesus. The monetary connection? Historically, we have failed to recognize the incomparable worth of Jesus' precious blood, by which, alone, humanity is saved. How tragic, we underestimate its value. Jesus was sold for the price of an adulterous slave.

5. Jesus would secure a bride just like Hosea, but it would cost Him everything. Although Jesus was a cheap commodity to Judas, we know otherwise. What this transaction accomplished spiritually is priceless. Just as Hosea purchased Gomer, Jesus ransomed us. We were rescued from captivity and bondage as well. We have eternity with Jesus and freedom from the power of sin! Pause momentarily and make this personal. From before the foundation of the world, Jesus has loved you with an everlasting love. In light of your salvation, you belong to Jesus. Your life is not your own. Prayerfully record the words of 1 Corinthians 6:19-20 below. Underline the phrase(s) which speak to your heart.

v. 19

v. 20

6. Hosea and Gomer's marriage was a picture of Israel's spiritual adultery and sin which mirrored his prophecy. It included Israel's rebellion and sin, their rejection, and ultimate restoration. How beautiful. Read Hosea 3:5 and record the verse below.

At the command of God, Hosea would again declare his unfailing love. Hosea 3:3. Obediently, he would reaffirm his vow of faithfulness to Gomer. In the midst of her shame and brokenness, Hosea made a public declaration of his unfailing love. He didn't care about her yesterdays or her feelings of inadequacy or unworthiness. He loved her regardless! Finally, her emptiness was satisfied. The void had been filled! At long last, she would know she was loved and accepted - just as she was. It was accomplished. Notice, Gomer brought absolutely nothing to the table. So, true with us! Jesus died for us when we were yet sinners with absolutely nothing to offer. From the cross, Jesus very last words were the public testimony of His unfailing love. "It is finished."

Epilogue.

After chapter Hosea 3, Gomer's name disappears. She was full and satisfied. She's the wife of a prophet and mother of three. I suspect she had her hands full. Commentators speculate Gomer is not mentioned by Hosea again as an example of what God would do to the northern kingdom if they continued in rebellion. He would put them away. Israel would be estranged from God.

Meditation
Hosea 3:5 Afterward the children of Israel shall return and seek the Lord their God and David their king. They shall fear the Lord and His goodness in the latter days.

Notes: Gomer - Perpetual Prostitute

Mary

Mary: Virgin Mother

Mary, the virgin mother, is perhaps the most commonly known woman in the Bible. One mention of her name and even the youngest church-goers can identify Mary as the mother of Jesus. Since mothers hold a significant place in all of our lives, kids get this. For centuries Mary's story has gripped our hearts. Even among the young, her story and the circumstances which surround the miracle conception and birth of Jesus captivates our hearts.

Sometimes you need to go back in time to move forward, and this is one of those times. As I prayed and prepared to write Mary's story, we are deep into Advent. I didn't plan it that way, but apparently, God did. What joy! I love Christmas, and the Christmas season is upon us. You can feel it in the air, and for the most part, my husband's hometown is teeming with excitement. Not over Christmas or Mary, specifically - but over Jesus. He is, after all, the reason for the season.

As I examined Luke's gospel, my earliest memories of Mary came to mind. These memories were delightful. Naturally, they were innocent times, more so than these. Pause for a moment and recall your earliest memories of Mary. When did you first discover the story of an innocent young virgin from Nazareth with such an extraordinary call from God? When did you first learn of her immaculate conception and her betrothal to Joseph?

I was introduced to the women of scripture through Mary, next Eve, and then Sarah and Rebekah and so forth. Like all the women of the Bible, Mary's life is significant to me. By now, if I've accomplished the task at hand in a way which glorifies God, you've recognized His redemptive work in each of their lives. Hopefully, you've seen it in your own life as well. It's my prayer you've identified familiar bits and pieces of God's work in their lives which mirrors yours. Women are women - always have been and always will be. I can promise you God's blueprint for us has not changed. His creative work in and through us has not changed much over the years either. Women still desire the basics, whether we're willing to admit it or not. Deep within us, God had placed the desire to love and be loved, and to nurture and partner with Him in His marvelous creation story.

This entire study is a vibrant testimony of God's amazing love for women and His profound plan to use each of us - yes, you too, in a way which glorifies His holy name. God has used every woman in scripture, their individuality, and uniqueness to reveal His love and plan for our lives, including Mary. How so? Let's take a look. My life first collided with Mary in a smallish town in the deep south. When I first met her, naturally it was Christmas time - my favorite time of year. My earliest memories of Mary are as follows.

Anne Nicholson

The Greatest Story Ever Told.

When I was in elementary school, we held a spectacular Christmas pageant. If you guessed all the girls wanted to be Mary, you guessed correctly. However, even back then I lacked the star quality of a leading lady. It appears I was much better suited for the choral ensemble which shared the biblical story through song and scripture. In some measure that was prophetic because many years later I am still telling the stories of Jesus through scripture. Today, I consider it a significant role with divine purpose. Writing about and teaching God's Word is not only an honor and privilege, but it's also my passion.

As I meditated my way through Luke's gospel, God brought to my remembrance the marvelous Christmas pageants of old. Looking back, I must say, this was quite a theatrical feat for elementary-aged kids. I wonder how we did it. Weeks and hours of preparation, practice, and memorizing lines occupied the fall months leading up to Christmas. For the teachers, this must have been somewhat like herding cats, but somehow, they did it. I find it interesting that no one objected. There was no public outcry, we had no protests, no one debated its political correctness, and we didn't make the national news. It was wonderful. I grew up in much simpler times than these.

As you might expect, during the weeks of preparation, much anticipation filled the air and on the night of our "great reveal," there was not an empty seat. Proud parents crammed into the make-shift auditorium which was a cafeteria that housed a large stage with velvet curtains at one end. High above center-stage, a wire held a large star of cardboard and glitter which twinkled above girls dressed as heavenly hosts. They wore long white tunics and headbands made of tinsel-covered wire which formed halos atop each head. We had it all. Shepherds, and three wise men bearing gifts, even a doll swaddled in a white blanket to lay in a manger. And, of course, there was Gabriel. You can't tell the nativity story apart from "the angel who stands in the presence of God" making his earthly visitation to Mary. Their picturesque encounter launched the entire story.

As you might well imagine, the most mature boy in the class played the angel, Gabriel. You know the guy I'm mentioning. There's one in every class who was only eleven but looked and acted like he was 14 or 15. He was a bigger guy with a more commanding voice than all the others. Not yet driving and shaving mind you, but someone who conveyed God's message to Mary in a confident tone which caused a hush to fall over the audience. The headliners of the performance were, of course, Mary and Joseph. Act three ended with a thunderous auditorium belting out, "Joy to the World," as Mary and Joseph stood in a life-size nativity complete with hay, flanked by the entire cast and some small animals on loan from a nearby farm.

I know the entire event would violate all the rules of today, but this was a simpler time. I long for days like this for my grandkids. Times when everyone said "Merry Christmas" freely and without fear or reservation. Times when celebrations of Christmas were welcomed and anticipated. I know God is in control and am confident He is working all things together for good because that's His plan. He loves us and He always - always wins. As I reflected over the Christmas pageant, I didn't recall one pouty face or any complaints as we filed out the exit doors. In our minds, we had launched the Christmas season as it should be - exalting our Savior - Jesus! Indeed, something about the miracle of Jesus always brings peace to the hearts of those who can hear His voice.

That's why in the late 1960's, the collective cultural decision was to worship and adore Him – unashamedly, publicly. To celebrate the miracle of Christmas and ring loud the bells of Advent - "Jesus Christ is born!" Jesus had come, and He alone is worthy! The greatest gift God could give - Jesus Christ who came and lived among us to die for us. That's all of us. Even those we might think too vile or evil, those we'd deem unworthy of His love, mercy, and forgiveness. Yes, even those, because He alone has the mind of God and loves as God. King Jesus, our Immanuel. He would say to us today, "No one is beyond my reach. No one is too vile or evil that my precious blood flows insufficient from the cross. My blood has covered it all! Come to me all who are weary and heavy laden and I will give you rest." God with us - Jesus, our Immanuel - He alone is worthy of our praise, worship, and adoration.

The Good Old Days.

With that thought in mind, when I was a girl, Christmas was a marvelous time of year. Not just in my elementary school, but everywhere. Back then Nativity scenes, Christmas parades, parties, and pageants were quite the norm. They were the predictable response to Christ's incarnation. Church windows and doors were not only dressed for the Yuletide season, but choirs of young and old heralded God's gift to man through beautiful music. Carolers, bell ringers, and choirs made a "joyful noise!" The living Nativity on the lawn of the largest church in town brought the miracle of Christ's humble birth front and center. Although I was much too young to participate at the time, I cherish this memory. Church members jumped at the opportunity to stand for hours in the cold night air - rain or shine - to portray a biblical role in God's greatest creation story - the miracle of Jesus. Of course, that would be the story of when God became man and dwelt among us. What could be better? Are other events in history worthier of celebration and remembrance? You get it, don't you - the reason for the season? God's love made like us, but perfect and holy to show us the way. Jesus introduced us to God in real time - living, breathing, and dwelling among us. Jesus said more than once, "If you've seen me, you've seen the Father." Think about it a moment.

God Is Love.

With divine purpose and humility, the King of heaven vacated His throne and became God made flesh and dwelt among men. He left heaven to be beaten beyond recognition, ridiculed and rejected because He is love. That's right, Jesus came to love us! Immanuel - God with us - came to reconcile God-haters, sinners, and thieves! Is this not worthy of celebration and fanfare?

God's love made perfect in the form of a tiny baby, born of poor peasants from an obscure place grew and matured to fulfill all scripture and find its climax on Calvary. That's where God's love collided with the depravity of man. That's where it was all settled and finished, and Satan was defeated! That's where the veil was rent from top to bottom and the everyday man - whomever, wherever gained access to God. The God of Everyman who is no respecter of people, who loves all humanity - regardless - even the unlovable and untouchable - He made a way. That was His purpose. He did what we could never do for ourselves. He saved us and reconciled us to God.

The King of all kings, our Lord Jesus, lived and died the way He was born. As scripture records, it was without pomp and circumstance and to fulfill all scripture. Immanuel - God with us - hung on a tree between two common thieves. At the cross, one found mercy and forgiveness, and the other rejected Jesus completely. How fitting? It always comes down to the cross. Jesus - Our Immanuel - came to bring a sword. In love, He came to divide us, to separate the real from the counterfeit, and replace religious ritual with real relationships. The great equalizer - our Jesus. He came to elevate the marginalized, to save the lost, heal the brokenhearted and set the captives free. Jesus! No other name can invoke such raw emotion. His name always calls for a decision. Yes, the road to the cross is paved with blood, the precious blood of the lamb - Jesus. Perhaps that's why Christmas has become such a blatant offense to so many. As prophesied, true love, God's love, was born in a manger and found its climax on the cross of Calvary. But before we go there, let's step back centuries to a hilly region of Galilee known as Nazareth.

Something About Mary.

God chose a human vessel to birth His only Son. It was His plan from before the foundation of the world. In fact, it was the only way. Who did God choose? Simply stated Mary, a young peasant girl from Nazareth born of Jews. When we first meet her, she is neither rich or famous. Nazareth was a city in the region of Galilee of which Nathanael once asked, "Can anything good come out of Nazareth?" (John 1:46). From his jaw-dropping question, we can assume Nathanael didn't think so. Among the more cultured Jews of Jerusalem, Nazareth was merely a poor farming village of lowly reputation located in the fertile Galilee. It was a three-day walk from Jerusalem, situated about 70 miles to the north. Of course, Jerusalem was the site of the Temple and center of all cultural and religious activity. Although the Jews of Nazareth were hardworking, kept all the feasts, and possessed a deep faith in God, to the Jews of the thriving city of Jerusalem, Nazareth was a nothing little village in the middle of nowhere. It's no coincidence its inhabitants were considered inconsequential and irrelevant. In Matthew's gospel Mary is identified as the wife of Joseph, "of whom was born Jesus who is called Christ." (Matthew 1:16). In Luke's gospel Mary is introduced with these words. "Now in the sixth month the angel Gabriel was sent by God to a city of Galilee named Nazareth, to a virgin betrothed to a man whose name was Joseph, of the house of David. The virgin's name was Mary." (Luke 1:26-27).

Although Mary's age is not revealed in scripture, Bible scholars believe she was between 12 and 15 years old when God's Spirit came upon her. Luke identifies Mary as a young woman who is betrothed to Joseph in Luke 1:27. The word *betrothed* must be examined for us to understand its contextual meaning. Let's take a quick look.

The word *betrothed* is *mnēsteuō* from the original text. It was much more than an engagement based on today's western culture or understanding. According to the *Greek-English Lexicon of the New Testament, betrothed* was *"regarded as binding, so that the breaking of a betrothal was legally equivalent to divorce."*[13]

A Binding Contract.

When Gabriel visited Mary, she had previously entered into a contractual agreement with Joseph. Although this may be difficult for us to grasp, the common betrothal period lasted about a year. During this time, both parties remained under the roof of their parents even though their marriage was legal and binding. I don't write these words to point out any failure or broken pledge on Mary's part toward Joseph, that's not my purpose. To the contrary, I believe careful examination of her circumstances reveals the beauty of her character, her heart, and her soul. She was not a lawbreaker. She was a young woman who knew and loved God. She was also a woman of noble character. That's why it's so fascinating she responded with confident poise and certainty when Gabriel delivered his riveting message of good tidings. She and Joseph were married, and in the legal sense, the only thing which remained was its consummation or their sexual union. They were *"one flesh"* in a legal sense, but not yet in the natural or physical sense. In other words, they were as good as married but had not known the joy and blessings of sexual intimacy. Mary was a virgin!

As a young bride can you imagine being married, yet living under your parent's roof - without your husband - without a honeymoon? Unique, isn't it? Parents were much more involved than that. It was a commonly held practice for parents to pick their children's mates. That's right. If your jaw dropped with the thought of that statement, you are not alone. I dare say, most of us could not imagine such a fate. But Jewish tradition holds that most marriages during Mary's day were contracts prearranged between parents. Generally speaking, grooms of today propose marriage by getting down on one knee, pledging their undying love and devotion, and offering a ring, usually containing a diamond or precious stone, as a symbol of their undying love.

---

[13] Louw, J. P., & Nida, E. A. (1996). Greek-English lexicon of the New Testament: based on semantic domains (electronic ed. of the 2nd edition., Vol. 1, p. 456). New York: United Bible Societies.

In most cases, it's an intimate moment between the two. That is unless a fiancée makes his profession of love a worldwide event through the use of social media or the widescreen television at a major sporting event. Nonetheless, in Mary's day, it was entirely different.

Will You Drink The Cup?

After a successful negotiation among the parents, father's primarily, all eyes turned to the potential bride. She would be offered a cup of wine which asked essentially, "Will you drink of this cup as a sign of your pledge and fidelity?" In so doing, it was accomplished. If she drank, her fate was sealed. His too! It was all legal and binding and their year separation proved not only their purity and fidelity in pledge but afforded the bridegroom time to build or secure a home for his bride. Upon its completion, their union would be celebrated. The bride would not know when that day of celebration and consummation would come. Often, they would not see one another during this betrothed period. When she ventured outside, she was veiled. That was a sign and symbol to everyone that she was betrothed and pledged to another. In other words, she was off the market. You may recall seeing this lived out in Rebekah's story. After traveling 500 miles to meet Isaac, she hopped off the camel and veiled herself in his presence, as was the custom. Her actions not only conveyed her respect for her future husband but offered a sign or symbol of her submission and purity as his bride.

All betrothed women waited until the appointed time. Every night before their marriage consummation, the bride would make herself ready and then wait upon the groom. She would lay out her wedding clothes and fill her lamp with oil. Since the Jewish day begins at sundown, the lamp was a necessity. It would be carried on the journey to light the way. As she made preparation nightly, she wondered, "Would this be the night?" Finally, the groom's father would say, "Go and take your bride, the time has come." What time? The preparation for his bride was complete - their home was ready.

At long last, the joyous time had come. The couple is united, with much celebration and feasting, including wine and joyous dancing. While guests partied, the couple retreated to their new home for the consummation of their marriage. After many months of waiting, their betrothal climaxes with something too beautiful for words. The two become one flesh and in an instant, a physical and spiritual exchange occurs, just as God has planned. In a love triangle with God, they begin their lives. They give of themselves and receive for themselves something unique - something so beautiful, meaningful, and tender only God could be behind it. He created marriage and all its accompanying joy, fire, and passion. If you are married, think back to this moment in time. Few of us can forget the unspeakable joy and unique tenderness of that moment or God's perfect plan. To love and be loved completely reflects God's passionate love for us. But much more. It reflects the beautiful love and eternal harmony of the Trinity. Scripture makes it clear. Our marriage is to reflect Christ's love for His Bride - the Church. (Ephesians 5:21.)

Who is Mary?

Mary is the one God chose to birth His son. She is the only human to witness Jesus' birth and death. Both life-changing events fulfilled prophecy. Only Mary witnessed Him arrive in the form of a helpless baby and die for the redemption of humanity. As a mother myself, I can grasp the exhilarating thrill and unspeakable joy she felt at His birth, perhaps you can too. To see and hold your newborn and nestle him or her against your breast for the first time is incredible. It brings an awe-struck satisfaction of wonderment and praise like none other. It's been many years since my first child, a son, was born. I can still remember what he looked like as I held him close and gazed into his eyes for the very first time. I have vivid memories of these moments with his two brothers and sister as well - I'll never forget. Each birth a miracle, each baby uniquely made in God's image and given unto my care and protection. I was not a born-again believer at the time, but even then, I recognized the hand of God at work. I knew it was a miracle. Even then, I could sense His presence in the miracle of birth and advancement of His plan.

On the other hand, motherhood and the love it awakens makes it difficult for me to grasp or imagine the pain Mary endured in the shadow of the cross. Thanks be to God, all of my children are alive and healthy as I write these words. In fact, as God ordained our family has expanded to include a marvelous daughter-in-law and three beautiful grandkids - two boys and one girl. Again, all miracles and blessings come directly from God. As a witness to His death, how did Mary endure such sorrow?

Within her name, we find our first clue. Mary - the name means *bitterness; rebellious; obstinate*. At first glance, those words don't sound much like Mary to me. However, the key is found within the meaning of the root word, *Maria* which means *sorrow, trouble, disobedience, or rebellion*. Here we see our answer in the word, *sorrow*. Yes, Mary will know pain and grief, much sorrow, as the mother of Jesus. It will be part of the package deal. I find that interesting. We know there's a lot of information embedded in the names of biblical characters. Most often, we see the character of the name deep within the nature of the person. So, for Mary, we must look closely at Luke 2:34-35. Our clue is revealed in verse 35.

After 40 days of purification, it was time for Joseph and Mary to dedicate Jesus to the Lord. (See Luke 2:22-24). The Temple dedication fulfilled the scriptural mandate of Exodus 13:2; 12-15. In obedience, they took their infant son and their offering of purification, (two turtledoves or two young pigeons) and traveled six miles to Jerusalem to dedicate their first-born son to God. Reading from Luke's gospel: Then Simeon blessed them, and said to Mary His mother, "Behold, this Child is destined for the fall and rising of many in Israel, and for a sign which will be spoken against (yes, a sword will pierce through your own soul also), that the thoughts of many hearts may be revealed." (Luke 2:34-35).

Look again at Simeon's prophetic words to Mary, "... (yes, a sword will pierce through your own soul also), that the thoughts of many hearts may be revealed." (Luke 2:35). As prophesied, Mary will know sorrow, indeed. According to the *Greek-English Lexicon of the New Testament*, her soul which shall be pierced (an idiom) literally *"a sword goes through one's soul"* meaning to feel the intense pain of sorrow; to feel pain and sorrow; to be sorrowful and distressed.

We read, "The virgin's name was Mary" (Luke 1:27). The importance of the virgin birth cannot be overlooked. A correct understanding of the incarnation depends on the truth; Jesus was virgin-born. The nature of Christ's conception testifies to both His deity and His sinlessness. The inspired words of Luke and Matthew assure us Mary was a virgin when Jesus was conceived. Through supernatural means, the Holy Spirit brought about this divine conception. It was the holy work of creation. Similarly, we become a holy and sacred work, a new creation, when Christ is supernaturally conceived in our hearts. That's when we are born of God's Spirit; commonly referred to as our rebirth. The results? Like Mary, we have Christ in us, the hope of glory.

God chose Mary.

So, God chose Mary. What made her so exceptional for this purpose? Let's state the obvious first. She was born for this, although she was no one of particular stature or privilege. She had a simple life as a small-town girl of Galilee, from Nazareth. She was from meager means. So was Joseph. That fact is noted in their sparse offering of purification at the Temple when Jesus was dedicated to God. (See Luke 2:22-38). The Law of Moses provided an acceptable offering from the poor - two turtledoves or pigeons as an offering of purification. It was acceptable if you couldn't bring a yearling lamb along with a dove or a pigeon. (See Leviticus 12:6). They were poor, and they knew it, and so did God. Choosing Mary was not a mistake or a wrong choice. I have an idea Mary's humility and humble lifestyle afforded her immense wealth in spiritual riches - Joseph too. In other words, what she lacked in material wealth was more than abundant in spiritual wealth. We shall see moving forward she had keen spiritual insight for such a young woman. The depth of her love and devotion to God is evident in Mary's Magnificat - her song of praise. She loved God with her whole heart, mind, soul, and strength. Mary was well on the way to fulfilling the greatest commandment and the one like it, loving your neighbor as yourself when God's Spirit came upon her. Although she was poor economically, she was never poor in the spiritual sense. It appears that Mary was richer than most, and blessed among women. To our basic description of Mary, we'll add one last thing. Mary was from the right bloodline.

A Family Connection.

Mary came from good stock, hailing from the family line of David on her father's side. Her mother's ancestry is linked to Aaron. Her unique partnership with God was about to change the course of history. Her life and obedience and what it yielded, a Savior, would unleash God's love on the earth. His life would redeem what was lost or stolen. It would reconcile and settle the hearts of humanity once and for all. That's radical! Her call was revolutionary, and her commitment was just as radical. Let's not overlook Joseph. How many men could step it up as he did? Would they be willing? Probably not, but God gave him a dream and Joseph had faith to believe God and got on board. His faith in God was the key. That was it. Joseph was upstanding, reliable - a man of intergrity. He was perfect for Mary. In fact, he was an incredible man from the right bloodline as well. Like Mary, Joseph was of good stock. (See Matthew 1:16). For further study, Matthew 1:18-24 reveals Joseph's dream.

Mary, a small-town girl, living a modest lifestyle in obedient obscurity was about to become the mother of our Savior and King. Jesus was about to fill her, literally - mind, body, spirit, and soul. He wants to fill us more abundantly, just the same. I wrote earlier, as I prepared to write Mary's story, we are deep into Advent. I couldn't help but think of her a little bit differently this Christmas season. When she yielded to God, His Spirit came upon her, and there was no turning back, no chance to say, "Oops, I've changed my mind. On second thought, I'd rather not."

Later, when labor pains overcame her on the outskirts of Bethlehem, Joseph was hard pressed to find a place for the incarnate God to be birthed. Frantically he searched, but guess what? There was no room in the inn. There was no place for Jesus to be born. He is still looking for a place to be born - even today. Is there room in your heart to receive Him? Are you open and available to have His love, nature, and Spirit overcome you as He did Mary? He wants to fill us with His presence and power, His promise and forgiveness, and His unfailing love. We all need more of Jesus. He wants to be born in our hearts anew.

Our question for the week becomes, "Is there room for Jesus in your heart?" Is God's grace inviting you into a deeper walk with Him? Do you sense His Spirit leading you in a new direction in the coming days, perhaps not too distant? If so, He will give you the grace to respond, just like He did Mary. Where God guides, He provides! He will help you yield your life to accomplish His divine plans.

Jesus Wants To Use Us.

Jesus desires to draw others to Himself through us. He wants to use us just like He did Mary as we go about our lives, and as we live for Him, exalt Him, and adore Him. Mary's world, as she knew it, was about to change radically and forever. Through her decision, so was ours, so was humanities. She was a humble servant who was available and willing. She had keen spiritual insight and was a ponderer. I would venture to guess she spoke with God more than anyone else. Even before Gabriel's visitation and news of good tidings. Her great hope was in Him, not her circumstances or surroundings. She looked to Him as her source of strength, power, and provision. I write these words because when Gabriel gave her the news of good tidings, she was ready. She stepped up immediately and yielded all her life wholly. Mary lay all of her plans, hopes, dreams - her entire agenda aside. She consented to God's sovereign plan. Mary was on board with God. Mary's yes has touched you personally. Her yes was authentic and genuine. Her yes was impeccable, and it was full of life and life-giving. Her yes ultimately birthed salvation and unleashed God's unfathomable love on the earth. How amazing! God used a poor peasant girl from Nazareth to help win our salvation. No one else in history has done on our behalf what Mary did. Our study guide will reveal the measure of Mary's incredible faith and deep love for God.

Where Is Mary In God's Redemption Story?

Mary was a devout Jew, and it's no doubt, she would have been looking for her Messiah. She would have known of His long-awaited, long-anticipated coming. All Jews did. At this dark, dark time in history, there was much oppression. They suffered under heavy taxation, governmental overreaching and regulation. In addition to much persecution, there was little peace and a prevailing evil was at work in the world. Just like today, there were many poor among them and much suffering. Therefore, all Jews longed for their Messiah, including Mary. Sounds somewhat familiar, doesn't it? Are we not living under much governmental overreaching, corruption, and injustice? There is much suffering all around us. ISIS is a threat to the entire world. Every day we see the evidence of its evil and hatred and brutal violence. Jesus, Himself, prophesied in His day the anti-Christ spirit had gone out into the world. Evil is not new, and it will continue until the Prince of Peace returns. As a result, tempers are short, and anxieties are at a fever pitch. Many souls are troubled. There appears to be little hope among the youth - worldwide. Things are out of control all over the world, or it indeed looks that way.

But God! As believers, we know God is in control, and He has a plan. Rest assured, don't despair. God wins - He always does! It's my personal belief the world is ripe for His second coming! Like the brides of old, which means being filled with His Spirit, are you ready? Are you looking up? Take heart, for our redemption draws near!

In God's Time.

When the world was ripe for a Savior, Jesus was born to a young virgin named Mary. Her unique, one of a kind story began before the foundation of the world. Long before "In the beginning God..." from Genesis 1:1, and it continued throughout the Old Testament prophecies. A Messiah was coming! Luke 1 introduces us to Mary. At God's appointed time, young Mary of Nazareth found favor with God and was blessed among women. "The Lord" was with her. (See Luke 1:28b; 30). The truth of these inspired words has been grabbing hearts for centuries. No one else in scripture is introduced in this fashion.

Additionally, no one else in scripture was invited to participate in God's work of salvation in such a unique way. Only one mother was needed to birth God's son, and God chose Mary. Perhaps that's one reason she has long captivated the hearts of God's people everywhere. Every time I read and study her story, I'm fascinated! Let's review those inspiring words again. The Lord was with her, she found favor with God, and was blessed among women. From her virgin womb salvation would come. Mary holds the esteemed honor and privilege of being the mother of Jesus, the one and only Savior of the world. She would be the first woman to be filled with God's Spirit as well as God's love. For deep within her protective womb, the love of God would grow and flourish.

Although every conception and birth is a miracle, Mary is the one with whom God partnered in His work of salvation for the most fantastic creation story in history. Only she could claim rights to the title *"mother of salvation."* A literal translation of Jesus' Hebrew name, *Jeshua*, is *"the Lord is salvation."* As prophesied, through the birth of her tiny son, God prepared for the deliverance of humanity. The inspired words of the prophet Isaiah neatly define that love for us. Sixty-six chapters reveal God's prophetic plan to love us into His kingdom, even though we are sometimes thankless, faithless, and prone to wander.

Expecting.

It is not uncommon for expectant mothers to hope their infants will change the world. Countless hours are spent thinking and praying about the fate of their unborn child. Not what they'll look like, but rather what they'll be made of - that's what truly counts. Their character and inner beauty, their overall courage and strength. Mary would be no exception. She would ponder God's love in light of Gabriel's message, as well as the fate of her unborn son. Most assuredly, the importance of His life and ministry came to mind. Mary had watched as her people struggled under the weight of high taxes and oppressive Roman rule. As she pondered the significance of the coming Messiah, peace and hope embodied Mary, and God's Spirit came upon her.

At Gabriel's departure, Jesus' coming was Mary's most treasured secret. She must have smiled shyly while gently patting her belly. In this moment of time, only God, Gabriel, and Mary knew of her call and purpose. Mary was on a mission with God! Can you imagine? She was in step with Him and acquiesced to His divine will and purpose, immediately, although she knew many obstacles lay before her. Did she think of Joseph and her pledge of fidelity? Did she take a deep breath and stand a little taller? Did her heart pound like never before? Can you imagine what she was thinking? How would her family receive the news? Moreover, how would Joseph receive the news of Mary's *good tidings*?

What a ministry and what a call! Deep within her virgin womb, God's lamb would grow and flourish. She would know much bitterness before the end, but it, too, would have a divine purpose and fulfill prophecy. As God had planned, she would face it with poise and grace because she was born for this. Mary knew, with God all things are possible.

From outward appearances, her pregnancy would follow the model of all pregnancies. However, God's Spirit and divine purpose would set it apart from all others. It's immaculate conception; its announcement, Joseph's vision, Jesus' lowly birth, and a guiding star would accompany it. In fact, everything about it from start to finish is divine and fulfills prophecy. We'll take a closer look momentarily. Suffice it say, Mary's pregnancy would be like none other. Because of its divine nature and eternal purpose, Mary received a preview of her coming child through a visitation from God's messenger, the angel Gabriel. Mary knew Jesus' birth would change the world and its course of history. How did she know it? She knew God, and she knew His Word.

We will examine this revelation through the inspired words of Mary's Magnificat on day three of our study guide. The Messiah, her Messiah, was coming. It was promised! All Jews looked toward heaven with great anticipation year after year. Most evidently, she understood the significance of the Messiah's birth! It would bring hope to the world in a dark and perilous time. When Gabriel departed, Mary looked heavenward with the scriptural surety Jesus' birth would change everything, including us! With awe and wonder, Mary, who found favor with God could move toward Nazareth and whisper, confidently, these familiar words:

> "For unto us a Child is born, Unto us a Son is given…. And His name will be called Wonderful, Counselor, Mighty God, Everlasting Father, Prince of Peace." (Isaiah 9:6).

From that moment, whatever the world thought about her circumstances became trivial. If God's Spirit could place the Savior of the world deep within her womb, young Mary was confident His keeping hand would preserve it, protect it, and keep her safe in the process. She knew God always wins. In circumstances which would have overwhelmed most of us, her scandalous pregnancy elevated her faith to greater heights. Unbeknownst to her, in the coming years, she would need deep faith more than now. When Jesus faced the cross, Mary's devoted love for God and saving faith would uphold and sustain her.

Walking with confident peace, Mary prepared to face Joseph and her family. With each step, her mission and purpose became more evident. Young Mary from Nazareth had received the most coveted call of women. It was a divine call of profound magnitude. It was indeed the call of a lifetime. Can you imagine? Young Mary, a poor peasant girl from Nazareth, had been singled out by God. Mary was on a mission with God! In an instant, she availed herself wholly to Him. Although many of us confessed, "I surrender all," when Mary said it, she meant it entirely. For this, Mary had been equipped by God.

In A Family Way.

Recalling Gabriel's encouraging words concerning Elizabeth's miracle conception, Mary made haste to Judah to visit her relatives. (See Luke 1:39-56). What a tender scene. Mary, the first woman to be filled with God's Spirit as Jesus grew and flourished within, and Elizabeth, the first to confess and identify Jesus as Lord. Surprised at Mary's appearing, Elizabeth tenderly inquired, "But why is this granted to me, that the mother of my Lord should come to me?" (Luke 1:43). Did you catch that? Elizabeth identified Mary as "the mother of my Lord."

Both women are pregnant at the same time. Elizabeth with John the Baptist, and Mary with Jesus. At Mary's appearance, Elizabeth greets her with this bold statement, "Blessed are you among women, and blessed is the fruit of your womb." (Luke 1:42). Mary responded, confirming her relative's words, "For behold, henceforth, all generations will call me blessed." (Luke 1:48). Mary spoke these prophetic words months before Joseph or her parents knew of her pregnancy; long before anyone knew of the call of privilege on her life. Except for Elizabeth, whom the Holy Spirit enlightened so she could pay tribute to Mary's amazing faith. Notice Elizabeth's words, "Blessed are you among women…" and Mary's prophetic response, "all generations will call me blessed."

These are prophetic words, indeed. Both women have made remarkable statements. Notice, Mary will be blessed *among women,* but not *above them.* We must understand she is undoubtedly due our respect and honor, but never our worship. Idol worship of Mary in any form is inappropriate and blasphemous. She was God's humble servant who never exalted herself. She was full of grace and would be horrified by inappropriate and unwanted exaltation or attention. Her desire would be we worship Jesus, her Lord, and Savior who died to save us. This week's lesson will outline our appropriate, God-honoring response to her life, as well as her astounding call.

What Did Mary Get Right?

As far as I can see from scripture, Mary got almost everything right! She was an amazing young woman who identified with God's call upon her life. Mary was willing and available. She had courage and faith - surprising faith. She knew God. Young Mary was fully persuaded God was guiding her steps. She feared not! What an amazing combination. God divinely made her for this purpose. In a way which honored God, she stepped into her call. Without flinching or hesitation, at Gabriel's news of good tidings, Mary's astounding reply was this: Then Mary said, "Behold the maidservant of the Lord! Let it be to me according to your word." (Luke 1:38). Mary was more than ready; she was steadfast, resolved, and confident.

As Gabriel departed, Mary's life-changing adventure began. God chose well! She would meet her destiny with poise and grace, strengthened by the hand of heaven. Although many challenges lie ahead, she would face her future with incredible courage, and unwavering faith.

Mary loved God much more than she feared man, and she knew the scriptural mandate of the psalmist. "It is better to trust in the Lord Than to put confidence in man." (Psalm 118:8). Mary's hope rests wholly in God. She was willing to suffer whatever assaults and insults lie ahead to do God's work, God's way. What a word for us. If this was God's plan for her life, Mary wanted it all - everything that God had planned and not anything less. Her faithful testimony unfolds through Mary's Magnificat in Luke 1:46-55.

What Did Mary Get Wrong?

According to scripture, the closest thing to an error occurred at the wedding of Cana, a village in Galilee. (See John 2:1-10). It was a family-related affair. Mary was there and Jesus as well as five of the disciples. Which disciples? Those called and traveling with Jesus from John's account in John chapter 1. They were Andrew, Peter (Simon), Philip, Nathanael, and an unnamed disciple who was undoubtedly John. He must have witnessed this miracle because only the Gospel of John records the miracle at Cana. What was the miracle? Jesus first miracle, turning water into wine.

What did Mary do wrong? First, she got ahead of Jesus. Second, she imposed her will upon Him. Third, she tried to help Him out. Dare I say, we are all guilty on all counts. I know I am. I've not only run ahead of Him; sometimes, I've flat out ignored Him. I am ashamed to confess this, but it's true. I have also imposed my will on people's lives, sometimes I've pried or meddled, and I've done more harm than good when I tried to help Jesus. He doesn't need my help, or yours either for that matter. He desires our obedience. Remember this. Blessings follow our obedience, and these spiritual blessings are invaluable gifts from God. And, let's not forget the words of the prophet Samuel, "Behold, to obey is better than sacrifice…" (1 Samuel 15:22). Ladies, obedience is always the better plan!

So, in a motherly fashion, Mary merely suggested to Jesus the wedding hosts had run out of wine. Sounds innocent enough, doesn't it? However, Jesus let her know, quickly, she was out of order. He responded to Mary: Jesus said to her, "Woman, what does your concern have to do with Me? My hour has not yet come." (John 2:4). By addressing her as "woman," commentators suggest Jesus moved beyond His position as her eldest son and stepped into His divine call as her Lord. In so doing, Jesus placed some distance between them. Although He loved His mother deeply the time had come for Jesus to establish some boundaries. He knew He had a short season of ministry to accomplish the will of His Heavenly Father - the one who sent Him. Nothing, not even a loving mother would cause Him to veer off track. He had come to act, do, and say, according to the will of His Father. So, a critical hour was upon them. It was time for Mary to let go. The time had come for her to recognize Jesus as the promised Messiah and the Son of God. She knew the prophecy. She knew for thirty years this day would come. From that moment, Mary saw Jesus through new eyes. He was indeed her Messiah and King. Even Mary would bend her knee to the incarnate God and worship and adore Him.

Women of the Bible and God's Redeeming Love

How Did God's Love Redeem It All?

Mary birthed the greatest blessing ever known to humanity! Mary of Nazareth yielded her life and was wholly abandoned to God. Let's review the words of the prophet, Isaiah:

> For unto us a Child is born, Unto us a Son is given;
> And the government will be upon His shoulder.
> And His name will be called Wonderful, Counselor, Mighty God,
> Everlasting Father, Prince of Peace.
> Of the increase of His government and peace
> There will be no end, Upon the throne of David and over His kingdom,
> To order it and establish it with judgment and justice
> From that time forward, even forever.
> The zeal of the Lord of hosts will perform this. (Isaiah 9:6-7).

Mary, Full Of Grace.

When I think about Jesus, it's hard for me to imagine an ordinary woman was used for such as this. But, it's all true. He saw something in her heart which made it all possible. As I pondered this thought, I recalled God uses anyone He chooses and always has. But something even more profound came to mind. From the words of Mary's Magnificat, Luke 1:46-55, it was clear that the Word of God saturated Mary's heart. I can't stress that enough. She knew and worshiped the God of Israel long before her call. In Luke 1:47, we see the word "savior." What honesty, what humility. Mary referred to God as "savior," her savior. An indication she recognized her own need for a Savior - for salvation. That occurred before His birth, long before God's plan to use her became public knowledge and most definitely long before the wedding at Cana. Mary confessed these beautiful words to the angel who stands in the presence of God – that would be Gabriel – upon receiving his message of good tidings.

We find no evidence in scripture Mary ever thought of herself as immaculate or worthy of exaltation or worship in any manner. She knew full well she was not someone capable of answering our prayers. She needed answers to prayers herself! I see humility in her words. To be part of the kingdom of heaven, even Mary had to confess Christ as her personal Lord and Savior. We all get to heaven the same way and Mary would be no exception. We must all confess, repent, and believe. There is just no other way. Jesus is the only way to salvation. And, Mary knew it. Jesus' own words to Thomas: Jesus said to him, "I am the way, the truth, and the life. No one comes to the Father except through me." (John 14:6).

Being Filled With The Spirit.

Mary's last appearance in scripture is found in Acts 1:12-14. In these verses, Luke records the Upper Room prayer meeting shortly after the death of Jesus, and what a remarkable meeting it was. A hundred and twenty believers gathered in the upper room and waited and prayed for the fulfillment of Jesus' promised Holy Spirit. When the Spirit was given or poured out, they were ready to be the witnesses of Acts 1:8. Immediately they were filled, empowered and encouraged. Following Peter's lead, Mary and the others burst out the doors and testified of Christ. It's perhaps the greatest sermon Peter ever preached. (See Acts 2:14-39). In my opinion, it was his finest hour. On the day of Pentecost, thousands who heard his words inquired, "what shall we do?" (Acts 2:37). Peter's powerful response:

Then Peter said to them, "Repent, and let every one of you be baptized in the name of Jesus Christ for the remission of sins; and you shall receive the gift of the Holy Spirit. For the promise is to you and to your children, and to all who are afar off, as many as the Lord our God will call." (Acts 2:38-39).

On this very day, Pentecost, the church was born. Three thousand came to saving faith and believed. It occurred to me, once again Mary had Jesus' Spirit deep within, having received it in the Upper Room. Think about it. The same spirit which overcame her at Jesus immaculate conception now embodied her again. How thrilling! His Spirit would remain with her the remainder of her days. Truly, He is the comforter! Mary, the only human to share in Jesus' earthly beginning and the end could now witness boldly of His unique purpose - the salvation of man.

At long last, Mary could look heavenward with peace and joy. It was finished - indeed! Mary blessed Mary, who partnered with God for the salvation of men had witnessed it. What a marvelous gift for Mary - to see the fruit of ministry. Missionaries worldwide, including us, have labored and toiled and prayed for fruit yet unseen. I can imagine once again Mary stood a little straighter, perhaps a bit taller. Most assuredly, as she smiled and looked heavenward, she whispered a prayer of thanksgiving as her heart overflowed with joy and gladness.

As we bring Mary's story to its close, remember this. When the angel Gabriel spoke these words to Mary, they were words of comfort. Gabriel said, "…you have found favor with God." (Luke 1:30). In essence, he said, "Mary, this is a good thing." The literal translation for *"favor with God"* is *"full of grace."*

Be blessed this week as you study about Mary who was indeed full of grace. May those words be spoken over each of our lives as well. In closing, from this week forward, and until He returns or calls us home, may we be found full of grace. And ladies, that's a good thing!

Mary's story is found in Matthew 1; 2; 12:46; Luke 1; 2; John 2:1-11; 19:25; and Acts 1:14

Mary: Virgin Mother

Day One: Who Is Mary?

Memory Verse: Luke 1:38 Then Mary said, "Behold the maidservant of the Lord! Let it be to me according to your word." And the angel departed from her.

We first encounter Mary on what appeared to be an ordinary day, but it will prove to be otherwise. On a quiet hillside overlooking Nazareth, Mary will have a divine visitation and receive the most coveted call of women. She will be chosen to bring forth the incarnate Son of God. At the appointed time, Mary, from the line of David, will supernaturally conceive the Christ-child through the Holy Spirit. An innocent peasant girl from Nazareth will be elevated to a position of privilege and honor which endures throughout eternity. In a moment's time, everything about Mary's future changes. I am sure the divine encounter took her breath away! How incredible and what a call! For most of us, an unexpected pregnancy is most welcome news, albeit surprising because it's God's plan. But, can you imagine what Mary thought when she heard these incredible words? Mary's body would nurture and nourish a King. Her arms would cradle Him and hold Him close. Mary would kiss His tiny face and pray over Him daily. To love and nurture greatness of such magnitude is unimaginable and awe-inspiring. God made flesh in the form of a helpless baby would be born of Mary! Through misty eyes and with a melting heart, a betrothed virgin from Nazareth said, "Yes to God." Instantly, she stepped into her destiny. Mary of Nazareth was called to birth a King - our Savior and King - Jesus Christ our Lord.

To frame our story and gain better insight into Mary, the woman, we will examine multiple passages which define and shape her character.

1. Most often, biblical names reveal the nature or character of its owner. The primary meaning of *Mary* is *bitter; rebellious; obstinate*. From what we know about Mary, the definition doesn't seem to apply. In this case, however, the key is in the root word, *Maria*, which indicates *sorrow, trouble, disobedience or rebellion*. There we see the answer in the word *sorrow*. Mary will know sorrow, much sorrow, as the mother of our Lord. Thinking biblically, can you identify times of possible sorrow in Mary's life?

Anne Nicholson

2. Read Luke 2:34-35 to find a clue about Mary's sorrow. What does Simeon prophesy in verse 35?

3. You are an original! Each of us has unique attributes because we are exclusively handmade by God. To discover a unique quality about Mary, read and record Luke 2:19 below. From this passage, it's interesting to see Mary was uniquely known for reflection. She was a deep thinker and thought things through. I'm convinced she prayed a great deal during times of solitude. Mary trusted in God and waited upon God. She was not an impulsive or scatterbrained young woman. As we move through the lesson, we shall see she knew God and His Word - well. Thinking biblically, what else might this verse suggest or reveal about Mary?

4. For greater insight, from the Greek *ponder* - συμβάλλω *sumballō, soom-bal'-lo*; to give careful consideration to various implications of an issue—'to reflect on, to think about seriously, to think deeply about.'[14] Have you pondered like Mary? If so, what heart change or revelation came through your quiet time with Jesus?

---

[14] Louw, J. P., & Nida, E. A. (1996). <u>Greek-English lexicon of the New Testament: based on semantic domains</u> (electronic ed. of the 2nd edition., Vol. 1, p. 349). New York: United Bible Societies.

5. Mary was from Nazareth. In Christ's day, it was an agricultural community located in the northern part of Galilee. At the time of Christ's birth, archeologists speculate 480 residents called it home. Today, the number of resident Israeli-Arabs is approximately 40,500. Of that number, 69% are Muslim and 31% Christians. Read John 1:46. What does the verse ask? Thinking biblically, why do you think this might be significant?

6. In Luke 1:26-33 Mary has an unexpected visitor. Who is it? This is his third visitation in scripture. Who else has he visited? For discussion purposes, identify and record a verse of reference for each visitation. *One is found in Daniel 10 and the others are found in Luke 1.

Who was the visitor? _____

Visitation 1

_____

_____

Visitation 2

_____

_____

Visitation 3

_____

_____

Anne Nicholson

7. Notice the visitor's initial words of comfort in each visitation. What were they?

8. These words of comfort reveal the heart of God - a command from the original language. Gabriel has given Mary wise counsel. He has extended the same words of *comfort* to Zacharias and Daniel during their divine encounters. Fret and fear are the devil's twins. How might fear discourage you from the purposes of God?

9. Read Luke 1:30. From this passage, something is *"found."* From the original text, the meaning implies, "the unexpected gift of the kingdom of God." What was it? Record the verse below and underline the phrase which identifies what was *"found."*

10. Review Luke 1:13-17 and Luke 1:26-33. What is the spiritual connection between Gabriel's prophetic messages of glad tidings?

*The visitation verses are: Daniel 10:12; Luke 1:13; and Luke 1:30

Meditation
Luke 1:30 Do not be afraid, Mary, for you have found favor with God.

Mary: Virgin Mother

Day Two: Where Is Mary In God's Redemption Story?

Memory Verse: Luke 1:38 Then Mary said, "Behold the maidservant of the Lord! Let it be to me according to your word." And the angel departed from her.

The timing of Gabriel's good tidings was perfect. Israel was eager to be delivered from the oppressive Roman rule. They had long awaited the prophesied Messiah. The good news of His coming would first enlighten Mary. Who was the messenger? Gabriel, a prominent angel and spiritual being whose divine purpose is serving God and supporting humanity. *Gabriel* means *man of God; God is powerful*. In the Old Testament, his appearance to Daniel was in the likeness of man. The passage reads in part, "yes, while I was speaking in prayer, the man Gabriel…" (Daniel 9:21). In Luke 1, when he appeared to Zacharias, Gabriel described himself as "Gabriel, who stands in the presence of God." (Luke 1:19). How fitting that God would use Gabriel to herald such good news! From God's lips to humanity's ears. Some Bible scholars list Gabriel among the seven angels mentioned in Revelation 8:2. He and the archangel Michael are the only two celestial beings named in the Bible.

God would make a way. Today's lesson will examine the astounding words Mary heard through Gabriel's Messianic prophecy. Our questions will come from Luke 1:26-33.

1. Read Luke 1:26-27. What can we discover from these two verses? List the important facts below.

v. 26

v. 27

2. Luke 1:27 twice declares Mary's sexual purity or innocence. She was a virgin! The importance of her virginity cannot be overstated. Thinking biblically, why is this important news?

Women of the Bible and God's Redeeming Love

Mary was *"betrothed"* to Joseph, meaning much more than you might think. A Jewish betrothal was as legal and binding as the marriage itself. From the moment of pledge or betrothal, the couple was regarded publicly and legally as husband and wife. The only thing which remained was their sexual union, which was generally delayed for about a year. During this time, the bride and groom stayed faithful to their pledge and lived with their respective parents until the appointed time. The groom had much to accomplish before consummating their marriage. Namely, securing a home for himself and his bride. Then and only then, were they prepared to begin their lives as husband and wife in every sense of the word. When the bride went outside, she was veiled. Her bridal veil signified to the world, "My life is not my own, it is faithfully pledged to another."

3. In Luke 1:28, what exciting news does the angel reveal to Mary? Record the verse below. Underline the last phrase.

4. Notice in Luke 1:28 the words, *"favored one."* A literal translation is *"full of grace."* From this verse, Mary is identified as a recipient of divine grace. Look closely at the verse. Notice, Mary is the recipient of divine grace, not the dispenser. She is exalted among women, but not above them. How does this make you feel? Have you ever prayed to Mary? If so, have you anticipated things or her favorable response? Please share.

5. Read Luke 1:29-31. In Gabriel's customary fashion, he brings comfort to Mary in verse 29. Highlight Gabriel's Messianic message in verses 30 and 31.

v. 30

v. 31

6. Mary is instructed to name Him Jesus. What does Jesus mean? What does it mean to you personally?

7. Luke 1:32-33. He will be _____, and will be called the _____ ____ _____ _____; and the Lord God will give Him the _____ of His father David. And He will reign over the house of Jacob forever, and of His kingdom there will be no end.

8. What does Mary's response reveal to Gabriel in Luke 1:34? Why is this significant?

9. In Luke 1:35, Gabriel reveals three very important things. Record them below.

1.

2.

3.

10. In the sixth month of Elizabeth's pregnancy, Mary learns her elder relative is expecting. Indeed, Gabriel heralds exciting news. A longtime childless couple, Zacharias and Elizabeth, are expecting. What a blessing from God! What was Mary's response to this profound news in Luke 1:37? Record the verse below.

11. Read and pray through Luke 1:38 several times. Can you identify the words of humility in this verse? If so, record the words which best express Mary's humility. Do these words reveal your heart as well?

Meditation
Luke 1:32 He will be great, and will be called the Son of the Highest;
and the Lord God will give Him the throne of His father David.

Mary: Virgin Mother

Day Three: What Did Mary Get Right?

Memory Verse: Luke 1:38 Then Mary said, "Behold the maidservant of the Lord! Let it be to me according to your word." And the angel departed from her.

Today's lesson will focus on some of the most beautiful words in scripture. Not only do they exalt the Lord, but they also reveal Mary's in-depth knowledge of scripture and her relationship with God.

1. Read Luke 1:39-40. Mary traveled hastily to a city of Judah. Who was she going to see? What was she hoping to accomplish?

2. Read Luke 1:41. In this verse, Elizabeth's unborn child causes quite a stir. Upon Mary and Elizabeth's meeting, something significant was accomplished. In your opinion, what occurred in both the natural and the spiritual realm at their greeting?

3. Read Luke 1:41-45. Elizabeth was filled with the Holy Spirit in verse 41. Verse 42 echoes the words of the angel Gabriel from Luke 1:28. Write the words of Luke 1:42 below. What question does Elizabeth ask in Luke 1:43?

Luke 1:42 -

v. 43

4. Review Luke 1:45. Who is blessed and why? Record the verse below.

5. Mary's words of Luke 1:46-55 are filled with Old Testament references and quotations. Mary knew scripture! God's word was written on her heart, as evidenced. Thinking biblically, why might her knowledge of Old Testament scripture be an asset to Jesus? How might it benefit Mary in the future as well?

6. Read Luke 1:46-47. Mary exalts the Lord, confessing her soul's delight in Him. She has lifted up words of adoration to and for her Lord. That should be the launching pad for all prayer - a humble heart. Mary's words express language typical of someone whose only hope for salvation is divine grace. Identify these words and record them below.

7. Catholics have long worshiped Mary and exalted her to a position which God never intended. She was a humble servant of God whom He favored for the esteemed honor of being the mother of Jesus. Nothing more and nothing less. It is evident from these verses Mary is worshiping,

not desiring worship. Looking at Luke 1:46-47, can you identify anything in these passages to support the notion Mary herself ought to be an object of adoration?

8. Read Luke 1:48. What does "…He has regarded the lowly estate of His maidservant;" mean? What, if anything, does it tell you about Mary?

9. Three important truths are identified in Luke 1:49-50? Record them below.

1._____

2._____

3._____

10. Complete the following verses from Luke 1:49-55. Mary's amazing words recite, point by point, the covenant promises of God! Nothing about Mary is exalted in these verses. As you can see, she is clearly a devout and faithful servant of God.

v. 49 He who is mighty_____

v. 50 And His mercy_____

v. 51 He has shown strength_____

v. 51 He has scattered_____

v. 52 He has put down_____

v. 53 He has filled the hungry_____

v. 54 He has helped_____

In remembrance of His mercy,

v. 55 He spoke_____

Luke 1:56 reads, "And Mary remained with her about three months, and returned to her house." This verse gives us a timeline. Mary arrived at the home of Zacharias during Elizabeth's sixth month of pregnancy, and remained "about three months." Bible scholars speculate she was with Elizabeth until the birth of John the Baptist. Afterward, she returned home to face her family and Joseph. Mary was approximatley three months pregnant when she departed for home.

Meditation
Luke 1:50 And His mercy is on those who fear Him From generation to generation

Mary: Virgin Mother

Day Four: What Did Mary Get Wrong?

Memory Verse: Luke 1:38 Then Mary said, "Behold the maidservant of the Lord! Let it be to me according to your word." And the angel departed from her.

1. Mary was an amazing young woman. She demonstrated God-honoring character well beyond her tender years when she spoke the words of this week's memory verse. Read Luke 1:38. These words display Mary's courage, but so much more. Her faith! She was willing to serve God in whatever capacity He chose. Even if she was betrothed to another, Mary was at peace with whatever God had planned. Do you think like Mary? Are you wholly yielded unto the purposes of God?

2. Shepherds came visiting after Jesus was born in Bethlehem and laid in His manger. These outcast Bedouins were the first to worship Jesus. The shepherds had received divine notification of the Messiah's birth. Read Luke 2:8-20. Pay particular attention to the words of verse 19 and record them below. What does this mean? What do you think Mary pondered?

3. Review Luke 2:10-13. We see in verse 10, while the shepherds watched their flocks by night, they received news of "good tidings of great joy" for all people. What else did they discover? Record the highlights of Luke 2:11-13.

v. 11

v. 12

v. 13

4. Read and review Luke 2:21-38 to learn of Jesus' dedication at the Temple in Jerusalem. Simeon and Anna were present. Who are they? What did they proclaim? What's significant about each testimony?

Simeon? (Luke 2:25-35)

Anna? (Luke 2:36-38)

5. As we saw from Mary's Magnificat (Luke 1:46-55), she was deeply spiritual with a commanding knowledge of God's Word. She was also dedicated, reserved, prayerful, worshipful, faithful, and resourceful. On the occasion of the wedding at Cana, her resourcefulness shone through. Read John 2:1-11. What did Mary ask of Jesus? Why?

6. Review John 2:1-11. Mary meddled! If she erred, this was it. At first glance, these passages reveal Mary's attention to detail which is a good thing - that is, until it isn't. Our unsolicited attempts to help God can be problematic. When we get ahead of God, we push against His grace and make our journey harder, not easier. The story unfolds at the wedding of Cana, on the occasion when Jesus performed His first miracle by turning water into wine. Mary's efforts to help Jesus were met with stern words from her son, according to John's account. The verse says: Jesus said to her, "Woman, what does your concern have to do with Me? My

hour has not yet come." (John 2:4). By addressing His mother as "Woman," commentators suggest Jesus moved beyond His position as her eldest son and stepped into His divine call as her Lord. Have you ever gotten ahead of Jesus? What was the outcome?

7. Thinking about the wedding at Cana, a critical hour had come! In loving rebuke, Jesus placed some distance between them. It was time for Mary to recognize Jesus as the promised Messiah and the Son of God. She knew the prophecy. Mary knew for thirty years this day would come. From that moment on, she saw Jesus as her Messiah, her King, and her personal Savior. What would this mean for Mary in light of eternity?

8. Review the words of Mary's Magnificat from Luke 1:46-55. Long before Jesus was born, Mary knew she carried the Savior of the world within her womb. In her prophetic words to Elizabeth, she had humbly confessed her need for a *"Savior."* (See Luke 1:47). What honesty and what humility. Mary referred to God as, *"Savior,"* her personal Savior. For clarity, let's review her words of Luke 1:47-48.

v. 47 And my _____ has rejoiced in God ____ _____.

    a. From the passage, who is rejoicing? _____

    b. In whom are they rejoicing? _____

v. 48 For He has regarded the _____ _____ of His

_____; For behold, henceforth all generations will

call _____ blessed.

      a. Who and what condition has been regarded? _____

      b. Who will be called blessed henceforth by all generations? _____

Meditation
Luke 1:47 And my spirit has rejoiced in God my Savior.

Mary: Virgin Mother

Day Five: How Did God's Love Redeem It All?

Memory Verse: Luke 1:38 Then Mary said, "Behold the maidservant of the Lord! Let it be to me according to your word." And the angel departed from her.

In today's lesson, we look at Mary at the end of Jesus' life. First, we will look at her salvation and then visit her at the Cross and in the Upper Room. God has truly blessed her life. She, alone, has the distinction of being the mother of our Lord. As an Old Testament saint, Mary would confidently recall the prophecies she knew so well, and echo the words of the prophet Joel: And it shall come to pass That whoever calls on the name of the Lord Shall be saved. (Joel 2:32). Above all else, Mary knew Jesus as Savior.

1. Mary recognized her own need for a Savior. We find no evidence in scripture Mary thought of herself as immaculate or worthy of exaltation or worship. She knew full well she was not capable of answering our prayers or hers! We find humility in her words. Read Luke 1:47. Do you think Mary knew salvation could only come through Jesus? Why or why not?

2. To be part of the kingdom of heaven, even Mary had to confess Jesus as her personal Lord and Savior. We all get to heaven the same way. By believing Jesus is our Savior and Lord, the Son of God. We must all confess, repent, and believe. There is no other way. Mary knew this! Jesus said it best, "I am the way and the truth and the life. No one comes to the Father except through me." (John 14:6). Does His Spirit reign within you? Are you born again? If not, take the time to settle the matter with Jesus. No one gets to the Father apart from Him. He is the gateway to our salvation and the one who died for you. It's the most important question you will ever answer. Your answer will shape your eternity!

Women of the Bible and God's Redeeming Love

3. Prayerfully read John 19:25-27. These words are almost too painful to read, particularly if you're a mother. What must Mary have felt during this anguishing scene? Can you identify with her sorrow? Her heart surely skipped a beat as Jesus spoke to her from the cross! In those moments, how did she stand? There is only one answer. God intervened and strengthened her to stay the course. In our hours of most profound need and sorrow, He is there to comfort, to strengthen, and to undergird us! Record a verse that assures God's comfort or presence in our times of need.

4. As we come to the cross of Calvary, it's painful and our emotions are stirred. For many, the temptation to turn away is great. But, if we do so, we miss the magnitude of these historical moments. If we miss them, we lose the purpose of the cross. We miss all God accomplished on our behalf, and on behalf of humanity. Of course, the overarching mission and focus of the cross is love! Can you see Mary there? Can you imagine her bitterness of soul and intense sorrow? Simply said, Jesus died because He loved us! (See John 3:16.) His sacrificial love activates a corresponding love from every believing heart. Prayerfully read John 19:25-27. As you survey the cross, what stands out to you from Jesus' words in John 19:26-27?

5. Every believer has an emotional response to the sufferings of Jesus on Calvary. Mary's soul was pierced; ours as well. The truth of the cross has caused wars, crusades, murders, and deep-rooted hostility, even within families - since Jesus said, "It is finished." Those three powerful words grip all human hearts, because the cross begs and demands a decision - it always has. It has become a blatant offense to many, but not to believers and certainly not to Paul. Read the words of Paul in Galatians 2:20. Paul has demonstrated an overwhelming determination to survey the "wondrous cross." Here we get a glimpse of Paul's passion and commitment to

the gospel. Can you see the wondrous cross? Prayerfully record Galatians 2:20 below. Take a minute and consider the cross. Jesus has given Himself up for you! Make it personal. What descriptive words come to mind as you survey the wondrous cross?

Galatians 2:20 -

As we turn to Acts, we find Mary in the Upper Room, waiting, watching, and praying. She never lost sight of God's plan. She was brave and courageous all the days of her life. Mary had left the scene of the crucifixion with John, and she would remain under his watchful eye until either she died or he was banished to the Island of Patmos. Scripture is silent on Mary's end. We saw in John 19:27, as Jesus died on the cross, He tenderly transferred the responsibility for his mother to John. In His last hours, He ministered love from the cross.

He Is Risen!

6. When Mary heard Jesus had risen, it must have been a tremendous shock – that is, until she saw Him for herself. After His resurrection, Jesus spent forty days preaching and teaching *"them"* about the Kingdom of God. (See Acts 1:1-3; 1 Corinthians 15:5-8). It's evident she had not only seen Jesus but was regularly in the company of those who saw Him. Now, gathered in the Upper Room, they're praying and waiting as commanded to receive the promise of the Father, His Spirit. We find Mary there. Shouldering the responsibility of being her Lord's witness. (Acts 1:13-14). She was in the midst of things, so to speak, praying and waiting as commanded in the company of the apostles and other believers. Again, Mary is called! Read and record Acts 1:8 below. We have a mandate! As believers, we are called to be His witness.

Acts 1:8 -

7. It appears Mary never retired to the background or sat it out. She would proclaim the truth of Jesus until her very last breath. How about you? Are you committed to sharing about Jesus until the end? If so, commit it to prayer in the space below. A written goal brings clarity and focus. In fact, we are 70% more likely to achieve our goals when we write them down. Unsure what to pray? Here are some examples to guide your thoughts. You might pray for courage, boldness, and divine appointments. You might ask Jesus to broaden your territory or sphere of influence within your family or at work, etc. You could pray for more vigilance, more discernment, and the "right words" at the right time. Pray for opportunities to minister to the

lost around you and love them into the Kingdom. Then, trust Him to use you mightily as He sees fit. Jesus is faithful to hear our prayers and respond. These prayers, He delights to answer.

The Upper Room.

Those who prayed and waited in the Upper Room were doing as Jesus commanded. Acts 1:4. They were waiting to be filled with the promised Holy Spirit, who among other things, would empower them to be His witnesses. When the 120 spirit-filled believers burst into the streets, they were in one accord. They shared a kingdom vision and kingdom purpose. Their united heart's cry was, "our lives for theirs." They were no respecter of people either. On this occasion, pilgrims from all over the world were gathered in Jerusalem. Peter didn't pick and choose who was "worthy" of salvation. He was Jesus' witness – period. He spoke the truth and left the results to God. On that day, Peter preached the most powerful message of his life. Some believe it may have been his finest hour. Look at the powerful results! On that very day - Pentecost, 3,000 were saved, and the Church of Christ was born!

8. Read and review Acts 2:1-47. These thrilling verses describe the birth of the Church. The one Jesus died to establish – Christ's church. What profound message and promise did Peter give to the multitudes in Acts 2:38-39?

The message –

The promise –

We Are Called.

Are you His child? Are you filled with His Spirit? Remember Acts 1:8 is still our call. To testify of Jesus, to share the good news of the gospel and be His witness. Our ministry begins at home. Stop now and pray for those in your family and immediate sphere of influence who have not believed in Jesus. Ask God to empower you with courage, gladness of heart, and conviction which says, "I will testify of my Jesus as Savior, the Son of God! I'll give my life for theirs!" As you pray these words, recall Mary's single-minded focus and undivided heart. When she came into agreement with God, all else paled except her part in God's mission. To that she was faithful! What could be better than partnering with God to pray for them daily and love them into the Kingdom?

We have much to ponder, as we conclude our study of Mary, who was indeed full of grace. Going forward, it is my hope and prayer something in her unique story has moved us to follow her lead and yield all we have for the benefit of the gospel – by His grace and for His glory!

Meditation
Acts 1:5 "…for John truly baptized with water,
but you shall be baptized with the Holy Spirit not many days from now."

Notes - Mary: Virgin Mother

More About the Author

Anne is a missionary, a graduate of Metro Atlanta Seminary, and the co-founder of Open Heavens Ministries, Inc., a nonprofit discipleship ministry established in 2004. Its mission is growing others in faith and practice through the study of God's Word. Ministry highlights have included varied outreach to the impoverished, establishing Bible studies in government-funded communities and homeless shelters, facilitating Laundry Love, launching feeding ministries, church planting, and urban city ministry complete with curbside prayer, preaching, and teaching.

She and her husband, Jimmy, have lived and ministered in four southern states as well as Mexico and Jerusalem, Israel.

Her more traditional work has included writing, developing, and teaching Bible college curriculum, bible studies, and women's retreats. She has served as a women's leader and facilitated countless small groups at home and abroad, as well as trained and mentored women who will serve as wives to tomorrow's pastors and missionaries, should the Lord tarry. Lastly, she has spearheaded prayer ministry and served as a community pastor in mid-town Atlanta.

Anne's life testifies God's Word transforms hearts, and she desires to share it with other women. Her love and passion for God's Word and literal approach to scripture, sprinkled with a bit of humor and frankness about the troubling times and circumstances in which we live, is not only challenging and inspiring but clever and refreshing as well. The Bible is not new to us, but who knew we might see Eve, Esther, Gomer, or Rahab as real people, possibly friends or perhaps even the girls next door? Anne did! In short, her inspirational teaching encourages women's faith. She's passionate about women trusting in Christ alone as they come to a fuller understanding of God's Word. Through in-depth Bible study, she motivates them to embrace God's Word – wholly, and challenges them to love it, live it, and trust it! Her passion is contagious.

To date, except for her study, *To Rome with Love*, all of Anne's studies and course curriculum feature biblical truths and insights from women of scripture. She has used the rich texts of their lives to shape and develop every lesson - every story. Her straightforward approach to the facts of scripture and strong faith and hope in God is mixed with heartwarming, true-life missionary tales and adventures, as well as antidotes and confessions from one woman's heart to another. Anne loves all the women of the Bible and hopes you will too!

After 14 years of full-time missionary service, she and her husband have returned to Auburn, Alabama. Their initial call in 2004 launched a vibrant college ministry on Auburn's campus. To date, former students passionately serve the Lord in their ministry endeavors worldwide. Anne and Jimmy have a blended family of grown children sprinkled throughout the southeast. They include five sons, one daughter, a daughter in law, and three energetic grandkids – two boys and one girl.

For information about teaching materials, future publications, or to solicit Anne for a speaking engagement, conference, or retreat you are invited to contact her at annecnicholson@gmail.com